portrait of
LAVENHAM

Suffolk's man-mad...
in the 21st century

A portrait of LAVENHAM
Suffolk's man-made wonder
in the 21st century

First published in the United Kingdom in 2008
by Hepworth Computer Services

British Library Cataloguing in Publication Data

A portrait of Lavenham — Suffolk's man-made wonder

Hepworth Computer Services
1 Ropers Court, Lavenham
Sudbury, Suffolk CO10 9PU

Tel: +44 (0)1787 248054
Email: javatony@uwclub.net
www.hepworth-computer-services.co.uk

Printed and bound in Great Britain
by The Lavenham Press

Front cover: Lavenham Little Hall, looking towards The Great House and The Angel
photo by the author

The publisher would welcome information on any omissions or inaccuracies

J A Hepworth FNI

Softback edition published 2008   ISBN 978-0-9545938-2-7

Tony Hepworth

Dedication

This book is dedicated to

Marjorie

and to

Lavenham

Together they make it

our

Suffolk Haven

Foreword — by Clare Teal

www.clareteal.co.uk

When I first visited 'Wonky Town', in 2004, I quickly realised just what a special place it is. I'd gone there at the invitation of Lavenham Merchants' Guild, to sing in the Lavenham Arts Festival.

It wasn't long before this first visit to Lavenham that I had signed a major contract with Sony Jazz.

In front of a wonderful tiered seating stand, and with the magnificent Guildhall as a backdrop I sang, along with my backing group, to a sell-out audience who demanded several encores.

After the concert we moved on to The Great House for a relaxing drink and discussions about further visits to England's finest mediæval town.

My second visit was in 2005 and this time my concert was held in Lavenham Church, a lovely building which also

happens to have excellent acoustics, helped by a superb sound system installed for the concert.

My third visit, in 2006, was another concert in the church, organised by the Merchants' Guild and again with a full house. It's the first time I've had a rector's vestry as a changing room! Makes a very interesting change!

Having had such warm greetings to Lavenham and lovely memories of the glorious beamed 'wonky' buildings it is with great pleasure that I welcome this new book by Tony Hepworth — one of the Lavenham Merchants' Guild members who helped organise my concerts and a fellow Yorkshire-born person.

In the book Tony has portrayed Lavenham — Suffolk's man-made wonder — at the beginning of the 21st century. It's not a history book, but a picture of the village as it is today, though it will, of course, be instant history after publication. Whether in the sections on the village, events, buildings, people or other items of interest there are lots of colour photographs and much detail of which even some residents will be unaware.

I wish the book, and wonderful Wonky Town, every possible success.

Lavenham, in my opinion, is a quintessential cocoon of Englishness

England's finest mediæval town lies in the heart of southwest Suffolk, in what was, hundreds of years ago, a very busy industrial region but which is now largely on the tourist trail.

It is a lovely place in which to live and work, within easy reach of London and surrounded by excellent places to visit, such as Bury St Edmunds, Cambridge, Colchester, Hadleigh, Ipswich, Newmarket and many lovely villages.

Stansted Airport is less than one hour away and Harwich port provides a close maritime link with the continent. Lavenham enjoys a wide selection of hotels, B&Bs, restaurants, shops and businesses — far more than any other place of comparable size in the county.

Lavenham rejoices in several titles, including 'England's finest mediæval town', 'Suffolk's man-made wonder', 'Food capital of Suffolk' and, perhaps unsurprisingly, 'Wonky Town'.

England's finest mediæval town

There are well over 300 'listed' buildings in Lavenham, mainly because the rich industrial past gave rise to really wealthy merchants and tradespeople, who invested in property. When the trade later disappeared the houses, fortunately, were not pulled down but were left to

age gently. Many of them have, in the past fifty years, been tastefully restored, often by 'incomers.' Lavenham is now classed officially as a village. Its population has hardly changed for hundreds of years, though the number of houses has risen markedly. The historic 'listed' houses lie happily alongside newer homes.

Suffolk's man-made wonder

In 2006 BBC Look East ran a competition for the seven man-made wonders of East Anglia. One of the top nominations, voted for by BBC audiences, was Lavenham.

Food capital of Suffolk

Lavenham has more rosettes, stars and recommendations in the Harden's guide for the number of residents than any other place in the county.

Wonky Town

I first heard that title when jazz singer-songwriter Clare Teal (*of million-dollar Sony contract fame and Michael Parkinson's favourite jazz singer*) gave a concert in the Market Place in 2004. That was her first visit to Lavenham, of three to date, and she had walked around prior to singing at the Lavenham Arts Festival, organised by the Lavenham Merchants' Guild.

Why this book?

There have been many excellent books about Lavenham before, but none so far have given a 21st century picture of how old and new currently fit together in this lovely place. Lavenham was, and remains, a working village, with over 130 'rated' premises of one kind or another, and there is a great deal more to it than just the crooked houses and timbered buildings.

My own first visit to Lavenham was by train in the 1950s. That was how Rev. Canon Scott envisaged every visitor would arrive, when he wrote his book in 1896. I travelled in uniform (*as a cadet in the Royal Navy*) to meet my parents who were spending a weekend at The Swan Hotel, then a Trust House.

I always recall a stroll down Water Street. Half way down, on the right, work was being done on one of the beamed houses. A notice read: "Cosford Rural

District Council. This house is unfit for human habitation." Little did I realise that when I came to live in Lavenham, in 1982, that very house would be my home. And what a happy five years they were. I rented it (three bedrooms, garden and garage) for just £25 a week !

Subsequently, I've lived in Prentice Street, Harwood Place, Hall Road, Church Street and Ropers Court. There have been quite a lot of changes since my arrival. I saw The Priory as a working farm, Lower Road graced by a large factory and the remains of Mortlock's Shed, and The Glebe as a ruined farm complex. They, along with the trains, have all changed.

As a newcomer to Lavenham — well I've only been here 26 years so far — it has been fascinating to see how it has developed. The village vitality depends largely on tourism these days. Visitors come to see the glorious 15th and 16th century buildings. The Church, Guildhall of Corpus Christi, Little Hall, The Great House and many other buildings remind us of a very rich working town of bygone days. Yet it

nearly wasn't saved. As Annex 3 shows, Mr Donald Insall, at the request of the then West Suffolk County Council, wrote a critique of what there was and what could be done about it. 'Smelly town',

as it was known to some at the time, was all set to be modernised. Mr Insall, the Lavenham Preservation Society, and others, helped to prevent what would be considered improper modernisation.

At the start of the 21st century tourism is somewhat less than it was some years ago and businesses work hard to try to ensure that people keep coming. As mentioned, the wonderful mixture of hotels, restaurants, pubs, galleries, shops and services is quite unlike most villages of the same size in Suffolk — a great advantage to residents as well as visitors.

One of the most iconic new buildings in Lavenham is the Village Hall. Residents

saved for it over many years and it finally opened in 2005. There are new estates — principally Lower Road and The Glebe. In the author's opinion these fit in well with the remainder of the village, particularly as the newer gardens and buildings mature.

Just why Lavenham grew up here is an interesting question, and one often asked by visitors. There are no river connections, no particularly obvious road connections, no specially obvious height advantages, so what was it? Clearly, it included a combination of factors, including very astute business people, progressive land owners and merchants and some very far-sighted gentry. Everyone will have a view on that but let us now concentrate on Lavenham today.

Acknowledgements

My most sincere thanks for their advice, support and for sharing their local knowledge, go to many, many people, including but not limited to:

James Andrews
Doris Bagnall (MacGregor, Canada)
Lionel Baker
Jacqueline Barrett (Suffolk Police)
John & Val Barry
Klair Bauly
Sue Hamilton Blyth
Eamon Boland
Michael Burn
Clare Calder-Marshall
Alan & Gwenneth Casey
Kate Chantry (Suffolk Records Office)
Harold, Jill & Richard Chrystal
William & Gay Clegg
Anne Coupland
Veronica Cowlin
Régis & Martine Crépy
Cyril & Evelyn Curtis
Terence Dalton
Ellie Darling
Chris and Gina Dawson
David & Joan Deacon
Lynda Dobbin-Turner (Lavenham, Canada)
Ivo de Jong
Alison Englefield
Paul Evans
Alan & Sue Fayers
Paul Ford
Jan Foster
Leonie Frieda
Philip & Wendy Gibson
Jane Gosling
John & Marylyn Gurling
Dougie & Annabel Hawkes
Nigel & Beverley Hensby
Michelle Hepworth
John Hipkin (Environment Agency)
Jacqui Hobbs
Mike & Gaye Hodges
Stephen Hogger
Robert Holmes
Ben, Simon & Stacey Howlett
Eileen Huffey
Elsie Hynard
Chantal Jackson
Dinah James
Christopher & Patricia Jay

Claire Jay
Jim & Carol Keohane
Marjorie King
John & Sue Knight
David Lane
Bryan Lapthorne
Matthew Manning
Amanda Mansell
Frederick Marshall
Marjorie Newman
Andrea Norman
Elizabeth Norman
Bryan Panton
Tim Partridge
Graham Pattrick
Alex Paul
John Pawsey
Jeremy Pembroke (Suffolk County Council)
Tim & Gilli Pitt
Martin Ransome (Suffolk Police)
Tony & Eve Ranzetta
Carroll & Barbara Reeve
James Robinson
Patricia Rockall (Babergh District Council)
Jean Rogers (LGWSD)
Sir Clive Rose GCMG
Robert Rush
Yvonne Skargon
Desmond & Frances Skinner
Nellie Smith
Tracey Sparling (EDF Energy)
Lizzi Stevens
David Tokeley
Richard Ward
Martin & Vickie Weaver
Tim West
Roy & Anne Whitworth
Derek & Maureen Wilding
Rev. Dr. Nick Woodcock
Jonathan & Susie Wright
Tim Yeo MP

and especially to all those who kindly read the various proofs and made constructive suggestions. I do hope most sincerely that I haven't left anyone out of this list but, if I have, I apologise unreservedly in advance.

Any mistakes in this book — in word or fact — are, of course, mine alone.

Tony Hepworth

About the author

Tony Hepworth has lived in Lavenham since 1983, and now with his partner Marjorie, to whom he owes so much.

His involvement in village life has included representing Lavenham on Babergh District Council for 11 years, winning three elections. He feels very privileged to have had that opportunity and it taught him much about the village, its people, its facilities and challenges.

He has been a bass chorister in the church choir and a member of Lavenham Tennis Club for some years. He sang and acted in Olde Tyme Music Halls in the old church rooms, splendidly organised by Desmond and Frances Skinner.

Closely associated with Lavenham Merchants' Guild, variously as Secretary, Treasurer and committee member, he is very keen to see the Guild continue its efforts to publicise the village and has produced most of their newsletters, concert programmes and leaflets, some of which ran to 100,000 copies.

From his first home in Water Street Tony subsequently moved to five other addresses — in Prentice Street, Harwood Place, Hall Road, Church Street and now Ropers Court. He has worked from home since arriving in the village, carrying out mixed computer work for local companies, including database management, payrolls and leaflet production (for the church and a number of local companies).

This varied local experience, combined with his earlier career in the Royal Navy and overseas consultancy work, has been the basis of his interest in producing a book about Lavenham in 2008. The project started in earnest about two years ago and has, of course, involved considerable research, meeting lots of people, web searches, visits to the Suffolk Records Office and numerous emails and telephone calls.

Tony's book production experience includes involvement with The Nautical Institute on some 38 books, monographs and other publications — design, layout, typesetting, editing and indexing. He was elected a Fellow of the Institute in 2006.

Tony was born in Dewsbury, Yorkshire. From the Wheelwright Grammar School he won a scholarship to Pangbourne Nautical College, and later won entry by open Civil Service examination as a 16 year old cadet to Britannia Royal Naval College at Dartmouth.

He then followed a career as an Executive Officer in the Navy, becoming a Lieutenant Commander at the age of 30. Retiring early from the Navy, Tony then  spent 13 years in the Middle East — Group Training Manager for Gulf Air, Training Manager at Jeddah Port, Saudi Arabia and Administration Manager of Port Khor Fakkan, Sharjah Emirate.

UK based again from 1982, he set up a small IT company and carried out a number of consultancy roles, including Project Manager for a World Bank Management Development and Training study of the Ethiopian Port Authority, work with the Crown Agents and Lloyds Register of Shipping in Pakistan, Jamaica and Trinidad, projects in Nigeria and Kuwait and several visits to Russia and Kazakhstan as part of a series of EU TACIS projects, working in Novorossisk, Perm, Nizhny Novgorod and Aktau.

Tony has two sons, two daughters and four grandchildren.

Contents

Introduction

- Lavenham in Suffolk, England

- England's finest mediæval town

- Man-made wonder

- Town or village?

- Coat of Arms

- Statistics

- Some media quotes

- Lavenham tourist information

- Lavenham 'Blue Badge' guides

- Lavenham village signs

- Local government

Looking down Church Street towards the Swan Hotel
and over the rooftops towards the Market Place
photograph by Mike Hodges of Lavenham Photographic Studio

Lavenham in Suffolk, England

www.discoverlavenham.co.uk

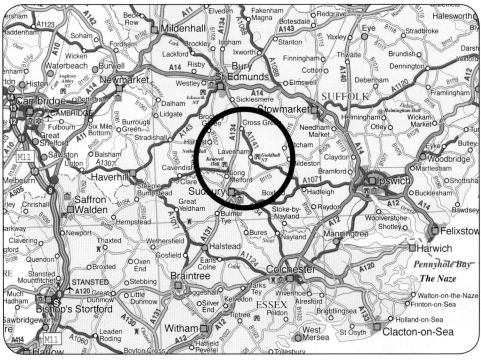

© MAPS IN MINUTES™ 2003. © Crown Copyright, Ordnance Survey 2003

*The new
village sign*

Lavenham in Suffolk — England's finest mediæval town — is situated on the A1141, about two miles East of the A134 between Bury St Edmunds and Sudbury. Sudbury is seven miles away, Bury St Edmunds 11 miles, Colchester 17 miles, Ipswich (Suffolk's county town) 20 miles, Harwich 25 miles, Cambridge 35 miles, Stansted Airport 40 miles and London 65 miles.

Lavenham is well placed as a centre for visiting East Anglia, lying midway between the university city of Cambridge and the beautiful coastal towns of Suffolk. Bury St Edmunds lies to the north and Colchester, England's oldest recorded town, to the south. Newmarket, the home of English horse racing is a short drive away and Gainsborough's House in Sudbury displays very fine paintings by the master painter.

Lavenham's wonderful history is ever present in its fine collection of timbered buildings and it remains a working village, although of a quite different type to its 15th century version. It sports a great variety of hotels, restaurants, shops, cafés and B&Bs.

*Entering Lavenham
from Sudbury Road*

3

England's finest mediæval town

www.discoverlavenham.co.uk

It is tempting to think of Lavenham as a lovely 'old' place — great for visitors — that just happens to have a few residents as well. It is true, of course, that Lavenham as we know it today would not exist in its present form without visitors, and they are all very welcome. Unlike almost any other village of the same size anywhere in England, Lavenham enjoys a wealth not just of old buildings, important as they are, but shops, businesses, pubs, hotels, restaurants, post office, pharmacy and much more.

Barn Street

Corner of High Street and Market Lane

Lavenham remains a busy working village as well as a tourist attraction, and both facets sit well side by side. Lavenham is an easy place to get to and is a great centre for visiting East Anglia. This book aims to record Lavenham as it is today, with an occasional look back at how it was and how it developed.

2007 was the 750th anniversary of the granting of Lavenham's Market Charter, on 15th September 1257, in the reign of King Henry III (1216—1272). The charter — to Hugh de Vere, Lord of the Manor — allowed the citizens of Lavenham to hold a Market on Tuesdays and a Fair on Monday, Tuesday and Wednesday of Whitsun week.

As the committee responsible for the celebrations wrote "This momentous event in the history of Lavenham was, perhaps, more significant than has been realised. Not only did it give the town (as we were then regarded) the right to hold regular fairs and markets, it provided the momentum for the woollen cloth produced here to be sold at markets all over the country and, less than a century later, to be famous in Europe too. It could, therefore, be reasonably argued that the great wealth generated here in the 15th and early 16th centuries, and the legacy of the wonderful buildings left by rich clothiers, stem directly from the granting of the charter."

Barn Street

Water Street

Church Street

Lavenham's position as a manufacturing town of national importance is hard to imagine when you see the quiet, rural charm of the village today. Lavenham was the 14th wealthiest town in England in 1524, with 33 cloth making businesses. It was richer than Lincoln and York during the period that the church was rebuilt (1486-1525) and the Guildhall of Corpus Christi completed (1529).

It was in Queen Elizabeth the First's reign (1558-1603) that refugees from persecution in the Netherlands came and settled a few miles away in Colchester. The lighter and cheaper cloth they produced meant that the traditional Lavenham 'dyed-in-the-wool' broadcloth had to seek alternative markets in colder climes — mainly north Europe and in Asia. The industry declined until, early in the 17th century, woolcombing and spinning took the place of finished woven cloth, supplying yarn to other places. This continued for some two hundred years until, in the early 19th century, poverty and decay meant that people migrated to other towns.

In the late 19th and early 20th century relative prosperity returned with the 'new industries' of horsehair weaving and coconut mat making. Five factories were built and, using traditional weaving skills, they employed hundreds of local people. Horsehair cloth was used to furnish railway carriages but, as demand fell and synthetic fibres were introduced, the factories closed and, by 1930, six hundred years of cloth manufacture had ended.

The first village sign

The legacy of Lavenham's history is the number of half-timbered buildings (grand houses to modest cottages), the wonderful parish church of St Peter & St Paul, the splendid Guildhall of Corpus Christi, Little Hall, the Market Place and, today, the excellent variety of hotels, restaurants, B&Bs, shops and galleries that benefit residents and visitors alike. Lavenham Tourist Information Centre is a very useful starting point for further information — 01787 248207.

Water Street

Man-made wonder

Lavenham was voted one of the seven man-made wonders of East Anglia by BBC Look East audiences in 2006. Weather presenter Julie Reinger visited some of the most awe-inspiring man-made wonders in the region. One of the top nominations, voted for by BBC audiences, was the historic town of Lavenham.

"The whole village is an amazing man-made wonder, it's not just one or two buildings," said Julie. She explored the town with Jane Gosling, who works for the National Trust at the Lavenham Guildhall. "Great wealth was generated in Lavenham," Jane said. "There were multi-millionaires that lived here and by 1524 it was the 14th richest town in the country. It paid more tax than York and Lincoln and all the big cities."

According to Jane, wealthy merchants rebuilt their houses with close studded timbers between 1450 and 1530 to show off their wealth: "They were saying 'Look at my building, look at my bank balance,'" she said.

Eileen Huffey, whose father used to be the blacksmith, has lived in Lavenham all her life and Nellie Smith, who was 99 shortly after filming took place (*who both starred in the production*) most of hers. "When I first came here the buildings were holding each other up," says Nellie. "They were all tumbling down. I know we grumble about people coming in from outside but at least they have saved the place and spent a bit of money on it."

Looking north east from the church tower

Town or village?

www.discoverlavenham.co.uk

Lavenham is known as "England's finest mediæval town" and by others as a village. Whether a town or village depends on when you are describing it. Lavenham was at one time the 14th wealthiest town in England, a busy and extremely prosperous centre based around the wool cloth trade.

Leaning houses — High Street

Now it is officially classified as a village. The OS defines this as "a centre of population with an area less than 2.5 square kilometres (*1 square mile*). A village will always have a church." Wikipedia offers "a clustered human settlement or community, larger than a hamlet, but smaller than a town or city." It makes quite a difference as far as local government goes, particularly on funding.

There were (2008), according to Babergh District Council, some 121 homes in Council Tax Band A, 211 in Band B, 177 in Band C, 113 in Band D, 125 in Band E 125 in Band F, 82 in Band G and just one solitary house in Band H.

The 2008 overall business rate value for businesses in Lavenham was a surprising £1,213,025 and the total business rates actually payable by Lavenham's rated business premises was no less than £484,228.

Within the current parish boundary there are 2,966 acres (1,200 hectares).

Coat of Arms

Until now (2008) Lavenham — unlike many other towns and villages — has never had a Coat of Arms. The very successful celebrations of the 750th anniversary of the grant of the Royal Market Charter inspired the idea that this situation should be changed.

The Coat of Arms, when agreed, will be an appropriate recognition of Lavenham's position as an outstanding example of a mediæval market town. It will be used in various ways by organisations in Lavenham itself and to promote the village's attractions to visitors.

An application has been made to the College of Arms for the grant of Armorial Bearings, which will include a Shield and Motto. With the approval of the Parish Council, a small group was established to investigate the project. The Parish Council may make a donation to the cost and residents and others interested in the project are being invited to contribute.

Fund raising events were also planned and the formal application should have been presented by the end of 2008. The group members involved were Sir Clive Rose, Philip Gibson (District Councillor), Marylyn Gurling (Parish Council Chairman) and Geoffrey Lindsey-Smith (fund raiser).

Statistics

The population shows little variation between 1732 and 2001, though it fell by 35% between 1901 and 1961, and rural depopulation was a significant factor leading to Insall and other studies, as well as the decline in housing quality.

1732 ... 1,776	1778 1,741	1838 1,870
1872 ... 1,823	1901 2,018	1931 1,454
1936 ... 1,400	1951 1,489	1961 1,305
1966 ... 1,310	1970 1,426	1971 1,444

2001 ... 1,738 (835 males, 903 females)

Of the 1,738 persons, 1,727 were recorded as living in households, 11 in communal establishments and 27 were students living away from home.

Houses (2008)

955 homes were recorded by Babergh District Council, with 39 second homes and 27 empty (unfurnished, unoccupied). For Council Tax bands see page 6.

Businesses (2008)

Babergh District Council recorded 132 'rated' businesses, ranging from very small to businesses with over 50 employees.

Traditional knitters outside Lavenham TIC

Shop on the High Street

An aerial photograph (from the author's collection) showing the sports fields, Church, Tenterpiece, Potlands Lane, Hall Road and — at the bottom — one of the Swan Hotel car parks

Some media quotes

The Times magazine — 10 May 2008

"All is not happiness here. The villagers love the place, but so does everybody else, and that's the problem."

Alan Franks wrote "First-time travellers to Lavenham in Suffolk find themselves questioning their sobriety. If they turn out not to be drunk, then it must be the houses because they are slewing all over the place. Roofs shrug and buckle on cock-eyed gables. Buildings lean over as if they are resting their head on a neighbour's shoulder. If the English village is a state of mind, this one trumps the most active imagination. Lavenham comes across as the village equivalent of a celebrity who has everything: looks, money, history, hard times, depression, recovery. Most of the timbered houses here were built in the second half of the 15th century. That it has survived in this form is due to three things: solid craftsmanship, a brilliantly waged war of preservation in the 20th century and the sometimes inconvenient truth of new money."

Alan also wrote "Traffic is an extremely hot potato in Lavenham. The street has the biggest unbroken run of homes of this epoch anywhere in Britain. Shake them to bits and you are destroying more than property.... Lyn Gurling, Parish Council chairman says that slapping a World Heritage Site designation on the village would staunch the lifeblood that keeps the village from turning into a full-blown museum."

Alan concluded by writing "It's the damaging indifference of incomers that is at the heart of the Battle of Lavenham, whether they arrive in human or vehicle form. They're not all bad. They never were. In the 21st century Poles come to work in the kitchens of the Swan, just as there were Flemish weavers coming to set up their looms in Water Street in 1335. (Author's note: There is no actual evidence that they did so!).

Suffolk Free Press — May 2008

Following his death, the Press wrote "The Rev. Rex Bird spent 10 years as rector at Lavenham, between 1965 and 1975, during which time he famously attracted Cliff Richard to sing at St Peter and St Paul's Church."

Daily Express — 3 November 2007

"Discover the village that time forgot"

Simon Edge wrote "The picturesque streets of Lavenham are a slice of living history. The medieval buildings are the perfect background to enjoy a lazy afternoon. One of the most astonishing heritage sites in England, ... if it weren't for the cars parked in the Market Place you would think you had travelled back half a millennium.

The Times — 4 October 2003

"The 1500s live on in Suffolk"

Nicholas Roe wrote "Five hundred years ago something rotten happened in East Anglia — and we should all be selfishly grateful for it nowadays. The place went bust.

Foreign wars, high taxes and overseas competition worked destructive tricks on the cloth and wool trades that under-pinned the booming economy of these eastern counties, and virtually overnight it all went belly up. Money fled. The place stagnated. And if you want to know why this is such great news for today's cultural tourist, you simply have to climb to the top of the giddyingly high, 40 metre (131 ft) tower of the St Peter and St Paul Church in Lavenham, Suffolk, and gaze out at the landscape we inherited from those poor old demoralised wool barons all those years ago."

Sunday Times — 1962

To tourists, preservationists, antiquaries or simply lovers of beautiful things, Lavenham is a remarkable survival of Tudor England: "The most complete example of a small mediæval town in East Anglia."

The fiercely contested issue is whether Lavenham should be frozen as a historical monument or be injected with the flotsam of new people and new industries so that it develops into a living, breathing 21st century community.

The 'antis' fear development, those in favour want a new prosperity brought to a town which, although lovely to look at, provides employment for less than 10% of its working population.

The preservationists are mainly settlers — people who have moved in or have escaped to a perceived rural idyll. The supporters are those who don't mind living in its overbearing charm — as long as it gives them a living.

Lavenham tourist information

www.discoverlavenham.co.uk

Tourist Information Centre

Lavenham has an excellent Tourist Information Centre, which is operated by Babergh District Council, at the top of Lady Street, just off the Market Place.

It is usually open every day from Easter until the end of October from 10.00am to 4.45pm and on weekends in November, December and March from 11.00am to 4.00pm. The telephone number is (01787) 248207 and the email address is

lavenhamtic@babergh.gov.uk

Services offered include:

- Holiday information covering Suffolk and the East of England, also London. Brochures of all parts of the U.K. can be ordered
- Events lists
- Walking & cycling maps and leaflets
- Theatre guides
- Souvenirs, inc. locally made arts & crafts
- Local bus timetables
- Accommodation booked anywhere in England (personal callers only)
- Bookings taken for guided walk of Lavenham

There is also an Information Point at the Cock Inn car park.

Lavenham Tourist Information Centre

The TIC has a very extensive range of brochures and leaflets about Lavenham and other Suffolk attractions — general guides, walks and cycle leaflets, OS maps and footpath maps.

The gift selection includes locally made preserves, fruit juices, fudge, locally crafted pottery, handmade Suffolk soaps, etc. There is a good range of books, DVDs, many Suffolk related. The TIC also stocks books on local airfields and hosts fund-raising activities from time to time.

Ready for customers

Guided Walks

Visitors can enjoy a guided walk around Lavenham with a qualified Blue Badge Guide — from end March to end October. Walks usually start at 2.30pm on Saturdays; 11am on Sundays and Bank Holiday Mondays (not the August Bank Holiday). Themed walks also run throughout the year. Group bookings can be made for other times by prior arrangement. Tickets and start point are at the Tourist Information Centre.

Frankie, the 'resident' TIC cat

Amanda (on left) and Veronica Cowlin (Manager)

Audio Tour

"Exploring Lavenham", an audio tour of central Lavenham, is available from the Pharmacy. For further information about the Audio Tour, including group bookings or reservations, you should contact the Lavenham Pharmacy direct in the High Street, telephone 01787 247284.

Veronica in costume

Local produce and gifts are on sale

Part of the leaflet range

An information point at The Cock Inn car park

Lavenham 'Blue Badge' guides

One of the best ways of seeing Lavenham today is with a Blue Badge Guide — and contact with them can be made through Lavenham Tourist Information Centre in Lady Street, just off the Market Place.

An initiative by Babergh District Council and Lavenham Tourist Information Centre established a team of eight Blue Badge Guides in Lavenham in 2001. The team — Barbara Butler, Caroline Bridge, Chris Hunt, Dinah James, Gill Templeman, Jim Robinson, Pam Pudney and Simon Gallup — all trained in Colchester, qualifying in either 1990 or 1994.

Dinah James

The history of Lavenham can't change but the guides have a way of bringing individuality to their tours, some having researched specific areas of interest.

Barbara and Gill can often be seen in 'costume', talking about the clothiers and weavers (Gill), the Tudors and the annual 'Lantern' walk and 'Mediæval Meander' (Barbara). Jim has written a booklet *Lavenham's Pubs, Inns and Beer House, Past and Present* and will happily undertake a themed walk on this subject.

Barbara and Pam are East Anglian Regional Guides and, like Simon, guide in Flatford and Dedham, based on John Constable. Chris lives in and can lead a very interesting walk around Nayland. Additionally Barbara, Caroline, Dinah, Gill, Jim and Pam can offer tours of Sudbury, Long Melford and Clare, all local places of interest and with special characters to hear about:

Sudbury (Thomas Gainsborough), Long Melford (Cloptons, Cordells and Martyns) and Clare (Lords of Clare and Elizabeth de Burgh).

The guides also work with the National Trust. Visiting groups are given an introduction in the Guildhall by manager Jane Gosling, followed by a guided tour of Lavenham and ending with tea and cake in the tea room.

In May 2008 the guides were involved with The South & Heart of Suffolk Walking Festival (organised by Babergh and Mid-Suffolk District Councils), with many of the guides leading walks for the programme.

The guides are an enthusiastic and active group of people, who enjoy sharing and helping visitors understand the history of Lavenham and the nearby area and will always do this to the best of their ability. A guide will happily walk with just one person or groups of up to 30, with bookings (as stated above) being made through the Lavenham Tourist Information Centre, or privately.

Lavenham village signs

The original Lavenham village sign is on the open green space between the Parish Church and Tenterpiece. Lavenham Women's Institute raised the funds necessary to commission the design and erection of the sign, to celebrate their 70th anniversary. Maureen Wilding was WI President at the time.

The designer chosen was Neil Rutherford of Lavenham. Made of oak (*some of which came from old Lavenham buildings*), the sign has three panels under the name of the village at the top. The upper panel represents heraldry — de Vere/Spring/Tudor Rose, the middle panel represents a weaver at a loom and the lower panel shows a relief of The Guildhall. The dates 1909—1990 appear at the bottom. To add interest for shorter visitors, Neil also carved a snail at the lower back of the sign.

A time capsule was buried beneath the sign before it was formally unveiled, containing a scroll report of how the money for the sign was raised. The sign now belongs to the Parish Council.

The second, and much newer, Lavenham sign stands at the junction of Bury Road and Preston Road. It was designed by Andrea Norman of Lavenham. Ironoak Forge of Buxhall, who created it, describe it as "the largest village sign in the country". They go on to say that "it contains more detail, historic or otherwise, than any others they know." Commissioned to commemorate the 750th anniversary of the granting of Lavenham's Market Charter by King Richard III in 1257, funds were raised by subscription from individuals and associations and it was unveiled on 20th October 2007.

The three steps represent the Market Cross and the sign has numerous features representing aspects of Lavenham including The Guildhall, the Parish Church, the Salvation Army, the US Airbase, the de Veres, the Springs, 'Bolton Billy' (a WWII bomb), sheep, a loom and a woad plant.

Local government

Into the 21st century

Currently (2008), a three tier local government system operates in Suffolk. There are plans to alter the system (*and in Norfolk*), yet again, described as a measure to save money (*probably — I suspect — over the very long, rather than short, term*), to end confusion, make access to services simpler, give clearer accountability for decisions made by councillors and to provide clear community leadership.

Following the Boundary Committee for England (BCE) review, it is probable that Suffolk's County Council and seven District and Borough Councils will be merged into unitary councils. Following consultations on the initial proposals, advice was to be submitted to the Secretary of State by 31st December 2008, with changes likely to be in force by April 2010.

Whatever the result, one of the biggest changes happening in local government is the growing extent of electronic communications.

Lavenham Parish Council

Lavenham usually has some 10 Parish Councillors (*either elected, every four years, or sometimes co-opted*). Normally, the Council meets on the first Thursday of each month, in The Guildhall, in the evening. All meetings are open to the public.

The Parish Council deals with local planning applications, street lighting, the cemetery, footpaths, First Meadow play equipment, walls outside the church, grass area maintenance and the recreation ground. If necessary, separate planning meetings are held to consider applications affecting the village.

The Council Chairman holds a Parish Surgery weekly in the Village Hall and it is fair to say that many representations have little or nothing to do with the Parish Council. However, they are — of course — redirected appropriately.

The Boundary Committee proposals are likely to mean more powers being delegated to Parish Councils.

Lavenham Parish Council meeting in The Guildhall — Thursday 3rd July 2008

left to right: Andrea Norman; Doreen Twitchett; Lesley Morrison; Joy Baker; Jane Bellward (Parish Clerk); Marylyn Gurling (Chairman); Philip Gibson (Vice Chairman); John Kemp; Derek Allen; Alan Fayers; Andy Cracknell;   (Not present: Christopher Sansbury)

Babergh District Council

www.babergh-south-suffolk.gov.uk

Lavenham is in the Babergh District of South Suffolk. Babergh District Council (BDC) is headquartered at Hadleigh and elections for councillors take place every four years. Lavenham has its own District Councillor amongst the 43 on the council (*the author was privileged to represent the village for eleven years*). The council has, for many

The Babergh District Council logo

years, been of 'no overall political control' and uses a streamlined committee model.

Chief Executive since 1999 is Patricia Rockall, who lives in Lavenham. She

Patricia Rockall, Chief Executive, Babergh District Council

thinks Lavenham is fantastic, being very aware of the privilege of living in such an historic, cosmopolitan, working village where it is possible to walk to so many first class amenities. On the plus side, the changes in the village she has noticed include the benefits of the new Village Hall

and the arrival of the French and Farmers' Markets. On the downside, she is concerned about the increase in traffic (especially large lorries) through the village.

She is keenly aware of the raised expectations on local councils to maintain high quality services whilst also keeping Council Tax levels as low as possible. 77% of the total Council Tax bill is for Suffolk County Council services; around 10% for Police and around 9% for Babergh services. The Parish Council raises a precept for the services they provide here in Lavenham, which is included in the overall Council Tax bill.

The total annual revenue budget at Babergh is £48m, of which £13m relates to council housing. 70% of the £35m balance is met by government grant,

18% by fees and other charges and just 12% (£4.3m) by Council Tax. Total salary, national insurance and pension costs account for less than 23% of Babergh's total revenue budget.

The council employs about 370 staff, of whom around 130 are part-time. The majority of employees are based at the Hadleigh headquarters. The make-up of the workforce changed significantly in the early 1990s. This was largely due to contractors being engaged to carry out work traditionally undertaken by their own workforce.

Council functions include Social Housing, Planning Matters, Council Tax collection, Food & Safety Licensing, Environmental Protection, Tourism & Arts and Economic & Community Development. Contractors undertake refuse collection, street cleansing, pest control, building and grounds maintenance (parks and open spaces) and the Leisure Centre and swimming pools.

Babergh District, created from five former local authorities in South Suffolk, takes its name from one of the old Saxon hundreds referred to in the Domesday Book. The district is wedge-shaped, with its point being the Shotley peninsula, which has the River Orwell on its northern flank and the River Stour (*which forms the county boundary with Essex*) on its southern side. The wedge extends inland for a distance of some 35 miles, embracing almost the whole of what is known as "Constable Country", the Stour valley, the valleys of the Rivers Box, Brett, and Glem and the historic towns of Hadleigh and Sudbury.

Babergh District Council at work

Suffolk County Council

www.suffolk.gov.uk

Lavenham is represented on Suffolk County Council (SCC) by the Councillor for the Cosford division. There are 75 County Councillors, elected in all divisions every four years.

Chief Executive Andrea Hill was appointed in 2008, on the second highest CE salary in England. This caused extensive press comment, considered rather 'over the top' by Councillor Pembroke (*elected in 2005 for Cosford division*).

Andrea Hill, Chief Executive, Suffolk County Council

Suffolk County Council is responsible for major services which are provided county-wide. These include:

- Business and trading standards — enforcing fair trading laws, protecting consumers and giving advice.
- Education and learning — schools, evening classes for adults, youth clubs and higher education grants.
- Environment — conservation of the countryside and public access to it, waste disposal and archaeological services.
- Leisure and culture — library services, archives and support for arts and museums.
- Public safety — fire fighting, rescue and emergency services, safety advice.
- Registration of births, marriages and deaths.
- Social care — care for older people who are physically or mentally infirm, or have a mental health problem, those with physical or learning disabilities and children and families who need protection and support.
- Transport and streets — maintaining and improving Suffolk's roads, footpaths and public rights of way, road safety, public transport co-ordination.

Suffolk
County Council

The Suffolk County Council logo

At present Suffolk County Council is rated best in eastern England and has been awarded 4 stars by the Audit Commission. The council view on the Boundary Commission proposals is that they would prefer just one unitary authority for the whole county.

The council's gross budget for 2008/09 is £1,032m, funded by £659 government grant, £101m fees, charges and contributions from other organisations, £2m from reserves and £270m Council Tax. Of the £1,032m, staff costs including pensions are budgeted at £502m. The council does not sell personal information about taxpayers to commercial companies.

Jeremy Pembroke regards Lavenham as a charming village, with a good school and a great head teacher. Having lived in Suffolk for some 40 years, he hasn't seen all that much change in the village, though he is keenly aware of the concerns about through traffic.

Councillor Jeremy Pembroke (Cosford), Council Leader

Suffolk County Council at work

The Suffolk structural review

www.electoralcommission.org.uk

From time to time governments decide to change local government structures — always ostensibly with a view to saving money and improving services. 2008 seems to be no exception to this process. The issue may be settled before this book goes to press, but that is unlikely.

According to their website, the Electoral Commission started its structural review of Suffolk on 3rd March 2008 and worked with local authorities and other stakeholders to identify potential concepts for the new unitary authorities. Those who sent in submissions — the County Council, local authorities, District Councillors, political groups, MPs and town and parish councils were all listed.

It appears, therefore, that the principal of unitary authorities had been decided in advance. The draft proposals were published in July, either for two unitary authorities — one for Ipswich and Felixstowe and the other for the rest of Suffolk minus Lowestoft — or a single unitary authority for the whole of Suffolk. These proposals were not final and were subject to representations from interested parties by 26th September 2008.

The initial proposals met a very mixed response, variously described as "hare-brained", "a messy nonsense", "very pleased that a joint bid with the County Council was one of the two options being consulted upon" and "extremely surprised", while David Ruffley MP (Bury St Edmunds) said this was "a truly bizarre decision." Babergh District Council reaction was posted on their website and also on the Boundary Commission website.

Interestingly, the Suffolk proposal (less Ipswich and Felixstowe) contained the additional idea of setting up Community Boards across the county, with a wide range of powers, bringing together citizens, unitary councillors, police, doctors and head teachers, with a devolved budget. In addition, the idea of Area Committees and Public Service villages was also included — yet more layers of local government. Personally, I fail to see how all of this would save money or improve governance.

The Mercury of 25 Sept 08 reported: "The battle over the future of local government in Suffolk looks set to become a bidding war after new claims that Council Tax could be cut by up to £250. Suffolk County Council, Babergh District Council and other councils are vying to gain the result. In Babergh, if the proposal is accepted, Council Tax might reduce by £145.

So many figures will be bandied about that residents will struggle to know who to believe. Babergh District Council has voted to support the BCE proposals, claiming it represented the best solution for "cost effectiveness and democratic accountability." Andrea Hill of Suffolk County Council said "the One Suffolk case was so powerful the BCE proposal would be dropped."

The consultation runs on until the end of December 2008. A further issue arising from all this is that if the Secretary of State accepts the proposals, the Electoral Commission would then be obliged, by law, to consider the need for an electoral review of the new authorities.

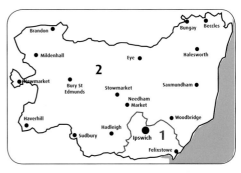

The draft proposal for Suffolk (less Lowestoft); an Ipswich & Felixstowe unitary authority (1) and a Suffok unitary authority (2). The proposal was made in July 2008 by The Boundary Committee for England, part of the Electoral Commission

East of England Regional Assembly

www.eera.gov.uk

Another body that affects us, largely un-noticed, is the East of England Regional Assembly, an unelected, unaccountable group of no less than 105 members (*72 from local authorities, 32 so-called Community Stakeholders and one representative from the Broads Authority*), who meet approximately twice a year. It exists to promote the social, economic and environmental well-being of the region.

The East of England Regional Assembly logo

Each year the 54 local authorities within the East of England nominate one councillor to the assembly. Political parties are then invited to nominate councillors from any part of the region to ensure that assembly membership reflects the political balance of the region. Stakeholder organisations are invited to nominate representatives to provide a minimum of 30% of the overall assembly membership.

Special responsibility allowances amounting to £74,120 in 2007/08 were paid to various post holders, plus £60 a day attendance allowance to each community stakeholder representative plus travel expenses. There are also, of course, large sums paid to the 54 permanent staff of the assembly (*based at Flempton, near Bury St Edmunds*).

The East of England plan, published in May 2008, sets out the regional strategy for planning and development to the year 2021. It covers economic development, housing, the environment, transport, waste management, culture, sport and recreation, mineral extraction and more — functions already dealt with to a considerable extent by the existing County and District Councils.

Member of Parliament

www.timyeo.org.uk

The Member of Parliament representing Lavenham is the member for South Suffolk. Since 1983, when he was first elected to represent us here in Lavenham, the member has been Tim Yeo (Conservative).

Tim Yeo MP
Member for South Suffolk

His website enables surfers to find out more about him, his role in Parliament, recent press releases and speeches, local campaigns and issues in which he is involved and how to contact him. He is always keen to hear from constituents, regardless of whom they vote for and will respond to any concerns they raise.

Of particular interest to Lavenham at the time of writing this book was his support for maintaining rural Post Offices open (and an alternative solution to the proposed Royal Mail closure programme), and support for the alteration of the proposed new flight holding patterns for Stansted and Luton Airports. He also welcomed the government announcement that Suffolk Primary Care Trust's plans for Sudbury would be referred to an Independent Reconfiguration Panel.

Tim Yeo is one of only 30 Conservative MPs to have won each of the last six elections. He was a member of the Thatcher and Major governments, serving in the Home Office, Foreign Office, Department of Health and Department of the Environment. In his last ministerial post, as Minister of State for the Countryside and Environment, he reformed planning law, helped to develop climate change policy and established the now thriving Energy Saving Trust.

The village

- Lavenham's streets

- Lavenham Community Primary School

- Lavenham clubs, societies and charities

- Lavenham Guild of Weavers, Spinners and Dyers

- Suffolk Preservation Society

- Lavenham Merchants' Guild

- Lavenham hostelries and restaurants

- Lavenham businesses

- Medical facilities

- Sports and recreational facilities

- Transport, traffic, parking and police

Lavenham's streets — sketch map

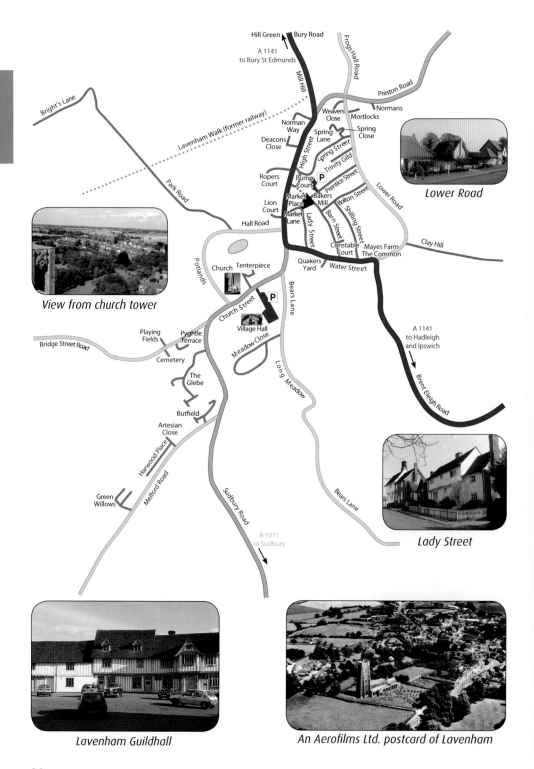

Hill Green
Bury Road
A 1141 to Bury St Edmunds
Frogs Hall Road
Preston Road
Bright's Lane
Lavenham Walk (former railway)
Mill Hill
Norman Way
Weavers Close
Mortlocks
Normans
Spring Lane
Spring Close
Deacons Close
High Street
Spring Street
Trinity Gild
Park Road
Ropers Court
Pump Court
Prentice Street
Lower Road
Lion Court
Market Place
Bakers Mill
Bolton Street
Hall Road
Market Lane
Lady Street
Barn Street
Shilling Street
Constable Court
Mayes Farm
The Common
Clay Hill
Potlands
Church
Tenterpiece
Quakers Yard
Water Street
A 1141 to Hadleigh and Ipswich
Brent Eleigh Road
Bears Lane
Church Street
Bridge Street Road
Playing Fields
Pyghtle Terrace
Village Hall
Cemetery
Meadow Close
Long Meadow
The Glebe
Butfield
Artesian Close
Harwood Place
Green Willows
Melford Road
Sudbury Road
Bears Lane
B 1071 to Sudbury

Lower Road

View from church tower

Lady Street

Lavenham Guildhall

An Aerofilms Ltd. postcard of Lavenham

Lavenham's streets today

Lavenham's streets — a mixture of old and new — tell a great story. Large timbered houses live comfortably with humble cottages and newer dwellings. The houses of the de Veres, Earls of Oxford and the merchant clothiers, shops, rooms for looms, weavers cottages, halls of the gilds and old inns, are much as they were when Lavenham was famous for its broadcloth. Streets at the beginning of the 21st century are:

Artesian Close

A fairly recent development of just four houses. It is so named for the artesian well there that was used by the local water company. The well still exists but is covered up and now forms the centre-point of a garden room in the back garden of one of the houses.

Bakers Mill

Leading off the top of Prentice Street, it is a conversion of a Flour Mill, with other new dwellings.

Barn Street

Formerly also known as Lynch's Street or Hockrill Street. The Old Grammar school towards the bottom of Barn Street was established around 1647, some 150 years after the building was erected. Five Lavenham boys were admitted free. John Constable, the landscape painter, was educated there briefly. The photograph shows the barn, now a private residence, after which the street takes its present name.

Bears Lane

Just off Church Street, the overhanging houses were where a master clothier lived and had his shop of looms. Emblems of the wool trade were there, including the Mitre of St Blaise, fleur-de-lys and spur-rowels. The lane also leads to Meadow Close and Long Meadow.

Bolton Street

Takes its name from Bolton's House, which belonged to John Bolton whose will is dated 1440. The house became the Wesleyan Chapel in 1811, and was demolished in 1911. Also known as Boughton Street and referred to in 1896 as Barbon Street.

Brent Eleigh Road

As the name implies, it leads towards Brent Eleigh from the village. In the sand pits near the road a complete skeleton (*in a crouching posture*) was found under a cairn of stones.

Bridge Street Road

Starts on a bend of Church Street/ Sudbury Road where the Old Police Station once stood (*whose foundations now lie under a garden plot*). Passing a few modern bungalows and the Sports Field, it leads past Slough Farm and then winds over the hills to Bridge Street, on the A134 road between Bury St Edmunds and Sudbury.

Bright's Lane (Drift)

Leading to Brights Farm from Park Road, it may have been Oxford Way (or Road) which joined Bridge Street Road.

Bury Road

Continues from the High Street, over the old railway bridge and on towards Mill Hill and Bury St Edmunds, via the outskirts of Cockfield and Sicklesmere. A lovely house by the name of Fiddler Simpson's is situated just before the high point of the road within the village boundary.

Butfield

Off Melford Road, before Harwood Place. A small development of modern houses, dating from the 1950s.

Church Street

Originally the continuation of High Street, later becoming Church End and then Church Street. The first Grammar School was here, which existed in the reign of Edward IV.

Clay Hill

Leads off Lower Road, just below the Common, across a small bridge over the River Brett.

Constable Court

Off Barn Street, where the old Stocko factory once stood, which has now been converted into residences and offices.

The Common

At the bottom of Water Street. North east of the Common is the entrance to the old brick field where pre-historic remains, fossils, Roman tiles and other Roman relics were found.

Deacons Close

Deacons Close, created in 1999, is on the site of a former coal yard and W.A. Deacons & Sons builders headquarters.

Frogs Hall Road

It takes its name from a medieval farmhouse called Frogs Hall. There is a ford across it.

The Glebe

A modern estate, replacing what was once Glebe Farm and surrounding fields A development of some controversy at the time it was started in the 1980s, it has matured nicely and enjoys some good views, including this one of the church.

It enjoys good green open spaces and, being relatively close to the village centre, is popular.

Green Willows

A relatively modern development, on the outskirts of the village, on the road leading towards Long Melford, just past Harwood Place.

Hall Road

Formerly Hall Street. From the Old Post Office to the junction with Park Road used to be known as Pound Lane. Victorian cottages in Hall Road are pictured here. The Hall itself is a timbered building of several periods, standing on the site of the Saxon Grange, head house of the Manor of Overhall, held by Unwin, in the reign of Edward the Confessor and where the Hall Mote (local court of Justice) was once held.

Harwood Place

Harwood Place is a local authority development along the road leading to Long Melford, just past Artesian Close.

High Street

The main artery of the village, with shops, hotels, galleries, the Pharmacy and the Post Office. The road, originally a track, joined the manors of Overhall and Netherhall. Roman artefacts were found there as recently as 2002 during a house renovation.

The Greyhound, dating from the late 15th century, is where Louis Napoleon stayed on his way to Brettenham Park as a prisoner of war. Numbers 87 and 88 were once the Pig and Whistle inn (a boar being the emblem of the Earls of Oxford and the whistle being the emblem of The Lord High Admiral of England — the 13th Earl of Oxford, Lord of Lavenham Manors 1485, held this office).

Hill Green

Opposite the water tower on the Bury Road, to the north of the village.

Lady Street

Really Our Lady Street, taking its name from the Gild of Our Lady (whose hall is now the Wool Hall, part of The Swan Hotel). Earlier known as Master John's Street and Baber (or Barbour) Street.

There were old Tudor shops at the bottom (now a residence). The Grove, the conjectured head house of Thomas Spring, the Rich Clothier, was where a Roman bath or crypt was discovered in the garden.

Lion Court

Lies off High Street, through an archway by the old Lion Inn.

Long Meadow

Recently built social housing, along Bears Lane and just past Meadow Close.

Lower Road

Passes what used to be the sugar beet factory and Holloways Cosmetics industrial site (which have been replaced by several modern housing developments).

Market Place

Used as a giant car park, and hosts many events, including Farmer's Markets, French Markets, jazz concerts and Morris dancing. Fairs were held here, dating as far back as 1290 and weekly markets. Bull baiting took place every 5th November during the 18th and early 19th centuries.

Market Lane

Leads into the Market Place from the High Street. The old Three Blackbirds Inn, a 15th century building, stands there. The lane is the only one way street in the whole village.

Mayes Farm

Off the Common, at the bottom of Water Street. A modern development.

Meadow Close

Sometimes known as Pit Meadow, Meadow Close is a large post World War II development by the local authority.

Melford Road

Leads off the Sudbury Road and passes in front of Artesian Close, Harwood Place and Green Willows.

Merchants Row

Is at the top end of Water Street, opposite The Swan Hotel. It comprises a group of shops in a delightful row of heavily timbered buildings. Restored from a very parlous state by Mike Hodges.

Mill Hill

On the road leading to Bury St Edmunds, taking its name from windmills that used to stand there. The base of one remains visible there.

Mortlocks

Part of the modern housing development on Lower Road that replaced the Holloway factory site. and where Mortlock's "Shed" once stood.

Norman Way

Leads from the High Street, at the northern end, to Deacons works and other small industries. It was named, I was told, after the route Selina Norman used to take her cows for milking.

Normans

Part of the modern housing development off Lower Road where there used to be Norman family cowsheds.

Park Road

Leading from the village to the site of the de Vere hunting lodge, whose masonry was there in living memory. Lodge Farm is just beyond Park Farm and it is recorded that a Roman urn was found there containing 197 silver denarii of 13 different emperors.

Potlands

Between Hall Road and Church Street. Medieval pottery ovens are behind the Hall, hence the name Potlands.

Prentice Street

A street featuring many angled roofs and houses (plus a lot of overhead wires). It is said that wool apprentices once congregated here. Behind the Angel is the site of the Guildhall of the Holy Trinity, whose charter was dated 1552. At the bottom of the street is Woolstaplers — the front is Tudor — which belonged to the last wool merchant in Lavenham, one Hitchcock. One of the steepest streets in the village, it provides good exercise.

Preston Road

Runs past the site of the Manor House of Nether Hall, which has now been replaced by a modern farmhouse.

Pump Court

A narrow lane running off High Street where there used to be a blacksmiths shop and a large water pump. It was later altered to make way for what is now the Spring Estate.

The Pyghtle *(a.k.a. Pyghtle Terrace)*

Part of the Sudbury road, between the Church and The Glebe

Quakers Yard

Runs off Water Street, half way down. A small development where once stood a carpenters workshop. Earlier it is thought to have been the site of the 'Dissenters Chapel', where Isaac Taylor and family worshipped.

Ropers Court

Leads through an archway, off the High Street, onto an area that formerly included Ropers Factory.

Shilling Street

Named after Shilling Grange, which belonged to John Schylling, whose will is dated 1476. In 1792, Isaac Taylor — father of Ann and Jane Taylor — rented the Grange for £6 p.a. — then later purchased Arundel House next door. Jane Taylor's cottage was built in the garden of Arundel House (but is no longer there, just a plaque on the gate).

Spring Street (Spring Lane, Spring Close)

The Spring Estate is a large modern development that was built between 1959 and 1962 by the local authority.

Station Road

So named as it led towards the railway station, running where numbers 56A to 56D High Street now stand. Later, it was merged into the High Street.

Sudbury Road

Continues from Church Street, leading towards Great Waldingfield and Sudbury.

Tenterpiece

An award-winning sheltered housing development of 1965/71 near the church, where tenter frames once stood.

Trinity Gild

Trinity Gild, another steep road,

Aerial shot of Lavenham, from 'Suffolk from the Air' website — photo by Chris Garnett
© Suffok County Council Education Dept SLAMnet

leads off Lower Road and has a footpath connection to Spring Street.

Water Street

Takes its name from the culverted stream flowing from Potlands spring down the entire length of the street under the houses on the south side. There is excellent pargeting on the Priory, where members of the Copinger family lived in the early part of the 17th century. The de Vere House dates from c1425 and was owned by them until 1671. The White Horse Inn, now residential, was built in 1425. The so-called 'Weavers Cottages' date from c1340.

Weavers Close

Off Lower Road and a relatively modern development.

Village centre from the air, from 'Suffolk from the Air' website — photo by Chris Garnett
© Suffok County Council Education Dept SLAMnet

Lavenham Community Primary School

www.lavenhamschool.org.uk

Currently (2008) Lavenham Community Primary School is owned and run by the Local Education Authority of Suffolk County Council, who decide the policy for admissions to the school. The current catchment area includes Preston St Mary and Kettlebaston. Children are admitted to the school in the year in which they become five. It is quite normal to have a reception year with children who are five at the beginning of the year and some who are not five until they are almost ready to begin year 1.

The school has developed a curriculum that is innovative and creative, relevant to children at differing stages of development. This makes provision to cover all areas of the National Curriculum, with teachers using a two-yearly topic cycle, accounting for mixed age classes and differing abilities.

As the headteacher, Mrs Jan Foster points out, "education is a partnership between home and school and Lavenham school places great emphasis on the partnership with parents and carers."

She goes on to say that the school vision is "to create an environment that

The school logo

inspires and stimulates children to achieve their full potential, enabling them to become confident, caring individuals with a life-long love of learning."

The building, pictured above and below, is a fine example of Victorian architecture, which has been modernised internally to provide a comfortable, bright and spacious learning environment.

The school staff, apart from the headteacher, comprises four teaching staff (classes depend on numbers, in 2008 there were three), one administrative assistant, a bursar, three teaching assistants, one learning support assistant, a caretaker/cleaner, a cleaner, a catering assistant, three midday supervisors and a playleader.

The school governors, apart from the headteacher, include two community governors appointed by the governing body, two representative governors appointed by the local education authority, and five elected governors (four parent governors and one teacher representative).

Children are encouraged to wear school uniform, preferably with the school logo. The school colours are navy, blue and white. There is a Home-School

27

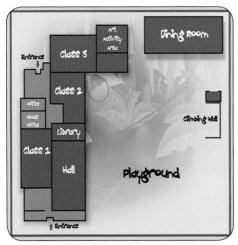

School plan, from their website

One entrance used to be half way down this side of the school.

Agreement, which is requested for every child, between the headteacher and parent/carer.

The school has an excellent brochure for the parents and carers of prospective pupils, which describes — in detail — the school staff, governing body and uniform, plus additional information such as policy for able (outstanding ability) children, accident and injury procedures, attendance, behaviour, internet use, parents' evenings, photo permissions, SATs, transport and welfare.

The school library

All children have regular access to computers in their classrooms, and each classroom is equipped with an interactive whiteboard, used as a teaching aid in a variety of lessons. All computers are linked to the school network, with a secure and monitored internet connection. The school teaches conversational French in Key Stage 2, religious education and sex education (with parent/carer consent), and caters for special educational needs.

Numbers

The school opened as Lavenham Board Schools (note the plural) in 1896, and had the capacity for up to 500 pupils. The builders were Messrs George Grimwood & Sons of Sudbury (who did many of the alterations to The Swan Hotel in the 1950s).

It will be noted that numbers at the school have dropped off markedly since it opened. This is due to a combination of factors, especially the fact that children now leave the school at age 9. The numbers listed on the school roll are:

Sep 2008	72	Dec 1991	58
Jan 2008	72	Apr 1991	80
Dec 2003	52	Mar 1991	78
Apr 2001	44	Mar 1941	299
Jan 2000	50	(Boys 147, Girls 152)	
Jan 1998	51	Jun 1939	184
Jan 1997	60	Mar 1938	200
Oct 1994	60	Sep 1899	473
Jan 1994	68	Sept 1896	415
Apr 1993	71	Mar 1896	210
Jan 1992	63		

Transfers

Transfers are normally made to Stoke-by-Nayland Middle School after leaving Lavenham, though the Middle School system is being abandoned in 2013.

Golden Jubilee scroll and certificate, prepared by the author in 2002

Friends of Lavenham School (FOLS), pictured above, is a group of parents who actively fund-raise for the school, helping to provide equipment, books and social events for the children.

FOLS are very fortunate to have the support of the parents and teachers at the school, as well as the people and businesses in Lavenham. Whether asking for adverts in programmes, raffle prizes, or batches of scones or biscuits they always receive a very positive and generous response.

Recently FOLS have raised money to improve and update the school's IT provision, have contributed to big improvements in the school playground and funded the annual leaver's disco, as well as things like providing crackers for the children's Christmas dinner.

FOLS was originally setup in 1997, to buy playground equipment (the climbing frame that the children still love) and to renovate the old toilet block. That fund raising was such a success that FOLS continued to help raise funds for, and awareness of, the school.

The school hall

The school playground

The school main entrance in Bolton Street

School staff (Mrs Foster, head teacher, on the right) in September 2008

29

Lavenham clubs, societies and charities

At the time of publication a large number of clubs and societies were operating in Lavenham. Some of them are noted here. If any have, inadvertently, been missed the oversight is regretted, and is certainly not deliberate. Some groups are noted elsewhere in the book.

Contact names and numbers for some of these clubs and societies appear monthly in *Lavenham Life*.

Lavenham Art Society

The Society was launched in May 2007 with an Open Art Exhibition, with 291 exhibitors, spinners and weavers from the Lavenham branch and paintings from Lavenham Primary School.

Its aim is to promote the development of and interest in the visual arts, by offering a programme of meetings for like-minded people in a relaxed and friendly atmosphere, in order to gain inspiration from demonstrations given by professional artists.

All meetings are in the Village Hall, with workshops and paintings days outdoors. The Society has a small ad hoc committee of volunteers.

Art for Fun

Run by a teacher on behalf of West Suffolk College Continuing Education Department, it met weekly on Wednesdays in the Village Hall. Students ranged from beginner to experienced and came from Lavenham and many surrounding towns and villages. Operated in Lavenham for some 14 years, though moved to Alpheton recently (hopefully temporarily) due to lack of space in the Village Hall.

Lavenham Badminton Club

Badminton is not a class activity, but an informal group of players who meet every week in the Village Hall.

Lavenham Bird Club

Founded in 1970, the club's aims are:

- To promote the study and enjoyment of birds by members and the general public.
- To assist regional and national organisations in matters affecting conservation of wild life.
- To encourage young people to take an interest in wildlife.

The club has a series of summer and winter programmes and activities. Indoor events are held in The Guildhall — with a small charge for non-members. Summer activities centre around the local area, plus occasional visits to well-know reserves such as Minsmere, Cley and Welney. On the first Saturday of every month the club conducts a survey along the old railway track to Sudbury, with results over the past 13 years being sent to the county recorder. Over 70 different species have been recorded. There is also close liaison with Lavenham Community Primary School and with the Lavenham Community Woodland Project.

Lavenham Bridge Club

The club meets weekly, and has met for many years, at The Swan Hotel.

Lavenham's Cambridge Extra Mural Class

 For over 30 years, Lavenham has held evening classes under the auspices of Cambridge University Institute of Continuing Education, based in Madingley. After trying various locations in the village, the class has settled happily in the splendid new village hall.

The classes, which attract young and old alike, have covered a surprising range of subjects. As always, local history and art are predictably very popular but in recent years subjects have included Astronomy, Genetics, the History of Philosophy, Musical Appreciation, Architecture and Latin. The latest course was the History of the Crime Novel and involved the possibility of writing a crime story oneself.

Most of the class members come from within the village, but courses attract people from villages around and from even further afield for some subjects. The membership currently stands at over 100.

Usually the courses are only held during the winter months. In September 2008 the subject was "The Englishness of English Art" and, for 2009, "European based Architectural History."

Lavenham Camera Club

 The Club's objective is simple — to promote the art of photography in all its forms. The Club meets monthly, in the Village Hall, where members take part in tuition sessions, workshops, talks by guest speakers, competitions, etc. Additionally, members take part in photo trips and visits. Membership is open to any member of the Lavenham or wider community

All aspects of photography, including digital and film technology, computer manipulation, composition, landscape, portraiture, studio work and much more form part of the monthly meetings.

Lavenham Carpet Bowls Club

 Lavenham Carpet Bowls Club (prime mover Brian Lapthorne) offers two weekly sessions, in the Village Hall, to accommodate individual time scales. It is a non-serious group who join in a relaxed, fun-loving, general wit-and-banter, social get-together. All ages are welcome, of any standard, with any disability — no impediments.

To broaden horizons, the club occasionally visit & play "friendlies" with other like minded neighbouring villages. In turn, the club reciprocates with "home" games. The club is a combination of meeting a wider variety of people, learning, and making new friends, and new members are always welcome.

A grant was obtained from the 'Awards for All' lottery fund.

Lavenham Community Council
Registered Charity 1106956

The aims of the Lavenham Community Council (LCC), formed about thirty years ago, are:

- To provide and maintain recreation facilities, playing fields and community centres within the Parish of Lavenham.

- To encourage leisure-time activities in the interests of social welfare for the inhabitants of Lavenham and its immediate neighbourhood.

- To raise funds for carrying out the Council's aims.

LCC is a company limited by guarantee, a non-elected body comprising representatives from the Parish Council, Parochial Church Council, sports clubs and Lavenham residents. The main sources of funds are annual events — the Open (Hidden) Gardens held in June, the Carnival held over the August Bank Holiday weekend and, at one time, the Christmas Street Fayre.

Lavenham Conservative Association

The branch has over 30 active members and meets regularly, visited by the MP whenever possible.

Creative Writing Group

Run, in the Village Hall, by Suffolk County Council Community Learning and Skills Development Section.

Lavenham & District Equestrian Club

www.onesuffolk.co.uk/LDEC

The club's aim is to provide well organised events (*most of which nowadays are based in the parkland of Melford Hall*) for any standard of competitor to come and have a fun day whilst keeping the atmosphere of the 'local show'. There are usually five events a year — open to members and non-members alike. Spectators are always welcome. LDEC was set up about 30 years ago to run horse shows in Lavenham.

Lavenham's Elderflowers

A group of ladies who meet monthly on a purely social basis for general enjoyment and some outings.

The Lavenham Exhibition Endowment
Registered Charity 310469

Young people, who reside in the Parish of Lavenham, may apply for a grant towards their further education, providing they are studying at any place of education, higher than elementary, including an apprenticeship or other professional or technical training.

Written applications must be sent to: The Clerk to The Governors, The Lavenham Exhibition Endowment, 19 Bolton Street, Lavenham CO10 9RG.

Lavenham Exhibition & Museum Trust
Registered Charity 1117997

Lavenham Exhibition & Museum Trust (LEMT) is a charity established to act on behalf of the people of Lavenham, as the trustee body for the many artefacts that have been gifted or loaned to Lavenham Guildhall Museum since its inception in 1971. It reports every year on its activities (usually in the *Lavenham Life* magazine).

The charity trustees are a nominee from Lavenham Parish Council, the chairman of the Museum Committee and two co-opted members.

Much of the collection is displayed in the Guildhall Museum (to which Lavenham residents have free entry) and, by special request, can make available facilities for viewing storeroom items.

LEMT's running costs are largely derived from the National Trust Guildhall Local Committee in recognition of the artefacts that are on public display, and some income has been derived from the sale of publications.

LEMT is always pleased in obtaining (or making copies of) documents and objects so that the archive can become a truly useful resource.

Felting and Weaving for beginners

Run, in the Village Hall, by Suffolk County Council Community Learning and Skills Development Section.

Lavenham 'Flix in the Stix'

 Films, usually in DVD format, are shown on the first Wednesday of every month in the Village Hall. Brian Lapthorne did a training course while the Hall was being built and suggested a connection to the PA system from the back of the Hall would be useful. Carroll Reeve obtained a grant to enable the purchase of a 16 foot remote controlled screen. Other projection equipment, housed at The Quay Theatre in Sudbury, is borrowed from Suffolk Digital Cinema Network, which is funded by Screen East, Suffolk County Council, Babergh and other District Councils. Based on audience requests and media reviews, Brian chooses the films which are hired from Filmbank, with a copyright licence.

The Friends of the Church of St Peter and St Paul, Lavenham

Founded some 50 years ago, the seven strong committee still has active founder members. The Rector is Chairman, the Honorary President is the Lord Bishop of the Diocese of St Edmundsbury and Ipswich, and the Patrons are the Master and Fellows of Gonville and Caius College, Cambridge.

The objects of the Friends are to assist in the maintenance of the fabric of the Church in order to preserve and protect it as a place of worship and to provide or contribute to the provision of such furnishings or equipment as are needed for the fulfilment of the Church's proper or parochial functions.

A sub-committee set up by the Friends raised a substantial sum of money that, with the Parochial Church Council, enabled a major project to be undertaken in the west end of the Church in 2007. This provided a Gift Shop, kitchen and lavatory facilities.

Lavenham Gardening Club

 The Club was originally Lavenham, Preston and District Garden Club, meeting in Preston St Mary. Now that the majority of members are residents of Lavenham, meetings are held in the Village Hall, on the last Tuesday in the month (except December). Average membership is in the region of sixty. The Club is not too professional in its outlook, so meetings are low key, enjoyable and sociable. The year follows a programme of monthly meetings addressed by a speaker, preceded by the usual notices and announcements regarding forthcoming events, plus three or four trips to places of gardening interest. A members-only Produce Show is held in August. The Club participates in community activities, such as the Village Fete, where it regularly has a sale of plants donated by members and a preserves and cakes stall. An annual quiz contest with Thorpe Morieux for a rose bowl is held in the autumn.

Lavenham Guildhall (NT) Local Committee

A group of the 'great and good' of Lavenham who advise the National Trust on the running of the Guildhall

Lavenham Guildhall (NT) Museum Committee

The Guildhall museum (first set up in 1971 to provide added interest for visitors to the building) is maintained by a voluntary group, a sub-committee of the National Trust Local Committee. The group maintains, revises and changes the displays from time to time. Most recently it has researched and mounted a temporary exhibition: 'a Lavenham timeline'. It is hoped that funding can be found to enlarge this into a semi-permanent display, acting as an introduction to Lavenham's history, some aspects of which are more fully covered within the museum itself.

The museum's artefacts and its documentary archive are held in trust, on behalf of the people of Lavenham, by the Lavenham Exhibition and Museum Trust (a registered charity), whose membership includes representatives from the Parish Council and the Guildhall Museum Committee.

Keep Fit 50+

Run by independent tutors on behalf of West Suffolk College. Welcomes a wide variety of ages. Normal comfortable fitness clothing recommended. The cost in 2008 was £39 a term (with reductions for the over 60s).

Lavenham Ladies 21st Luncheon Club

Meet every third Thursday for luncheon. A purely social gathering, and an opportunity for the ladies to dress up. A menu is distributed in advance, usually with four main courses and six desserts. Sometimes a speaker is arranged.

Lavenham Library

The library is operated by Suffolk County Council Library Service, is situated in the Village Hall and is open five days a week (though not all day) — usually Tuesday, Thursday, Friday, Saturday and Sunday. If not in stock, books can be ordered from any library in Suffolk. If not available there, other county libraries are approached and finally the British Library, though a small charge is made for out of county service.

Free public internet access is available, which can be booked or used on a drop-in basis. CDs, DVDs and audio cassettes can be provided on request.

The library also arranges activities for children, including Reading Game, Totrock and Bookstart.

Lavenham Local History Recorder

Suffolk Local History Council (SLHC) administers a Local History Recorders Scheme throughout Suffolk and maintains a network of people in the county to ensure the survival of valuable material for future local historians by:

- Seeing that the present is adequately recorded at local level.
- Being on the look-out for items of historical interest that might be overlooked or lost for ever.

To do this, recorders are asked to note significant happenings in their area, especially the changes going on around them, and also to be on the look-out for older records and to record reminiscences of their area in the past.

The normal arrangement is that the Recorders are asked to keep the collected items at their home, "but the aim is that all material of permanent value will be offered to the County Records Office."

Because we have a museum in Lavenham, SLHC accept that our collection will be deposited there (the Museum

Trust is a 'corporate' — if that is the correct word — member of SLHC). Any queries are answered personally by the Local History Recorder or in the name of the Museum Trust, whichever seems the most appropriate.

Recorders are asked to send in a short report at the end of each calendar year, giving an account of activities in their community and the changes which have taken place. The reports are kept on open shelves in the nearest branch of the Suffolk Record Office. When Recorders resign, the material they have collected is deposited for safe keeping with the Record Office in the name of the Suffolk Local History Council.

Lavenham Natural History Group

 The group was formed in 2001 to organise a series of talks on a variety of natural history topics during the winter months (originally October to March but now October to December and February to April). The talks are held at Lavenham Guildhall and are open to anyone at a modest cost to cover expenses (school students are given free entry). The meetings generally attract between 30 – 40 people, not only from Lavenham but from other villages in the area.

In the summer months the group has merged with the Sudbury Flora Group to carry out a series of weekday evening plant surveys in the district in preparation for a New Flora of Suffolk being prepared by the Suffolk Biological Records Centre in Ipswich. The surveys have also been welcomed by landowners who have been able to use the results to help towards various environmental schemes. In 2008 the group hoped to update earlier work done a decade or more ago and to make extra efforts to completely map the flora of Lavenham itself.

The 2007/8 winter programme included talks on: Butterfly Conservation in Suffolk, British Wildlife and its Conservation, Some Interesting Plants of Suffolk Woods, Joseph Andrews and his herbarium, and Spiders.

Lavenham Neighbourhood Watch

 The scheme was started in 1998 and covers the whole village. A list of names and telephone numbers is included in the village contact page within the monthly *Lavenham Life* magazine, and the scheme constantly seeks additional people to volunteer and help spread important news bulletins around the community.

The Police Direct Leaflet — "What's going on in your neighbourhood? — Get it direct" — is recommended. It encourages individuals to register and receive information about crime and policing issues in the area by email, text and voice messaging, direct from the police. This functions across the county and is FREE. Leaflets are available from the contacts listed, the village library and, of course from the local Police Station in Sudbury.

Information is then received by those registered concerning local crimes, warnings of bogus callers and distraction burglaries, crime reduction advice, details of major traffic disruption, personal safety tips, details of missing persons and latest information from your "Safety Neighbourhood Team."

Lavenham Oddfellows (Babergh Branch)

 They meet at the Village Hall.

The Oddfellows (*originally set up in 1810 to help protect and care for its members at a time when there were no Trade Unions, no welfare state and no NHS*) is a not-for-profit friendly society with members nationwide.

Lavenham Old Codgers

A group of friends who get together once a year and organise a rally to raise funds for charity.

Lavenham Over 60s Friendship Club

Meetings are held in the downstairs room of Royal British Legion Club on alternate Tuesdays, in the afternoon. New members are welcome at any time.

The club, which is affiliated to Age Concern, raises funds by 'bring and buy' sales and raffles at their meetings. Sums raised go to charity. Membership in 2008 was 39, both ladies and gentlemen. Meetings start with club business, notices of planned outings, news of events in and around our village, news of friends who are sick and others that may need a helping hand. Then there is a guest speaker. Tea and biscuits follow with time to chat and socialise. Members birthdays are remembered and those who are sick. Outings are organised and there is a Christmas lunch. All functions are subsidised by the revenue created by the club, which is entirely self-supporting.

It is, indeed, a friendship club reaching out to all over 60s in the community and beyond. The community bus does an excellent job in bringing disabled and housebound members to meetings to enjoy an afternoon that could otherwise be lonely.

Pilates

Weekly classes in the Village Hall.

Lavenham Royal British Legion

"If not for them who fought and fell
What would life hold today?
That we might live in peace and love
They gave their yesterday"

 The Royal British Legion (RBL) building stands back from the High Street, down a narrow lane between St Pauls Hall and a shop. It was founded in Lavenham in 1928. A wall plaque in the club room shows all the names of the men who worked so hard to form the branch and club. In 2008 there were some 160 members (people do not have to be ex-service to join).

 The women's section was inaugurated in 1945. They hold meetings monthly, with invited speakers and demonstrators, quizzes and — once a year — a cheese and wine party. The section works to raise money for benevolent funds. The main business concerns ex-service women and young widows with children who need help.

The RBL Lavenham Branch at Church

The branch fills shoe boxes to be sent to troops in Iraq and Afghanistan, who are very grateful. The branch also collects for the Poppy Appeal, has done so since 1945, and many members have received awards for this.

The Poppy Appeal is closely identified with Remembrance Day (always the second Sunday in November). The annual appeal takes place during Remembrancetide, traditionally the 13 days before Remembrance Day. By donating to the appeal, people all over the world are able to express, in a practical way, their sense of commitment to the welfare of ex-Service men and women, widows and dependants who are disabled or in need.

Lavenham Rambling Club

Founded in 1989, the club has as its object the pursuit of good health whilst enjoying the beauty of the countryside with its wild plants, animals and birds.

Anyone is welcome to join in the walks. The club has tended to widen its membership over the years, so that it now has walkers from surrounding villages and the town of Sudbury. Regular members now number about 50 but others come along occasionally. A link has been formed with another group based in Leavenheath.

Rambles usually take place on alternate Sunday afternoons throughout the year and normally last for about 2 hours over a 4 or 5 mile route. Members take turns to lead walks which they have previously reconnoitred to check for obstructions or dangers. Numbers on any particular walk can vary from a handful to as many as high 30s.

The programme of walks is posted or emailed to all members and is displayed on the Community Council notice board and listed in the parish magazine.

Lavenham Scottish Country Dancers

This group meets every Monday evening, in the Village Hall, during the winter. Beginners are very welcome to join the group of varied talents.

1st Lavenham Scouts

www.lavenhamscouts.org.uk

Meetings are on Friday evenings in the Village Hall. Scouts are for boys and girls from 10 to 14, Cubs for boys and girls from 8 to 10 and Beavers for boys and girls 6 to 7.

Silk, Ceramic and Glass Painting Group

Run, in the Village Hall, by Suffolk County Council Community Learning and Skills Development Section.

Lavenham Sinfonia

www.lavenham-sinfonia.co.uk

 Leader Jessie Ridley and Conductor Frederick Marshall founded the Sinfonia in 1979 as a small string orchestra and it quickly expanded it into a full symphony orchestra. Further information is shown in the Events section of this book.

The Lavenham Society

The Lavenham Society aims to obtain early knowledge of development proposals, to consider their impact and to give effective expression to reasonable observations and objections about such proposals which may present a threat and on which local opinion may not have been consulted; to encourage good standards of planning and architecture within the Lavenham area; to establish good working contacts with local government at parish and district levels and with other amenity bodies whilst retaining its independence to promote the views of Lavenham people. The Executive Committee meets approximately four times a year in the Guildhall and the AGM is in February.

Lavenham Table Tennis Group

An informal group who meet from time to time in the Village Hall.

Taoist Tai Chi

Classes run weekly in the Village Hall by the British Association of Taoist Tai Chi.

Lavenham & District Theatre Group

 The group was formed several years ago and has grown to about 200 members of all ages, with a wide variety of tastes in theatre, opera and ballet. They pay a nominal annual subscription. The group's aim is to encourage theatre going to local theatres by coach from Lavenham Market Place and visits a dozen or more evening or matinee events each year. Travel by comfortable coach is welcomed by members who do not drive long distances or at night, and car parking problems are avoided. The group is particularly attractive to single members who enjoy the company of others on these outings. Many popular events have to be booked well in advance — for example, those for "Carmen" at the Albert Hall in 2009, "in the round", had to be finalized in May

2008. The Group A.G.M. in March is always very well attended, and offers entertainment and refreshments, elects officers and confirms the choice of events recommended by the Committee. Proposals from members for possible theatrical events are always welcomed.

Watercolour Workshop

Run by a teacher on behalf of West Suffolk College Continuing Education Department. A chance for people to learn techniques and to build up to proficiency. Participants range from beginner to experienced. Ran in Lavenham for some seven years, though moved to Alpheton recently (hopefully temporarily) due to lack of space in the Village Hall programme.

Weight Watchers

This group meets weekly, in the evening, in the Village Hall

Lavenham Women's Institute

 Lavenham W.I. was re-formed in 2007 after a break of several years. The first President of the re-formed W.I. was Marjorie King (a retired Health Visitor for Lavenham and resident in the village) . Meetings take place on the first Monday of each month, in The Guildhall.

Women's Royal Voluntary Service

 The W.R.V.S., together with Suffolk County Council, organise the Meals on Wheels Service in Lavenham. Meals can be delivered every day to eligible recipients. This service is supported by a dedicated group

of volunteers who provide drivers and helpers twice a week throughout the year, many of whom have assisted for a great number of years.

The At Home Library Service (AHLS) is organised by the W.R.V.S. on behalf of Suffolk County Libraries. Currently there are two AHLS groups operating in Lavenham. One group serves residents of Cockfield and the residents of the sheltered accommodation in Tenterpiece, where a selection of books is taken fortnightly for the residents to make their choice. Once a month the other group takes, to the homes of individual clients, a selection of books, which have been chosen according to the individuals expressed preferences. From those, the clients make their selection of which books they wish to have on loan until the next AHLS visit. This group visits four residents of Lavenham, one in Monks Eleigh and twelve in Laxfield House, the residential care home in Brent Eleigh

Lavenham Woodland Project

A Trust set up to plant and maintain Dyehouse Field Wood (see separate article). They enjoy close relations with the Parish Council, who provide some financial support. They also have generous support from Mr David and the late Mrs Pauline Norman.

The trust initiated a Dawn Walk in 2007, and attended a Babergh District Council training day introducing new systems to support community charities such as the Woodland Project. They also attended discussions with Suffolk County Council, Babergh District Council and the Green Light Trust on alternative developments in the management of Lavenham's Railway Walk.

Good relations have been established with the class teachers at Lavenham Primary School. The Cubs, too, are being introduced to the woodland.

Woolcombers Bridge Club, Lavenham

Rubber bridge is played on Tuesday evenings, singles welcome. Membership is available on a limited basis.

Yoga

Run by independent tutors on behalf of West Suffolk College. Welcomes a wide variety of ages. Normal comfortable fitness clothing recommended. Cost in 2008 was £59 a term (with reductions for the over 60s).

Lavenham Youth Club

 An active club, run by volunteers, with two groups. One meets on the first Monday of the month and the other weekly on Thursdays. Additional leaders are always welcome, as the club currently has nearly 40 members.

Activities include adventure games, rounders, table tennis, craft work, pool, table football, theatre visits, circus trick training, drama workshops. A tuck shop operates each week. The club has also run a stall at the Carnival and been bowling in Sudbury. There are end-of-term party nights with karaoke

Sunset over Lavenham

39

Lavenham Guild of Weavers, Spinners and Dyers

Lavenham Guild of Weavers, Spinners and Dyers (LGWSD) — some 40 persons from a wide area around Lavenham — are affiliated to the Association of Weavers, Spinners and Dyers, whose objectives are the preservation and improvement of the craftsmanship in hand weaving, spinning and dyeing for the benefit of the public and the promotion of public education in such craftsmanship..

'Lavenham Blue'. Today indigo is normally used to produce the colour, though in the 14th and 15th centuries woad was used.

LGWSD are a small 'doing' Guild with no fixed programme of speakers. They arrange special interest events and workshops, not necessarily directly connected with weaving, spinning and dying but all textile related and, more importantly, fun! Meetings are held in the Guildhall or the Village Hall, with Open Days in March, June and September for The National Trust in the Guildhall.

More and more spinners seem to be coming forward (and beginners are welcome), probably because knitting is fashionable again. Members say that weaving, spinning and dyeing is very relaxing and a great social activity.

Some members have sheep, some have a business, but none make a living out of these weaving, spinning or dyeing skills, although some of their work is sold. There has been a dramatic decrease in the demand for wool in this country and consequently fleeces are very easy to come by from local farmers, many of whom keep rare breed sheep.

The Guild exhibit and demonstrate at local country shows, including Lavenham Carnival, where members of the public can see the crafts in action or try their hand at spinning and weaving.

There are a number of ways of weaving, including Card weaving, Inkleloom, Pegloom, Tapestry, Stick weaving, Rigid heddle loom, Table and Floor loom, normally with four or eight shafts and Tablet weaving.

'The Four Seasons of Suffolk' tapestry — presented by the Guild to the Village Hall

Flyer spinning wheel

Four shaft table loom with stand

The flyer spinning wheel is the most commonly used today but drop spindles are also popular. Great wheels, an example of which can be seen in the Guildhall museum, are used less often due mostly to their size. There are many different makes and models of new spinning wheels available costing up to £1,000 but a new spinner can buy a second-hand wheel and associated equipment for around £200.

Dyeing gives a new colour or tinge to material. Natural dyes are derived mostly from plant sources — leaves, flowers, fruits, barks or heartwood chips, though some insects (e.g. Cochineal) can be used, and soil pigments. Many require a mordant to enable the dye to be accepted by the fibres. Apart from natural dyes there are many different types of synthetic dyes available today that are easier to use and do not require mordants. The colours are not quite so subtle but with careful mixing a wide range of colours can be achieved.

Spinners and Dyers have woven two pieces for the Guildhall, one of which hangs in in the entrance. The other hangs in the tea room and was commissioned to celebrate the millennium. A wide range of fibres was used to depict the progress of yarn production over the years — cotton, linen, wool, horsehair, nylon, metal, silk and recycled polythene bottles. Another piece woven by the Guild hangs in the St Peter and St Paul room in the Village Hall, to mark its opening.

Tapestry by the LGWSD in the Guildhall tea room

Four shaft loom

Lavenham Guild of Weavers,

Inkle loom

Lavenham II bookmark, by Alison Swann

41

The rear of Bakers Mill, from Bolton Street

The rear of the Guildhall

Suffolk Preservation Society

www.suffolksociety.org.uk

The Suffolk Preservation Society (SPS), established in 1929, is the county branch of the Campaign to Protect Rural England. Little Hall is the home of its Director and staff. Although East Anglia is one of the most rural regions in England, the traditional rural-based system has changed vastly in the last forty or fifty years.

The Society works to protect and enhance the countryside, towns and villages of Suffolk. It has volunteers in the Districts with a Chartered Planner at Little Hall in Lavenham. They combine effective local action through the planning system with the promotion of building conservation projects, encouragement for sustainable planning, and campaigns and awards which support this ethos.

The Society is currently campaigning to ensure that the planning system is more reflective of what local communities want and need, rather than it being a delivery mechanism for national and regional government.

These issues include:

- Affordable Housing — The Exemplar Affordable Housing Project — Elmswell
- Review on local Government
- Challenging Aspirations on Design
- Climate Change — reducing our carbon footprint

Richard Ward

Richard, the Director of the Society, came to Suffolk some 20 years ago and has been working from the Society's offices in Little Hall, Lavenham, since 2003. As a former Conservation and Design Officer with Babergh District

Council, he knows Lavenham well and is acutely aware of the importance of preserving the best without setting things in aspic. Richard says "Shaping the future of Suffolk as well as respecting the past is the key to the Society's work." A small number of staff combined with many dedicated volunteers help to deliver the Society's work.

Richard Ward

photo Archant Suffolk /East Anglian Daily Times

Some of Richard's quotes (as recently published in *The Mercury*), include:

- "The bar of gaining planning permission is very low and we want to encourage developers to raise that bar. It's important that Suffolk retains its character and avoids looking like any other county."
- "It's important that town planners visit the towns they're responsible for and walk about to get a feel for the place. You can't appreciate a town from an office miles away." Suffolk Preservation Society regularly runs workshops and training days for its members, town and parish councils and amenity society members. It does this as it believes "the more people involved in planning that understand the process and procedures, the better chance they have of securing what they want from it."

Richard is keenly aware of the controversy surrounding the recent redecoration of Little Hall, using limewash, but insists that it is in the best long term maintenance interests of the building.

43

Lavenham Merchants' Guild

www.discoverlavenham.co.uk

Lavenham Merchants' Guild has been much more active this century than in the recent past and works hard for the village as a whole and its members. It has also set up the new village website.

The Guild's aims are:

- Promoting Guild members' businesses as widely as possible.
- Speaking for members with one voice on issues affecting their business and the village.
- Ensuring that members' business activities have a desirable impact on the village.

In 2008 there were 46 members, with a rateable value of over half a million pounds, ranging from one-man niche businesses to businesses employing substantial numbers of people, including hotels, inns, restaurants, B&B and self-catering accommodation, galleries, gift shops, clothes shops, professional services (computer services, photographic studio, estate agents, insurance agents and builders), antique shops, a pharmacy, tearooms, a specialist tea supplier and an outdoor clothing supplier.

 The Guild publishes thousands of copies of leaflets, publicising the village and members' businesses, issues newsletters (with copies to the press), provides identifying window stickers, arranges concerts and the French Markets and supports other village activities including, when possible, contributions to Lavenham School and Lavenham Church.

Tim West, the Chairman (since 2005), said: " The Merchants' Guild provides a wonderful pool of talent and experience to pull together for the benefit of all businesses, which are the life blood of modern Lavenham. As well as standing up for the interests of the businesses, the Guild has brought all sorts of exciting events to the village in recent years.

These include a regular French and Continental Market (the first proper use of the Market Place for over a generation), arts festivals with open air concerts and

Lavenham Merchants' Guild Committee at work, 28th August 2008

(left to right) Mike Hodges, Lavenham Photographic Studio [who took this photograph]; Dinah James, Erindor B&B; Bob Notley, Lavenham Cottages; Tim West [Chairman], Sworders Estate Agents; Tony Hepworth, Hepworth Computer Services; Philip Gibson, Angel Gallery and Angel Gallery B&B; Roy Whitworth [Treasurer].

drama and concerts in the wonderful historic church with leading names such as renowned cellist Julian Lloyd Webber, and star jazz singer/songwriter Clare Teal

(three times) who now also presents Big Band Special on BBC Radio. The Guild also provides a wonderful forum for people to get to know each other and for new arrivals to make friends in the village."

Other artists who have performed at concerts organised by the Guild include well-known organist Carlo Curley, the Deutz Trio, Jacqui Dankworth, jazz band Sax Appeal, Anna Calder-Marshall in 'The Wild Girl' and Elizabeth Norman in 'Anne of Cleves', Heartbreak Productions performed Shakespeare's 'Comedy of Errors' and 'Macbeth', Hatfields of Colchester Band played in the Market Place and there were very interesting talks by Leigh Alston and Brian Hicks.

Danielle Perrett, who lives locally, who is one of Great Britain's leading harpists, featured in two concerts run in conjunction with The Swan Hotel.

Harpist Danielle Perrett

LMG leaflet 2004
70,000 copies

LMG leaflet 2005
75,000 copies

LMG leaflet 2006
80,000 copies

LMG leaflet 2007
100,000 copies

Each of the above leaflets was prepared by the author

Programme covers for concerts in the church arranged by Lavenham Merchants' Guild

Lavenham Merchants' Guild contribute towards a whiteboard in Lavenham School

45

Lavenham hostelries and restaurants

Lavenham today enjoys a wide variety of excellent hotels, pubs and restaurants. There used to be at least nine pubs (some say 15), though many of them are now converted to other uses. Along with hotels and restaurants, those pubs open today are listed first, followed by some brief details of former premises.

The Angel Hotel

www.maypolehotels.com/angelhotel

Operated by The Maypole Group.

 The Angel has a large bar (open all day), serving a wide range of beers, wines, whiskies and other beverages. The restaurant menu changes daily, with food prepared on the premises, using locally purchased ingredients wherever

 possible. Seating is available at the front outside, giving great views of the Market Place and Guildhall. There are eight en-suite bedrooms (6 doubles, 1 twin and 1 family room). The residents sitting room has a splendid pargetted solar ceiling

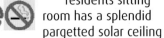

(probably early 17th century) and there is a large patio/garden at the rear. Free wireless broadband is available. The Angel was the first pub/hotel in Lavenham to go completely 'non-smoking', on 1st January 2004. The hotel, first licensed in 1420, is believed to be Lavenham's oldest inn. Much altered over the centuries, The Angel retains much of its Tudor character. In 1527 it is said to have belonged to Thomas Sexton.

The Cock Inn

 The pub (which is a free house) has two bars, a large restaurant and two gardens. The present building replaced an earlier one, destroyed by fire in 1950, which was much nearer the road. The front was plastered and the appearance much improved later on. Some believe that the name relates to the fact that the pub stands where an enterprising landlord

 used to hire out a horse to assist heavy loads coming up Church Street — hence a 'Cock' Horse. This was reflected in the sign that stood outside until recent times. The current sign shows a cockerel, said to relate to cock fighting once held nearby.

The Greyhound

 The Greyhound has two bars, a restaurant, a beer garden and patio area. The front of the pub (which is a Greene King establishment) has been extensively restored. Pub food is served in the bar and restaurant. There is a beer garden. Built in the late 1300s, Louis Napoleon is said to have stayed there on his way to internment in Brettenham Park.

Memsaab of Lavenham

www.memsaaboflavenham.co.uk

 The latest addition to Lavenham's restaurant scene is an Indian restaurant — as the name might suggest — which opened in 2007. Well situated near the corner of Water Street and Church Street. Apart from lunch and dinner, it offers a takeaway service.

Former premises included:

The Anchor

It was originally known as the Crown & Anchor and was probably, at one time, a Greene King pub. It closed in 1952 and is now a residence.

The Black Lion

Closed in the 1920s as a pub/hotel, it is now a residence. There are some carved beams in front and on the gables, once overhanging, some exquisite examples of pargeting. A band of fleur-de-lys is over the downstairs windows. The building operated as a greengrocers shop up to the 1950s and during World War II was the HQ of the local Home Guard. Later, up to the 1960s, it was King's Garage and taxi service.

The One Bell

This pub is thought to have been on the side of the High Street building known as One Bell, until recently a shop. It closed as a pub probably in the 19th century, though exact details are not known.

The Pig and Whistle

This pub closed about 1860 and is now a residence. The name probably derives from the sign of the de Vere family (a boar) and the whistle, sign of the Lord High Admiral, once a certain Earl of Oxford, a de Vere.

The Three Blackbirds

Now a residence. There is some difference of opinion over whether it was called The Blackbirds or The Three Blackbirds. Known to have been operating in the early 1730s.

The White Horse — Water Street

Built in the early 1400s, it closed as a pub around 1980. Like other buildings in Water Street the old brick water culvert runs underneath it. The building is now a private residence.

Jim Robinson's interesting book, *Lavenham's Pubs, Inns and Beer Houses, Past & Present*, published in 2006 and available at the Tourist Information Centre, gives further details.

The Great House

www.greathouse.co.uk

Often referred to as a little bit of France, nestling in England, The Great House is a multi award-winning restaurant with rooms. The restaurant offers superb modern cooking served with warmth by a young French staff,

at very competitive prices. The French cuisine is outstanding, with inspired flavours and textures using locally sourced seasonal ingredients.

The restaurant

a boutique five-star hotel. The ancient timbers of this 15th century building are retained and blend well with muted colours and modern art. Each room is elegant and unique with the finest bed linen and mini-bar, espresso machine, plasma screen TV, wifi, complimentary fruit and a welcoming decanter of sherry.

It was in 1985 that Régis and Martine Crépy, the current owners, converted the house into a restaurant, with the five bedrooms being opened in 1986. Both of them trained at the University of Lausanne, in Switzerland, the finest hotel and catering university in the world.

The Great House today is considered to be one of the best places to eat out in

The new Great House frontage in 2008

A stunning face-lift to the restaurant and rooms took place in January 2008 and the restrained, modern elegance that has resulted is a testament to the foresight and taste of the owners. The new look with wooden floors, comfortable leather chairs and white clad tables creates a distinctive yet relaxed atmosphere.

 The five handsome bedrooms offer sophisticated contemporary chic with taste and comfort. Each bedroom is en-suite, of course, with its own bathroom and four of the rooms have seating or a separate lounge. All are sleekly designed, light and elegant with the cosseting luxury of

The patio — for outdoor dining

One of the bedrooms

East Anglia — an opinion shared by the *Which? Good Food Guide* who rated The Great House 'East of England Restaurant of the Year 2009'. It was also voted the Great Britain & Ireland's 'Best Restaurant with Rooms of the Year 2009' in *The Good Hotel Guide*.

The Great House was built in the 14th and 15th centuries by the Caustons, an important family of clothiers. The house had its imposing Georgian facade added in the 18th century to keep up with the times. In the 1930s, along with Little Hall next door, it was restored to much of its original splendour by Colonel Gayer-Anderson, who sold it separately in 1938. Famous people have lived at The Great House, including the poet Stephen Spender in the late 1930s with his brother Humphrey and the writer Christopher Bush, known for his numerous detective novels, who lived there 20 years until his death in 1973.

The Swan Hotel

www.theswanatlavenham.co.uk

(Operated by Thorpeness and Aldeburgh Hotels Limited)

Today, The Swan is a quintessential English country hotel and restaurant, proud of its achievement of an AA four star 81% rating and two AA Rosettes.

Ancient oak beams and inglenook fireplaces blend beautifully with rich furnishings and fabrics to create the perfect ambiance for rest and relaxation.

Michael Burn, the current General Manager, previously with THF, Choice Hotels and The Moat House at Cambridge, likes the informal, relaxed nature of the village and feels at home. He has renovated all the bedrooms, doubled the garden in size and plans a possible change of the reception area.

The hub of the hotel is the historic Old Bar, once the haunt of RAF and 487th Bomb Group 8th AAF American servicemen who were stationed in Lavenham during WWII. Memorabilia

The hotel layout

remains in the form of cap badges and a collection of signatures that can be found on the wall next to The Boot Record. The latter records the names of servicemen who had successfully drunk 3½ pints of ale from a boot shaped glass in the shortest time, the record being 40 seconds! The servicemen had painted a nude pin-up girl on the ceiling, but this was prudishly painted over after the war. The floor of The Old Bar is made of bricks brought to Lavenham after being used as ballast on the old wool ships. Above the bar is a set of bells, used by Lavenham's renowned bells ringers, but sadly no longer in use.

The Swan was built in about 1400 and comprises three houses dating from the same era. The oldest part dates back to

The Swan Hotel exterior front

the late 14th Century. It is not known when conversion to an Inn took place, but it was well established by 1667, when the then Landlord, John Girling, issued a 'Trader's Token'. The Gurling family still live in Lavenham.

In 1830, The Swan was a flourishing trade post and had stabling for fifty horses. At that time, the Inn consisted of no more than the gabled part at the corner where Water Street enters the High Street. At that time, it was known as The Capital Old-established Free Public and Posting House. The entrance, which is now used for deliveries, led to the stables and was built just high enough to take the baggage wagons. A coach — known as the Lavenham Machine — operated three days a week between London's Gracechurch Street and Lavenham.

The Wool Hall, a former guild hall built in 1464, was used for trading cloth and was divided into three houses when the cloth industry went into decline. It was dismantled in 1911 and there were plans to re-erect it in Ascot, but its fate was saved by the Rev. Henry Taylor, who was determined to preserve Lavenham. The Wool Hall was re-erected in its original position and became a convalescent home for railway women. It was bought in 1963 and incorporated into The Swan.

Afternoon tea in the garden

The main restaurant

Above — the Old Bar, Below — Old Bar memorabilia

One of the lounges

One of the bedrooms

51

Lavenham businesses

There are well over 100 'rated' businesses in Lavenham at the time of writing. Some are included here and some elsewhere (*for various reasons*) and some businesses appear separately, rather than in the alphabetical section.

Any omissions are entirely inadvertent.

 Current members of Lavenham Merchants' Guild are shown by the LMG logo.

Adonis Ecology Ltd

A rapidly growing business, offering ecology services to businesses and individuals, particularly developers, throughout the UK. The company helps clients comply with wildlife legislation and policies and enhance biodiversity where possible.

David Alexander

Portrait photographer.

Antique Renovations

Experts in antique furniture renovations.

Beauty Gallery

Electrolysis and beauty salon. Gifts for all occasions.

Blocks Meadow Joinery

Carpenters and joiners.

Brett Farm B&B

www.brettfarm.com

A riverside bungalow about five minutes walk from the village centre.

Burnerserve

Central Heating installation, systems, repairs and services and boilers and radiators servicing.

ByChoice Estate Agents

www.bychoice.co.uk

 One of the fastest growing Estate Agents in East Anglia, selling quality homes across South Suffolk from five prominently located offices (one of which is in the centre of Lavenham).

Byes Barn B&B

www.byesbarn.co.uk

 Bed and breakfast in a beautifully converted barn with original features and exposed beams. Accommodation is a double room with private bathroom and full English breakfast is served.

Bruce Casey

Specialist building services. The owner has extensive experience of work on older properties in the village.

Paul Charles Recruitment Ltd

Executive search and selection.

Chilli & Chives

Offers a wide range of freshly prepared food made with quality ingredients.

Soups, patés, main courses, desserts, cakes, snacks and sandwiches, all ready to take home. Kitchen essentials, plus culinary gifts and utensils. Coffee/tea & snacks.

J.R. Clare

Underwriting agency.

Clark & Willcocks

Estate agents, surveyors and letting agents.

Cloud Nine

Hairdesser.

Coco — Shilling Street

www.coconuthouse.co.uk

Coco has been established since 1999 and specialises in decorative lighting including a fine range of quality lamp bases and beautiful lampshades in both contemporary and traditional designs. Moved to Lavenham from Long Melford in 2008.

Computer Systems & Software

Home and business IT support.

Curiosity Corner

www.curiosity-corner.com

Probably East Anglia's leading bear and doll shop, with over 1,000 pieces in store, including Steiff, Deans, Rubin Rive, Hermann, etc. The shop is spread over two floors. Gifts include Moorcroft pottery, silver items, jewellery and bags.

D & G Fayers & Son

Pet foods, animal and wild bird food, soft water salt, compost, Calor gas, LPG, wood and coal. Delivered locally.

Dallmer

Drainage wholesalers.

R. Darvell

Upholstery specialists.

Elizabeth Gash Knitwear

 Beautiful silk and lambswool knitwear designed and made in Suffolk, together with knitwear by other leading British designers and a comprehensive range of exclusive linen clothes.

Erindor B&B

www.erindor.co.uk

 Your host is a Blue Badge guide offering B&B in an 1820s house on the High Street. A minute away from The Guildhall and all amenities.

Grannies Attic

An Aladinn's cave of china, glass, metal ware, small furniture and so on. A cornucopia of gifts, collectables and crafts.

The Guildhall Tea Room

An excellent tea room.

Guinea House B&B

www.guineahouse.co.uk

 Very comfortable accommodation in a heavily beamed Grade II mediæval house, formerly a village doctor's house.

Tim Harbord Associates

Town planning consultants.

A.R. Heeks & Son

One of Lavenham's oldest established family businesses. A traditional grocers offering cheeses, bacon, confectionery, cooked meats, general groceries and an Off Licence section. John Heeks and staff provide a great local service.

It is the local National Lottery outlet.

Hepworth Computer Services

www.hepworth-computer-services.co.uk

 Combines desktop publishing, membership services, payroll agency, genealogical charting and typesetting with consultancy in human resource development, training and small business computing.

Publishers of this book and of the Lavenham Tourist Guide, on sale — like the book — at the Tourist Information Centre, the Guildhall bookshop, the Church gift shop, The Chapter House and other outlets.

Hogg@Home

A large china and glass store (*previously known as Martin Hogg's China Shop*) with many other dining, living and giving items, on the High Street.

Hour Cottage

www.hourcottage.co.uk

 A 4* Grade II listed Victorian cottage, now a B&B. Fully renovated and beautifully furnished throughout. Original features boast character and charm, giving a warm, cosy atmosphere to the property.

Instepshoes

Shoes and accessories.

J & J Baker Antiques

www.jandjbaker.co.uk

 One of England's leading general dealers, specialising in quality antiques (mainly English). Has 18th and 19th century furniture, oils and watercolours, collectors items, silver, metalware and 19th century English porcelain.

Kazuri

www.kazuribeads.co.uk

 Their hand-painted ceramic jewellery is made in Kenya. Every bead which makes up a necklace or bracelet is shaped by hand by one of the 300 local women employed by Kazuri (which means small and beautiful in Swahili).

Kemp's Printing Service

Stationery, printing and electrical. A long established local company.

Lavenham Army Surplus

http://armysurplusandcampingstores.tripod.com

 A retail shop with an unlimited supply of Army surplus and a wide range of camping equipment.

Lavenham Co-op

We are extremely fortunate here in Lavenham to have an excellent store that opens seven days a week (0700 to 2200 on Mondays to Saturdays and 0800 to 2100 on Sundays). It is a food retailer with Fairtrade goods, healthy options, fruit, vegetables and frozen/chilled foodstuffs. It also sells newspapers, wine and household products.

Usually has a good selection of flowers and cards and bakes a wide variety of bread products daily.

Lavenham Cottages

www.lavenhamcottages.co.uk

 Lavenham Cottages and The Hayloft are Grade II listed luxury 5 star self catering cottages situated in the heart of the village, overlooking the Market Place.

Lavenham Joinery

 Specialists in hand crafted kitchens, bathroom and bedroom units.

MLJ Associates

 Architects, specialising in residential, hotels and restaurant work, house extensions, barn conversions and miscellaneous renovations.

Services include dimensional surveys and survey drawings, conditional surveys, statutory consent applications, tender invitations, design coordination, contractor appointments and construction contract administration

Munnings Tea Rooms

www.munningstearoom.co.uk

 A traditional tea room in a lovely period setting. Offers fresh home baking using organic ingredients. B&B facilities.

Newman (Butcher)

P.C. Hobbs trading as Newmans. Apart from the main business of butchery, it is also a coffee shop, delicatessen, internet cafe and greengrocery provider.

NFU Mutual

www.nfumutual.co.uk/lavenham

 The firm insures commercial organisations, from business to fleet insurance to risk management services. The Lavenham branch is an agent of The National Farmers Union Mutual Insurance Society Limited.

G.S. Parker Construction

Groundworks company specialising in agricultural projects.

Pauline's Poky Parlour

Surely one of the most mysterious names of shops in the village. It is actually a ladies dress shop.

Process Instrument Sales Ltd

Distributors of process instrumentation.

Renaissance Coffee House

Coffee and snacks. B&B en-suite room.

Dr Rolfe & Associates

 Provides dental implants, tooth whitening, root fillings and general dental surgery.

Solitaire

Ladies and gentlemen's hairdressers and beauty salon.

Sparling & Faiers

A long established family and village business. Bakers and confectioners with a steady customer base.

Spirit of the Andes

www.spiritoftheandes.co.uk

 On the High Street, a specialist shop offering finest knitted products from Peru and Bolivia.

Sweetmeats

Sweets, chocolates and ice creams.

The Wool Room

Exclusive handmade designer knitwear in natural colours.

Tickled Pink Tea Room

 A 15th century building with original features, on two floors. Serves light snacks, home-baked cakes and hot & cold drinks.

The Timbers

An antiques & collectables centre on the High Street, with an interesting and ever-changing range of quality antiques and collectables. Over 40 dealers show there. It is open seven days a week.

Tudor Landscapes of Lavenham

All aspects of landscaping, working with you to create your ideal garden from design to completion.

Tudor Rose

One of East Anglia's leading florists. The owners specialise in cutting edge floristry, sourcing the best quality Dutch flowers coupled with regular buying trips to Belgium, Germany and Holland.

Vestry Tearoom & Bistro

Tea room and bistro. Sunday lunches.

Victoria Cottage

www.victoriacottage-lavenham.co.uk

A Grade II listed, beautifully refurbished cottage, sleeping 2–6. Centrally heated, it has a well equipped kitchen, two double bedrooms, TV and a pretty garden, with cot and bikes available.

~~Vintage Pink~~ The Village Fete

Renamed late in 2008, offers general giftware with a country feel, and a particular interest in children's items, "gifts inspired by life in the country."

Vintage Pink ~~2~~

Ladies wear and jewellery and accessories. Beautiful clothing with a vintage twist. Renamed late 2008.

W.A.Deacon & Sons Ltd

The company provides a full range of building services, specialising in timber renovations, property refurbishment and new builds, both domestic and commercial. Recent contracts include the refurbishment of the new Pharmacy in Lavenham. William Amos Deacon founded the family firm in the early 1950s. Employing local tradesmen, they carried out a wide range of building work using traditional methods and materials. When "Bill" retired in the early 1980s the firm was taken over by his two sons David and Roger and the business became a limited company in 1988. The company moved to its present offices and workshops in 1998.

W.A.Deacon Funeral Services

Provides high class funeral services. Has a small Chapel of Rest plus three refrigerator spaces.

The Wildlife Art Gallery

www.wildlifeartgallery.com

Housed in a former (but beautifully altered) cinema and shooting range on the High Street, the gallery was opened in 1988 to specialise in 20th Century and contemporary wildlife art. Over the years they have held retrospective exhibitions by artists such as Peter Scott, Eric Ennion, Donald Watson and R.B.Talbot Kelly and have had exhibitions by many of the best artists working both here and in Europe.

They also have a strong representation of paintings depicting the countryside, its landscape and work. Epitomising these have been exhibitions by artists George Soper and Harry Becker.

48 Water Street B&B

An attractive and selective B&B in a former butcher's shop.

Angel Gallery

www.angelgallerylavenham.co.uk

Angel Gallery, in the Market Place, is a 15th century Grade II wool merchant's residence, with a wealth of oak beams, overlooking the Guildhall. It is both a gallery and a B&B.

The gallery, a splendid beamed area with historic arches, houses exhibitions by local, national and international artists.

Permanent collections are held of the work of Leslie Gibson ARCA (1910-1969) and costume drawings from the 1930s by Mary Wild ARCA. Signed exhibition pottery by John Leach is also on display.

The Gallery specialises in and exhibits stage and costume drawings, including etchings and original work by Alan Barlow, Etienne Drian, Leslie Hurry, Peter Rice, Carl Toms and David Walker. The owners also support and encourage young artists to develop and show their work.

The interior of the gallery

For bed & breakfast there are three charming, beamed, very well equipped bedrooms — a double room and twin room with en-suite and a twin room with a private bathroom.

Superb breakfasts are cooked by mine host.

One of the Angel Gallery B&B bedrooms

www.crookedhousegallery.co.uk

Alison Englefield

Possibly one of the most photographed buildings in the High Street, the Crooked House Gallery is a 14th century building where Clare Calder-Marshall (*former film maker and journalist*) and Alison Englefield (*artist, textile print designer, sculptor and poet*) specialise in paintings, ceramics, jewellery, textiles, sculpture, prints and glass — chosen for originality, beauty and wit.

Clare Calder-Marshall

The Crooked House

Alison creates the jewellery and paints in her garden studio, being primarily known for her painterly paper-pulp work based on ancient frescos (*viewable on her website*: www.artwaves.co.uk).

Recently, Alison designed the mugs and painted the banners for the village's 1257 Market Charter celebrations. Together, Clare and Alison make a compelling team. They feel that Lavenham needs to inform the public about itself in an entertaining way — a great notice board in the Market Place and clear signage — time to blow its own trumpet, loudly!

They came to Lavenham some five years ago from Cornwall, to be nearer to families and friends and because they had fallen in love with the eccentric nature of The Crooked House (*which suited their artistic leanings!*) the historic village and the friendly people.

They first met in Wales about 20 years ago, where they wrote a film script together and then went into business, running art & craft workshops for all ages in schools, museums and galleries. Clare is the driving force in the gallery, meeting the public, working with artists and organising the exhibitions (*and Alison!*).

The interior of the gallery

Howlett of Lavenham

Howlett of Lavenham showroom and forecourt

www.howlett-ltd.co.uk

Howlett of Lavenham is a family owned and family run business, founded in Lavenham in 1958 and thus celebrating its 50th anniversary this year. The company moved into new, purpose built premises 40 years ago, which have grown as the business has expanded.

The business is run by partners Ben and Simon Howlett and four family members work in the business. Many of their staff have been with them over a long period of time and they have a number of customers who have been loyal to them since the business started 50 years ago.

As a family run business they have seen many changes over the years. They believe that they achieve continued success through fair trading plus good customer and staff relations.

The company were a Peugeot Main Dealer for many years but became an independent Peugeot Specialist four years ago. The business comprises many facets. They pride themselves on being Peugeot Professionals and sell new, pre-registered and used cars. They don't have to be Peugeot — they deal with all models and specialise in sourcing specific cars for customers.

Howletts have a large well equipped workshop with the latest technology and offer servicing and MOTs. They can service all makes and models of cars, including 4x4s and motorhomes, not just Peugeots. They have the latest diagnostic equipment and offer aircon recharging and fit batteries, exhausts, etc.

They have their own 'on-site-bodyshop, equipped to repair all types of damage, to any make of car. Using the latest equipment, skilled technicians complete quality repairs that exceed manufacturer's requirements. Those repairs are then guaranteed to meet the manufacturer's warranty standard.

Howletts work in partnership with major UK and international insurers to provide prompt repair completion times. Digital imaging and electronic estimating over the Internet allow them to speed up a process that has, traditionally, been slowed by the need to have an insurance engineer view a damaged vehicle.

A Howlett of Lavenham workshop

Daily car hire is available at Howlett of Lavenham, with vehicles ranging from small hatchbacks to vans and 7-seaterMPVs. Rates are competitive and this is a very convenient local service for both residents and tourists

Howletts also carry out cosmetic repairs, glass replacement and air conditioning maintenance and car and van hire are available.

Howlett Leasing

Stacey Howlett receives the Premier Partner Award 2007-2008 from Christophe Displace, Director and Head of Network Vehicles Ltd.

Business customers are well provided for. Stacey Howlett of Howlett Leasing was delighted to be voted winner of the prestigious title 'Premier Partner 2007-2008' given by Network Vehicles Ltd during their annual award ceremony at the Belfry Hotel. Howlett Leasing, a vehicle leasing

brokerage based in Lavenham (*and sister company to Howlett of Lavenham*) took top place from more than 100 national franchisees.

Stacey, who started the brokerage in 1988, commented "Our success has been primarily due to very hard work, determination and being able to offer our customers regular 'Special Offers' on a wide variety of vehicles including cars, vans and double cab pick-ups. Through the years we have built up a very good relationship with our customers who have stayed extremely loyal."

Howlett's motor racing activities

The photo below shows a Peugeot 306 GTI rally car driven by Ben Howlett and navigator Simon Howlett, who entered several European rallies in the autumn of 2008 and have enjoyed success at top class level in previous seasons.

The photo below shows Bradley Howlett (Ben's son) at age 19, competing in the DEP 125 National Motocross series, in third place in 2008 in the Junior Section after a succession of good results.

Lavenham Pharmacy & Perfumery

www.lavenhampharmacy.co.uk

Christopher and Patricia Jay moved the Pharmacy & Perfumery across the High Street to its current location, opposite The Swan, in 2006. Large, sympathetic alterations were undertaken, including a herb garden at the rear, designed by Janey Auchincloss of Lavenham.

Christopher and Patricia made huge efforts to retain all the best of the old while putting in superb modern facilities and it was interesting to observers that a Planning Officer from Babergh District Council, apart from other curious demands, made a huge song and dance about the outside sign being hung two feet too high (*in his opinion*). A considerable amount of the Jays money and Council Taxpayers money was expended on the matter.

Christopher and Patricia Jay at the pharmacy counter

An outline historic building survey and impact assessment was prepared by noted architectural historian Leigh A. Alston MA(Oxon) prior to alterations to the building. His survey said that "the early 19th century rendered facade conceals a typical timber-framed merchant's house of the 14th and 15th centuries. It contains a rare and unusually intact smoke bay that heated an attached kitchen."

The front interior

This cross-wing Grade II hall house, with its preserved mediæval frontage, was brought into the 21st century with an extension and sympathetic conversion of the interior, to accommodate a full-service pharmacy. The beautifully integrated style and quality is evident throughout, with a visually appealing, streamlined and contemporary look, while still conveying a traditional and welcoming atmosphere. "It's fantastic", says Patricia (the managing director). "Never a day goes by when people don't come and say: Wow, this is the best pharmacy I've been in."

There is a huge amount of directional lighting in the shop, which works very well. Strolling through the shop, the space suddenly fans out into a spectacular circular form. It provides access to the consultation area and a curved wall of custom built units, bathed in tasteful lighting from the overhead lamps.

The Jays came to Lavenham in 1988 and bought the old pharmacy in1990. The new Pharmacy & Perfumery provides a health screening service, and large ranges of medicines, equipment, health foods, fragrances, gifts, jewellery, beauty accessories and luxury toiletries. Business splits about 50/50 between professional health care and beauty care retailing.

A leaflet prepared for the pharmacy by the author

Looking from front to rear

There is a private consulting room where patients can, privately and confidentially:

- Discuss medicines with the pharmacist
- Enrol in the NHS Suffolk 'Stop Smoking Scheme'
- Have blood pressure, blood sugar and cholesterol levels measured, as well as being offered advice on ailments.

The Pharmacy & Perfumery stocks an extensive range of ladies perfumes and gentlemen's fragrances and luxury bath products from Crabtree & Evelyn and the quintessential English Floris range.

There is Italian hand-made glass jewellery by Antiqua Murina. A wide range of luxury gifts include Vagabond bags, Kent and Mason & Pearson hair and

shaving brushes, and Stratton compacts, all of which are made in England.

The Pharmacy & Perfumery will gift wrap your purchases, free of charge, and mail order is available.

Mr Jay has formulated his own cough mixture (Formula J), known affectionately as 'Jay's Fluid.' Christopher's brand of pharmacy is based on care in the community. The Jays good reputation has spread far beyond Lavenham.

The impressive curved interior near the dispensary area

The changes the Jays have noticed include improved pavements, the Glebe and Lower Road housing developments, and more people, all of which are good for the community as a whole. Changes they hope to see, like so many others in the village, is more affordable housing and they would like to see Lavenham continuing to grow as a thriving village.

26th November 2006 — Nellie Smith (99) cuts the ribbon at the official opening

The main window onto the High Street

Lavenham Photographic Studio

www.lavenham-photographic.co.uk

Specialising in wedding, portrait and social photography, Lavenham Photographic enjoys the privilege of being part of both the business and social community, working from a beautifully renovated 15th century timber-framed building in the centre of Lavenham.

With its state of the art digital camera equipment, computing and lighting, a visit for a sitting is an enjoyable and rewarding experience. Being able to view the results on a large display monitor ensures complete satisfaction that the precise images have been captured. Prints can be framed or canvas mounted. to suit all tastes. Alternatively, a digital CD is also available or loaded into a digital photo frame slide show.

The studio is an inviting location for couples to discuss their future wedding plans. Past weddings can be viewed that have been taken at the many churches and venues in Suffolk and surrounding counties. This enables prospective brides and grooms to see how their day will be captured and also provides some photo ideas that they may not have thought of. The whole family often enjoy a follow up visit to the studio to view the results of the wedding day on a large screen monitor, often extending their visit to include lunch or afternoon tea at the many places to eat in the village or enjoying visiting the many points of interest that Lavenham has to offer.

Commercial photography is also undertaken and, over the years, commissions for a variety of local businesses for promotion and advertising have been taken — from creating inviting images of hotel rooms, gardens and conference facilities, to tempting food presentations for pubs and restaurants.

The design and construction of web sites is another service provided, keeping in step with rapid developments in this growing technology.

Being actively involved in the community, photographing village events is all part of the service; from documenting prestigious Royal visits by Prince Charles and Camilla, to the annual carnival and rare breeds motor show. Lavenham recently provided a wonderful backdrop to a very popular international classic VW exhibition.

LAVENHAM PHOTOGRAPHIC STUDIO LTD

Historic Lavenham Merchants' Guild
MEMBER

Always on the lookout, a photographer is often to be seen around the village, camera in hand, to capture opportune scenic shots, such as a spectacular snowfall in winter or hanging baskets during the summer blooms for the annual Hidden Gardens.

For several years photography for a Lavenham calendar has been produced, with themes ranging from 'Lavenham Then and Now', where past images were reproduced side by side with current day images, to 'Lavenham Buildings & Flora'. The proceeds of the calendar sales went towards the recently constructed Village Hall.

As well as photographing the many weddings, christenings (and even requests for funerals), images for Church publications and postcards are provided when required with compliments, as a little 'thank you' for the benefit we enjoy from this amazing much revered building.

Between 1987 and 1989 saw the business on the 'back burner', during which time a building renovation programme was undertaken which included the current purpose-designed studio, shops and family home.

Lavenham was very popular with US personnel from the many air force bases that were in the area up until the late 1980s. The famous Crooked House was purchased and, after total renovation of the building, opened as a studio specialising in 'Bygone Days' portraits. A wardrobe of mediæval and Victorian costumes were put together and much laughter, fun and frivolity was enjoyed by both clients and photographer alike

The closure of the air bases saw the end of this episode and focus moved to specialising in weddings and portraiture.

Returning in 1984 to live in the UK after spending 15 years in Botswana, Mike Hodges decided to spend time developing his hobby of photography. Now, over 20 years on, it has proved to be a very rewarding and worthwhile decision.

Lavenham Press

www.tlg.uk.com/lplweb

Lavenham Press, based around Arbon House (a former silk weaving factory, later horsehair factory) in Water Street, is an independent, family-owned and run company and has been in business for over 50 years, being established in 1953.

 The Press is the largest local employer, with more than 50 staff, and takes its social responsibility seriously. Lavenham Press is an Investor in People and extremely pro-active about training. It also has an impressively green environmental policy, using the latest products, designed to minimise its impact on the environment.

Mr Dalton, Managing Director, told me: "Company philosophy revolves around the customer. We support the customer at every stage, being both flexible and responsive and have a special understanding of the publisher's viewpoint in that we have also published in our own right for many years.' This understanding certainly seems to have paid off as many of the customers have been with the company for 10 or 20 years and, in one case, for over 40 years."

Terence Dalton,
Managing Director

Press equipment currently includes three Heidelberg Speedmasters and a battery of digital presses. Lavenham Press services include — besides printing — binding and mailing. The company uses Apple Macs and PCs in its work. Pre-press data is processed in a variety of formats and there is a fast turn-round bindery and 'print-on-demand' service.

While the company handles some commercial print, about 80% of the output is books and periodicals. Lavenham Press has an extremely varied customer base, numbering many institutes, associations and societies within the medical and environmental sectors. Commercial publishers are also well represented, as are various independent publishers, including self-publishers.

Lavenham Press operates a highly sophisticated digital workflow system. The company can receive finished pdf files; however, it also has the capability to help out at any stage of the earlier work and is often involved in typesetting

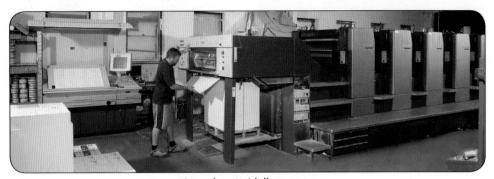

Five colour Heidelberg press

The Studio

or specialised scanning on behalf of customers.

One area that has seen growth in recent years has been stock holding and single order fulfilment for a number of publishers with titles that do not offer enough turnover to interest the major distributors. "We started this to help us distribute books that we publish of local interest in East Anglia, and it's growing steadily," said Mr Dalton.

"We do not market these titles, just offer a fulfilment service, and the process is operated in such a way as to make us invisible to the buyer. The bookshops call

Polywrap mailing line

a dedicated line as if to the publisher, and they send us payment in the name of the publisher."

He continued: "We provide a service to our customers, supplying books and journals where required, on time. The means of production and the chosen logistics are secondary to how effectively the customers' needs are

met. We have considerable flexibility with digital capability and a range of B1 litho Heidleberg presses (one, two, four and five colour). TPL produces all sorts of book, mono or full colour throughout, although the colour element is growing as the unit costs of four-colour litho are falling, and most membership magazines are predominantly colour. We also produce many technical journals."

Computer to plate making machine

Regarding the appropriate use of digital and litho printing, Mr. Dalton sees the gap closing in that while cost-effective digital runs grow, corresponding improvements in modern litho machines and digital work flows, reducing front end costs, make litho increasingly competitive. "We can make over 100 B1 plates a day, and the set-up time and costs on modern machines have come down dramatically. This increased productivity means litho costs for smaller runs have become far more viable. It is not just the cost factor with colour digital, but also the quality. There is now little to choose between litho and digital" comments Mr Dalton.

Planning meeting in progress

69

Sworders Estate Agents

www.primelocation.com
www.rightmove.co.uk
www.property-platform.com

Tim West, proprietor

Sworders are long established as an independent firm of estate agents, surveyors, valuers and auctioneers. Specialists in the sale of period and historic properties for generations, there can be few of the wonderful old houses in Lavenham that have not been dealt with by the firm at some time.

Sworders have a wonderful office in the historic Toll Cottage in the middle of the Market Place, perfect for promoting Lavenham's splendid listed timber houses. With their main office in Sudbury, backed up by an office in London W1, they attract clients and purchasers from all over the country, and indeed the world, to England's finest medieval town.

The 2008 housing market

Tim West, proprietor of Sworders, says "After a period of fantastic growth, the housing market peaked in 2007 and the financial crisis this year has brought about a sharp downturn, with prices falling back around 15% to 20%. However, once again history shows that the best

Houses sold by Sworders

period houses in Lavenham, the jewel of Suffolk, hold their value better than most properties when times are difficult. There will always be those who can see how wonderful it is to live in Lavenham and remain determined to make it their home. Supply is always limited, particularly of medieval timbered houses, large or small."

Sworders office in Lavenham Market Place

Tapestry Gallery

www.tapestrygallery.co.uk

Tapestry Gallery is the UK's leading retailer of reproduction mediæval and contemporary tapestry wall hangings, cushions, bell-pulls, footstools, table runners, firescreens and handbags — in short, everything tapestry!

They offer a magnificent collection of Jacquard woven artwork encompassing the skills of Flemish, French and Italian weavers. These richly textured tapestries add classical elegance and timeless beauty to any home, period or modern. Thanks to modern weaving techniques, they are able to bring together some of Europe's finest tapestries, making them both readily affordable and available in a range of convenient sizes to suit today's interiors.

Most of the tapestries are reproductions of the originals you see in historic houses or museums.

Tapestry Gallery is one of only two specialist tapestry shops in the UK. Since 1996, the gallery in Lavenham has been providing customers, both local and worldwide, with a unique and affordable alternative to traditional forms of artwork — a stunning selection of genuine Flemish Jacquard woven reproduction artwork ranging from copies of The Bayeux to mediæval through to William Morris.

Coincidentally, some of the 14th century buildings in Lavenham are reputed once to have been home to Flemish Weavers who fled Flanders to escape persecution and brought their weaving skills with them to work and settle in England. Whether or not they actually lived in Lavenham is a matter of some dispute.

Several hundred years later Tapestry Gallery is proud to offer reproductions of these exquisite pieces of woven artwork.

The Chapter House

www.thechapterhousebooks.co.uk

The Chapter House is an excellent bookshop with an amazing collection of second-hand books, as well as new publications. It also includes the village Post Office, a coffee shop and art gallery.

Behind the Post Office counter — the owners

The Chapter House from the outside

Books and cards

decorative plasterwork and ceramics with Nigel. She works very closely with Nigel on the computer sales and inventory side of the book business.

Nigel and Beverley Hensby started the business in 2007, having decided on Lavenham as their base following a reading of John Appleton's *Suffolk Summer*. The main business is the book trade, and their card sales business is also gradually being expanded. In addition, they also offer a wide range of artists materials.

They run the book business via the internet as well as local sales, and have part-time staff to assist with the shop on days off and for the Post Office at times. The Post Office provides an extremely vital service to the community — long may it last!

Above — three of Nigel's local paintings

Nigel is an artist with a very distinctive style, clearly reflected in his 2009 Lavenham calendar. He has always been avidly interested in drawing and painting, studied under well known Canadian artist Alice Waywell and ran an art gallery and painting supplies business in Toronto.

Beverley, following a career as a riding instructor, learned pottery and plaster techniques and formed a business selling

The Post Office prior to 2008

The Rather English Co.

 Specialist tea and coffee merchants, offering a wide range, including Lavenham Breakfast and Lavenham Afternoon blends and a range of what you drink tea and coffee from. Also, a showroom for new designs in clothing, leather goods and accessories, inspired by the owners' past work in period film and television.

On a personal note, I've taken to a special tea made for me by The Rather English Company — WellBeing — which consists of a mixture of two rare China green teas and two rare China white teas. As a cancer sufferer, I have been very pleased at how my well-being indicators have improved since I started drinking it. Of course, neither I nor The Rather English Company can prove that it is the main cause of the improvement, but I certainly feel that it has helped.

Dougie and Annabel Hawkes
photo courtesy EADT Suffolk Magazine

Visiting traders

Butcher & Poulterer

Brian Dowse's refrigerated mobile shop — butcher and poulterer — has been visiting Lavenham for many years.

Fish van

The fish van sets up in the Market Place every Friday, offering a wide range of fresh fish.

Greengrocer

Staggy's Mobile is in the village on Thursdays offering, amongst other things, fruit and vegetables, seafood, eggs, bread and cakes.

73

Medical facilities

First Responders

If you suddenly become ill in Lavenham, and call 999, be very grateful that a trained volunteer could be just three minutes away to render medical assistance, before the ambulance arrives. Those volunteers are called First Responders. Lavenham is extremely fortunate to have a First Responder Scheme in place. The local coordinator is Bryan Panton (a Serving Brother of the Order of St John), who — apart from his

business management activities — has 32 years experience with St John Ambulance, including being a First Aid instructor and running the Sudbury division.

The East of England Ambulance Service NHS Trust wanted to start a First Responder service and picked Lavenham as a rural location. Bryan was asked to join because of his experience. The service was started in 2002. Currently (2008) he is the only one involved though two or three others are under training.

Much of the necessary funding comes from village residents, directly or through fund raising events, with help from the Community Council and Parish Council, or from grateful recipients of the service.

If a 999 call is made for medical reasons it is classified in terms of severity — A, B or C. After summoning an ambulance, the controller will then call the First Responder by mobile phone, who should be at the scene within three (yes, three) minutes. Calls may come at any time of the day and the responder carries a first aid kit which includes oxygen and a defibrillator. Additionally,

the First Responder can administer cardio-pulmonary resuscitation (mouth-to-mouth). First Responders are not required to attend road traffic accidents, fights or childbirth.

In practice, about 1 in 25 calls are really serious. Cases have involved persons collapsing, persons getting entangled in a zimmer frame, worsening of chronic conditions and general reassurance. One of Bryan's cases involved an ambulance driver who arrived to help and, in his hurry, fell out of the ambulance and broke his ankle.

In the 12 months to April 2008 the Lavenham group attended 59 emergency calls. On 32 of those oxygen therapy was administered and on one occasion the automatic external defribillator was used. The average attendance time at a call is 45 minutes.

Lavenham Surgery

Lavenham Surgery

Lavenham Surgery is part of The Long Melford Practice, whose practice area covers Acton, Alpheton, Borley, Brent Eleigh, Cockfield, Foxearth, Glemsford, Great Waldingfield, Lavenham, Lawshall, Little Waldingfield, Long Melford, Preston St Mary, Shimpling, Stanstead, Sudbury and Thorpe Morieux. Lavenham surgery, which lies just off the Church Street/Cock Inn car park has a large waiting area and three consulting rooms. It is designed for wheelchair access.

The practice currently has seven doctors, including two salary GPs, supported by more than a dozen staff, including the practice manager (who now works from Lavenham) and two nurse practitioners. It has assisted the training of doctors for many years. Three new rooms were added in 2008 — one for consulting and two for administration.

A practice nurse works at Lavenham Surgery most weekday mornings and a phlebotomist from West Suffolk Hospital works there most Thursday afternoons. Consultations are by appointment only. Minor operations can be performed.

The Lavenham Surgery is open weekdays 8.30am to 6.30pm (closed for lunch). Repeat prescriptions can be arranged by leaving a repeat slip into either Lavenham or Long Melford, by telephone or by fax or email.

In August 2008 there were approximately 9,300 patients registered, with numbers growing slowly. Phone and computer systems are linked between Lavenham and Long Melford, and all records are recorded electronically.

Additional services available include long-term condition reviews, emergency contraception, counselling and a wide range of others. Patients have donated to a practice equipment fund, enabling the practice to buy equipment they could not otherwise have afforded. This includes a defibrillator and a 24 hour ambulatory blood pressure machine.

Lavenham Pharmacy

An excellent Pharmacy operates in the High Street, open six or seven days a week (see separate pages for Lavenham Pharmacy and Perfumery).

Dentists

Lavenham has two dental practices. One operates from Church Street premises and the other in the High Street.

Lavenham Osteopathic Service

Based in the High Street, the practice claims a safe and natural approach to detecting and treating damaged parts of the body such as muscles, ligaments, nerves and joints and is for all ages.

Hospitals

The nearest main hospital is the West Suffolk at Bury St Edmunds. At Sudbury, Walnutree Hospital and St Leonards are both slated for closure, after repositioning of their current services to a new facility.

Very occasionally, a more dramatic type of medical facility is used in the village
photo courtesy of Lavenham Photographic

Sports and recreational facilities

Lavenham enjoys very good sports and recreational facilities, especially for a village of its size.

The recreation ground

The recreation ground (off Bridge Street Road), with its pavilion, football and cricket fields and four tennis courts, is owned by the Parish Council and managed by the Community Council. Each of the sports are run by independent clubs who contribute to the maintenance of the facilities by payment of an annual rent. The ground and pavilion can also be hired for general use, children's parties, music practice and Pilates classes amongst others.

The Recreation Ground from the church tower. Top — the football pitch, centre — tennis courts, foreground — the cricket pitch

The old pavilion was demolished and replaced by an excellent new building that opened in May 2003 at a total cost of £90,000. The funding was obtained by sourcing grants and from the Community Councils fund raising efforts over previous years. Although subcontractors carried out certain essential work, much of the labour was obtained by inviting voluntary help from Lavenham residents, ably led by Ian Gammage, and a total of eighty men women and children assisted in its construction.

The Sports Pavilion

The Football pitch

The Cricket pitch

The Tennis courts

Lavenham Football Club

The football (soccer) club play in the Treadfirst Sunday League and are sponsored by The Royal British Legion.

Their players currently range in age from 17 to 29 and they play about 20 games each season.

In 2007, the team were winners of the Division 1 knockout cup.

Lavenham Cricket Club

http://lavenhamcc.hitscricket.com

The Cricket Club (affiliated to the Suffolk Cricket Association) have a delightful venue at the sports field, in the shadow (*no, not literally*) of Lavenham church. In 2008 they played in the Hunts County Bats Suffolk League, Division 4, finishing second. They were Champions of Division 5 in 2007. The club's strength in younger players has paid dividends as senior players retired.

The current club (of which the author was a sponsor for five years) was formed in the mid-60s. At that time, matches were played on a field off Brent Eleigh Road. The current pitch was developed later in the 1960s and the club moved there as soon as the pitch was playable. The then pavilion even provided home and away dressing rooms complete with showers!

The new facilities helped improve club fortunes and in the 1976 season the club played 33 competitive friendly matches, losing just two and drawing one. The club joined the local league in the early 1980s and since then have played in all five divisions of the league, obviously always trying to win but, most importantly, being able to enjoy the game.

Once a year Lavenham Cricket Club play The Bunbury All Stars — the world's number one charity cricket team. There are more details of the 2008 game in the events section of this book.

Lavenham Lawn Tennis Club

www.lavenhamtennis.org.uk

At the Recreation Ground, the club has four excellent artificial grass courts, three with floodlighting and a first rate clubhouse with changing and shower facilities. Club nights are held throughout the season on Tuesdays and Fridays for all adult members, with junior coaching on Thursday evenings during the main season. There is an internal knock out competition as well as numerous tournaments and social events during the year.

Tennis finals — 2008

The club runs three mens, two ladies, two mixed tennis teams throughout the summer and two winter league teams. All teams compete in the Halstead and District League, against teams as close as Sudbury and as far away as Wickham Bishops.

Play Areas

First Meadow Play Area

Just off The Common and designed to provide interest for younger children. Designed by Bethany Whymark (aged 7 at the time, of Lavenham School). Equipment provided by Playquip. Paid for by a grant from Babergh District Council with the remainder paid by Lavenham Parish Council. Maintained by Lavenham Parish Council

Above — the Meadow Close Play Area

Designed to provide lots of interest to younger children. Maintained by Babergh D.C.

Harwood Place Play Area

Designed to provide a special place for energetic youngsters to play ball games. Maintained by Babergh D.C.

Children's playground at the school

Transport, traffic, parking and police

Transport

There are two main forms of public transport in Lavenham — Chambers bus services and the LAMBS (Lavenham Area Mini Bus) Community Buses.

The Chambers 753 service (Bury St Edmunds to Colchester, via Sudbury) runs through Lavenham approximately every hour — Monday to Saturday — between 0810 and 1845 to Sudbury and 0735 and 1740 to Bury St Edmunds.

The LAMBS scheme, started by Marylyn Gurling (the current Parish Council Chairman), provides transport to those unable to use conventional transport or when there is no public transport available. The vehicles are equipped for wheelchair users and those with walking difficulties and the drivers are trained to assist.

LAMBS offers Cosford Connect and Dial-a-Ride journeys, both of which must be pre-booked. The fare is charged at a set rate, calculated on the mileage at the completion of the journey, payable to the driver at the time of the journey.

LAMBS also operates a scheduled bus service every Thursday to Sudbury for market day. Buses are authorised to go off route to collect passengers unable to walk to a designated pick-up point. Free bus passes apply. LAMBS employs three part-time drivers but a great deal of the work is carried out by a group of willing and generous volunteers.

Cosford Connect provides transport to link up with onward bus services at places like Lavenham, Bildeston, Boxford and Hadleigh for jurneys to Bury St Edmunds, Ipswich, Sudbury, etc. Journeys must be pre-booked at least one day in advance.

LAMBS is supported by Lavenham Parish Council, Suffolk County Council and other donations. The scheme is self supporting and, on Mondays, the bus takes people to the Salvation Army lunch.

Traffic

A great deal of traffic passes through and visits Lavenham and there is considerable discussion about it in the village. My own recollection, shortly after coming to Lavenham over a quarter of a century ago to live in Water Street, was being passed a large folder containing extensive correspondence with the police and local authorities to see 'what could be done about it.'

There is quite a lot of traffic to supply the businesses, without which we would all be poorer. Also, due to some extent to the growth of SatNav, large lorries often drive through the village on the way from A to B because the voice in the SatNav says that is the shortest route.

One solution would be to downgrade the A1141 to a B road, but apparently this would mean a sharp decrease in repair and maintenance funding, so the County Council are reluctant to take that action.

Not all our visitors come by car

Naturally, and increasingly over the past twenty or so years, nearly all residents have at least one car, often two, though interestingly they seem rarely to put them in their garages, which have become spare rooms, offices or workshops.

Parking

Car parking is an interesting subject in Lavenham. There are two public car parks, operated by Babergh District Council. One

is off the top of Prentice Street and the main car park, near The Cock Inn, also has some coach parking spaces. Until 2008 these parks have always been free of charge, despite several attempts by the officers of Babergh District Council to turn them into paying parks.

Why use the road to park?

Main car park (adjacent to The Cock Inn)

What double yellow no parking lines?

Prentice Street car park

Rolls Royce in the High Street

On road parking in the centre of the village is in regular use, not least by residents and shop staff. The Market Place, except for special occasions, acts in practice as a large car park. There are over 350 of these central on-road parking spaces, plus many others in the less accessible side streets.

Despite extensive double yellow lines, many motorists seem to treat them as only applying to other people, and the pavements, increasingly, are used by those who do not wish to walk more than a few yards to where they live.

One strange advantage of the parking in the High Street is that it tends to act as a self-limiting funnel, reducing traffic speed except in the early mornings and late evenings. The 30mph speed limit often appears to be disregarded at those times.

Road repairs in Water Street — October 2008

It's not just cars on the roads

Police

www.suffolk.police.uk
www.suffolkpoliceauthority.org.uk

When I first came to live in Lavenham there used to be a Sergeant and a Constable, based at the Police House at the junction of Sudbury Road and Bridge Street Road. Sadly those police have long gone, the police house has been dismantled and these days, from time to time, a Police Community Service Officer calls by. That person has to share time between eight villages — Lavenham, Brent Eleigh, Chelsworth, Cockfield, Kettlebaston, Monks Eleigh, Preston St Mary and Thorpe Morieux.

Safer Neighbourhood

Lavenham is in the West Babergh Safer Neighbourhood Team (SNT), which is one of three teams in the Babergh District. The number of officers in each team varies, dependant on the volume of crime and geographic nature. In West Babergh the team comprises a Sergeant, two Police Constables and four Police Community Support Officers. This ensures that if one of the officers is away on leave, for example, there is always someone on the team who can be contacted to provide advice and reassurance as well as dealing with any crimes reported.

The team members have been selected for their local knowledge, helpful

The PCSO for Lavenham from the West Babergh Safer Neighbourhoods team

nature, communication and problem solving skills, amongst other attributes.

Whilst not all the officers live in Babergh the Police are committed to making sure that officers selected for Safer Neighbourhood Teams do remain on their teams for some time to build up local knowledge and provide a familiar face to see. Whilst they no longer have the police house they have invested in a mobile police station which they will be using in all Safer Neighbourhood Teams from September 2008 onwards.

Whilst it is true that crime is blessedly low in Lavenham, it is always a pleasure to see real, live police officers or PCSOs as they make occasional visits here, either by car or on foot.

The Lavenham liaison PCSO (*who is on a 37 hour week*) tries to make a brief report at each Parish Council meeting and is accessible by telephone (*via the main police switchboard*) and by email, if important. When visiting the village she often gets comments from local residents such as "Are you lost" and is frequently asked by American visitors to have their photograph taken with her.

Our PCSO (*who actually lives the other side of Colchester*) and was appointed in the summer of 2007, describes Lavenham as having a "very good sense of community, with people willing to get involved." She describes crime in Lavenham as "very, very low and the village as a very safe place to live."

The apparel a PCSO has to wear these days is interesting. It comprises the uniform, body armour, high visibility jacket, a utility belt (mainly paperwork), a radio, a torch and a resuscitation mask. Note that PCSOs do not carry a truncheon.

Chief Inspector Ransome, District Commander, Babergh — in the Babergh

Local Policing Summary (LPS) 2008 said that "the police are working towards:

Chief Inspector Martin Ransome, District Commander, Babergh

- Reducing crime associated with the night-time economy
- Tackling anti-social behaviour and engaging with young people
- Addressing alcohol and other substance misuse
- Taking action to prevent and tackle domestic violence and abuse."

He went on to say that "central to achieving those aims are the SNTs, launched in 2007. They will be increasing the time they spend on patrol and will be working to come up with solutions to problems identified by local people."

In addition to the SNTs we are very fortunate in Babergh to have uniformed response officers working round the clock from Sudbury, Hadleigh and Capel St Mary police stations to respond to emergency calls, and calls where a quick response is required. A Crime Investigation Team also works from Sudbury, led by a a Detective Inspector. Furthermore, there are a number of specialist resources available, including the helicopter, dog handlers, roads policing officers and scenes of crime officers, amongst others.

The Suffolk Police helicopter

According to the 2008 LPS, crime fell in Babergh for the third year in succession. There were 149 fewer crimes in 2007/08 in the district compared with the previous year — but the police solved more of them. The detection rate increased by 2% to 28.7% (*meaning, presumably, that over 70% of crimes were not solved*).

The 2008 LPS goes on to say that as well as reducing and solving crime, the police are also concentrating on improving the quality of service they offer local people. They aim to pay particular attention to keeping people informed about police progress after crimes or incidents have been reported to them.

Police dog, with handler, jumping

Additionally, the police are developing closer working relationships with local councils, voluntary organisations and other agencies, in order to make their service even more effective.

A relatively recent aspect of policing is Police Direct. This is a high-tech messaging system provided by Suffolk Constabulary, the first force in the country to use this technology to keep people informed about local policing issues. Subscribers receive specific

The Police Direct logo

information from the police, direct to their computer, mobile phone or landline. It is free to join and subscribers can choose how to receive information.

Beamed house in Prentice Street

Junction of Bears Lane and Church Street

> "For houses in towns and villages there is nothing in England to beat Lavenham in numbers or variety."
>
> *Sir Nikolaus Pevsner (1902-83)*

Buildings

- The Parish Church of St Peter & St Paul

- The Salvation Army in Lavenham

- Lavenham's other religious centres

- Lavenham Village Hall

- The Guildhall of Corpus Christi

- Lavenham's 'other' guildhalls

- Little Hall

- Lavenham Hall

- Lavenham Priory

- The Old Grammar School

- Lavenham Old Rectory

- De Vere House

- Building close-ups

- Pargeting

- Market Place and Market Cross

- Listed buildings

- Other buildings

The Parish Church of St Peter & St Paul

"This is, needless to say, one of the most famous of the parish churches of Suffolk — rightly so, for it is as interesting historically as it is rewarding architecturally."

Sir Nikolaus Pevsner (1902-83)

Lavenham's wonderful Parish Church is often one of the first things visitors (and residents) see as they approach the village. It stands as a beacon and was, indeed, known as 'Thank God tower' by American airmen based here in WWII.

Today the church is not only the centre of Christian worship but hosts concerts and events, has a thriving book and gift shop and welcomes visitors of all faiths or none. Once a year the tower is open so that those who make the climb can admire fantastic views across the lovely Suffolk countryside.

In summer the church is open 8.30am to 6.30pm daily (services permitting), and in the winter from 8.30am to 3.30pm daily. Evening visits and guided tours can be arranged by special appointment.

The Parish Church of St Peter and St Paul, built between 1486 and 1525 and widely acknowledged as one of England's finest parish churches, is a splendid example of 'late perpendicular' style. It is the third church on the site.

Approaching through a unique avenue of trimmed box hedges, you can admire a building recording the wealth of the 15th century local wool cloth industry and thanksgiving for a Tudor victory at the Battle of Bosworth. The nave, tower, (Spring) Lady Chapel (south of the altar), (Branche) Holy Trinity Chapel (north of the altar) and eastern vestry replaced a 14th century church of which only the chancel remains. The chancel and 'spirelet' are the oldest parts of the present church,

dating from about 1330 and built in 'decorated' style. The tower is 141ft high and may originally have been intended to be completed with spirelets. It is said that the architect was killed by falling from the tower at its present height and it was thought unlucky to continue his work further.

John de Vere, Lord of the Manor of Lavenham, was a commander in the Duke of Richmond's winning army against King Richard III at the battle of Bosworth in 1485. Richmond became King Henry VII and de Vere (13th Earl of

Oxford) came to Lavenham, deciding to build a new church, helped by Thomas Spring II, who had built the vestry, where Thomas Spring I (died 1440) has a brass memorial. The new tower was begun in 1486. The nave was rebuilt (almost entirely of expensive limestone from Northamptonshire) and the north chapel, a gift of clothier Simon Branche, was finished in 1500. The building was completed by Thomas Spring III (the "rich Clothier"), who added the south chapel.

Inside the church are two intricately carved wooden enclosures (parcloses), made for the tombs of clothier Thomas Spourne (south side) and Thomas Spring III (north side). Puritan zeal and Victorian restoration carried out in the 1860s, directed by the Rector, Joseph Croker, have altered much of the original splendour of the interior.

The de Vere symbols of a star and a boar are very prominent on the exterior, as are the merchant mark of Thomas Spring, who was granted a coat of arms by King Henry VIII. The patrons of the church, who have its advowson, are the Master and Fellows of Gonville and Caius College, Cambridge. The memorial on the wall just north of the main altar is in memory of Dr Henry Copinger, rector for 45 years, who

died in 1622. The fine tenor bell, widely renowned, was made in 1625. The church currently costs over £1,600 a week to maintain (insurance, heating and lighting, etc) and is nominally insured for £20 million (though it could, of course, never be re-built for that sum).

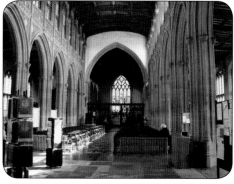

Photographs

This page: (left) the main porch; (above, top to bottom) general view; the nave; the north east aspect

Previous page: (top) the church tower from the south and (bottom) the box tree pathways to the church looking from the tower

A notice outside the porch welcomes 'Dogs with careful owners'. The church staff includes a Verger, an organist/Director of Music, a Reader, six Servers (ranging from 16 to 89) and a Cleaner. There is also a large number of Church Welcomers, who greet visitors, make them feel welcome and try to answer any questions they may have. There is a parish choir of ladies and gentlemen. The newly created gift shop is run by volunteers.

The Rector's ministry includes Preston St Mary as well as Lavenham. At Lavenham attendance is fairly good by comparison with many other villages of similar size. 8-o-clock communion on Sunday often attracts over 20 worshippers and the main Sunday service sees over 120. The Salvation Army, in particular, are partners in many major celebrations.

The church from overhead, photo taken by the author from a microlight aircraft piloted by Brian Wates of Lavenham

The northern aspect

The tower from the west, looking east

Above — the north east corner

Left — the font

The cemetery chapel near the church

Ground plan of the church

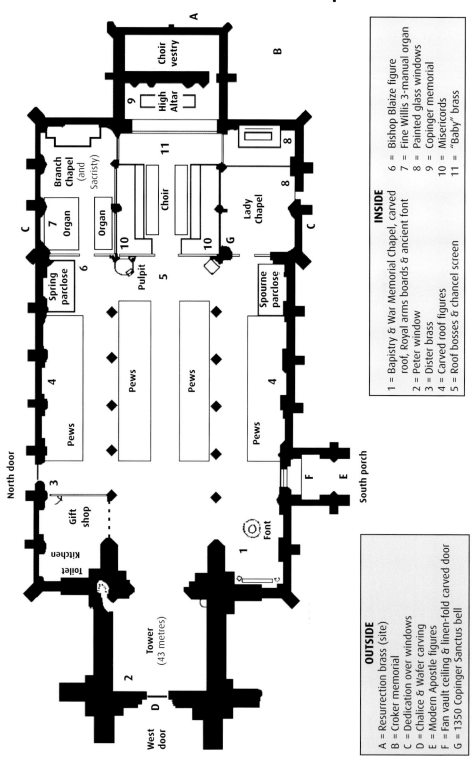

INSIDE

1 = Bapistry & War Memorial Chapel, carved roof, Royal arms boards & ancient font
2 = Peter window
3 = Dister brass
4 = Carved roof figures
5 = Roof bosses & chancel screen
6 = Bishop Blaize figure
7 = Fine Willis 3-manual organ
8 = Painted glass windows
9 = Copinger memorial
10 = Misericords
11 = "Baby" brass

OUTSIDE

A = Resurrection brass (site)
B = Croker memorial
C = Dedication over windows
D = Chalice & Wafer carving
E = Modern Apostle figures
F = Fan vault ceiling & linen-fold carved door
G = 1350 Copinger Sanctus bell

Timeline of the de Veres, the Spring family and the monarchs

before, during and after the re-building of Lavenham Parish Church

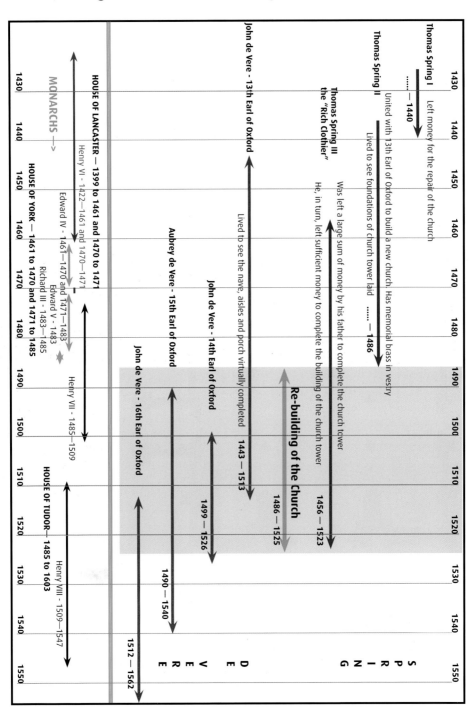

The church team

The new church gift shop, opened in 2008, in what used to be the choir vestry

Under starter's orders for the annual Suffolk Historic Churches Trust sponsored bike ride. (left to right) Cyril Curtis, Belinda Curtis, Pam Evans and David Sneaden

The church altar prior to the 8-o'clock service

Harvest supper in the church

Director of Music — Stephen Hogger BA (Hons) FGMS FASC ALCM ACertCM

The Church Organ

The earliest record of an organ in Lavenham Church was the bequest of money for it's repair in the 15th century. This was probably destroyed during the Commonwealth period and a replacement stood at the west-end and was moved to a gallery position under the tower before 1834, when David Davy says that seating was included for a robed choir.

This instrument was replaced by Peter Conacher & Co. in 1867 with a two manual and pedal organ in the Branch Chapel and the choir was moved to the chancel at this time. This organ was sold to the church at Collingbourne Kingston in 1996 when the present three manual and pedal Willis instrument was acquired from St Swithin's Church, Bournemouth. This is currently being enlarged to four manuals and fifty-one stops.

3 Manual Willis/Degens & Rippin

Couplers:
Swell to Great, Swell to Pedal, Choir to Pedal, Great to Pedal, Great to Choir

Pedal:

1	Open Wood	16	
2	Bourdon	16	
3	Violoncello	8	
4	Choral Bass	4	
5	Mixture	IV	19.22.26.29
6	Bombarde	16	
7	Fagotto	16	(Swell)
8	Trumpet	8	
9	Clarion	4	

Choir:

10	Lieblich Gedacht	8	
11	Dulciana	8	
12	Principal	4	
13	Wald Flute	4	
14	Piccolo	2	
15	Mixture	II	19.22
16	Krummhorn	8	
17	Tremulant		
18	Harmonic Trumpet	8	
19	Harmonic Clarion	4	

Great:

20	Contra Geigen	16	
21	Open Diapason	8	
22	Stopped Diapason	8	
23	Claribel Flute	8	
24	Principal	4	
25	Harmonic Flute	4	
26	Fifteenth	2	
27	Mixture III		15.19.22

Swell:

28	Open Diapason	8	
29	Rohr Flute	8	
30	Salcional	8	
31	Voix Celeste	8	
32	Gemshorn	4	
33	Fifteenth	2	
34	Mixture	IV	26.29.33.36
35	Contra Fagotto	16	
36	Cornopean	8	
37	Clarion	4	

Accessories:
4 thumb pistons Great, 4 Swell, 4 Choir;
4 toe pistons pedal
3 general thumb pistons
thumb and toe pistons to sw-gt, gt-ch, gt-pd
Great and Pedal pistons coupled

The Church choir

The church now boasts two choirs. The parish choir sing a wide range of music from plainsong to modern worship songs at the Parish Eucharist and the St Peter & Paul Singers sing Choral Evensong on the second Sunday during the summer months at 3.30pm.

The parish choir — October 2008

The church tower is open to the public for just one day a year (unless special arrangements have been made for a private visit). It is possible to see the ringing chamber and belfry, hear bell ringing demonstrations and gain wonderful views over Lavenham and surrounding areas from the church roof.

The church clock mechanism. There are no external clock faces

The church clock of 1775 bears the name of Thomas Watts II of Lavenham. It strikes the hours and operates the quarter chimes installed in 1887 for Queen Victoria's Golden Jubilee. Unusually, there is no external dial.

The ringing chamber

The tenor bell of the ring of eight, weighs 21cwt 7lbs and was cast by Miles Graye I of Colchester, adjacent to the church. Its birthday used to be commemorated on 21st June. The musical tone is exceptional and is reputed to be one of the finest in England. For peals rung at Lavenham, see:

www.felstead.org.uk

*Views from the church tower
top: Lavenham Hall and buildings
bottom: towards Ropers Court*

The belfry

Church Kneeler Millennium Project

In March 1996 a small committee was set up to carry forward an idea submitted to the Parochial Church Council. This was to furnish the church with hand-stitched kneelers on the theme: 'The history of Lavenham church and village 1000—2000 AD' as a millennium project.

Suggestions for designs were sent in, adapted for stitching charts, wools and canvas were chosen, and the project launched in May. This self-funding venture, involving designs, needlework and upholstery was accomplished by people in and around Lavenham, by January 2000. Altogether, 261 kneelers were completed using 150 different designs.

The steering committee comprised Eileen Watson, Barbara Pearmain, Patricia Hardie, Jane Bean, Doreen Brinkley and Sheila Stiff. Miss Lilla Page was the needlework consultant and Jay Craft of Bury St. Edmunds were the main suppliers.

146. Lavenham Guildhall

The building of the Guildhall was completed in 1529, when the Gild of Corpus Christi was granted a Royal Charter for its use as a centre for religious and welfare activities. The Gild also set standards for workmanship and wages for the cloth industry. Designed by Margaret Offord.

The 261 kneelers in the body of the church are eye-catching and deserve time to be appreciated fully. Eighty seven people undertook the challenge to sew the kneelers, and an estimated 26,500 stitches were needed in each one, taking many hours of work. Whether a stitcher was multi-talented, or without experience, all who were interested were encouraged to participate with outstanding results. Some were so pleased with their first attempt that they went on to do two, three or, in one case, thirteen! Individuals, clubs and businesses were able to sponsor the kneelers and their huge support enabled the project to be self-financing.

Kneeler 146 on special display in the church

003. Thomas Spring's Woolmark

The trademark used by Thomas Spring III, the rich clothier, who gave large sums of money in the 16th century to complete the building of the church. Adapted by Jane Bean.

The project spanned all generations, from primary school children to pensioners, and the enthusiasm of all concerned brought this community effort to a successful conclusion.

The details of all the needleworkers and sponsors are recorded in a special commemorative book on view in the church. Each kneeler has a number, matching the pictures in the book and in the kneeler leaflet, which is available for sale at the church gift shop.

051. The de Vere Shield

From a carving in the church. Albert de Vere was created Lord of the Manor in 1086. Designed by Jane Bean.

050. Friends of Lavenham Church

The Friends of Lavenham Church provide generous help with the furnishings of the church. Their emblem was adapted for stitching by Margaret Offord.

164. St Peter Shield

Adapted by Lilla Page from the church inventory, depicts St Peter's choice of an inverted cross for his crucifixion.

Left — the Kneeler Leaflet, available from the gift shop

Below — the Kneeler Book — available to all church visitors

Both items were prepared by the author

225. The Shield of St Paul

Emblem of our patron saint, adapted from the church inventory by Hilary Law.

95

The Salvation Army in Lavenham

The Salvation Army Hall

The Salvation Army (SA) is very active in Lavenham, with a variety of functions and events, run by a group of committed volunteers as well as a designated officer (though the post is currently vacant).

The Army hold services every Sunday; Morning Service at 10.30am, Evening Service at 6.00pm. On Remembrance Sunday each year a united service is held in the Parish Church. For some 50 years, during this service, bandsmen — currently Derek Wilding, Eric Walker and Robert Holmes — have been responsible for playing "The Last Post" and "Reveille."

The Pastoral Corps Council

The SA Home League is a social ladies network, with some 50 members, that meets weekly. The SA Ladies Fellowship meets fortnightly in the evenings, for craft work and keep fit sessions. The SA Luncheon Club — a community project — meets on Mondays and currently over 40 persons attend (not all from Lavenham). Participants can be collected by the LAMBS bus. It is aimed at anyone in need

or just to enjoy the fellowship of other people. The SA Parents and Toddlers Group (limited to 25, aged up to 4) meets weekly in school term time and is an opportunity for the children to carry out activities together.

Other events organised include Songs of Praise at the Carnival weekend (usually in the marquee), Christmas Carols in the Market Place and a Pentecostal service on the Common. The SA Band practices fortnightly, sometimes with other bands and the SA Songsters (choir) sing at morning services.

The Songsters

Fund raising activities include the annual May Fair, the July Coffee Morning, a Christmas Fair (in the Hall), a Flower Festival (held every three years) and 'Betty's Boutique' (a sale of bric-a-brac and other items from the building next to the Hall), the annual Harvest Festival Supper (enjoyed by over 90 people in 2008) and the annual Corps Christmas Dinner — very popular and very well attended for many years. In 2008 a Christmas Tree Festival, with decorations by various groups, was organised.

Another SA activity is their work with the Family Shoebox Appeal. Linked with children in Romania, Albania and Moldova, Lavenham SA provided 27 shoeboxes in 2007 for children who otherwise would not get presents.

Lavenham's other religious centres

There have been several churches and chapels in Lavenham at various times, apart from the Parish Church. Brief details, as far as they are known, are:

The Dissenters Chapel

Believed to be on a site standing back from Water Street (such chapels were not allowed to front a main road at the time). It is recorded that a Sunday School operated there as early as 1790.

The Primitive Methodist Chapel

Now in use as the Guildhall tearoom it was used as a chapel in the 19th century. Note the initials PMC on the wall outside.

The Congregational Chapel
(United Reformed Church)

Now a reproduction furniture exhibition and salesroom and home to

The Vestry tearoom and bistro, the former Congregational Chapel was built in 1827.

The Wesleyan Methodist Chapel

Where the Wesleyan Chapel stood is now a private residence. Formerly the site (a magnificent timbered building dating from about 1440) was home to John Bolton and became a chapel in 1811. In 1911 it was demolished to make way for the new chapel, which opened that year.

The Catholic Church

Deacon Tony Ranzetta is spiritual leader of the Roman Catholic Community in Lavenham.

Although there isn't a building in the village, the Catholic Community is active in Lavenham. It occasionally uses Lavenham Parish Church for services but the community mainly supports their Parish Church of Our Lady and St John in Sudbury and the churches in Hadleigh, Bury, Clare Priory and Coldham Cottage (Lawshall).

There is also a monthly Mass celebrated at Long Melford church on the 2nd Wednesday of the month, in Lavenham Guildhall on the 4th Wednesday of the month and at St Andrew's church, Great Cornard on the 3rd Wednesday of the month.

Details of Catholic services are in *Lavenham Life* monthly magazine.

Lavenham Village Hall

Village Hall floor plan

Lavenham Village hall — which has proved a great success since its opening — provides extensive community facilities, hosts the meetings of numerous clubs and societies and puts on farmers markets and other activities. It has

Jacqui Hobbs — Village Hall Manager

accessible entrance for people with disabilities, disabled car parking, accessible lift, toilet facilities for people with disabilities, wheelchair spaces available and an induction loop/infrared. Guide dogs are admitted.

The facilities are available for hire for meetings, wedding receptions and family functions amongst others, and Farmers Markets are frequently held there. New clubs such as carpet bowls, badminton, table tennis and a Youth Club have been formed and are thriving. Suffolk County Council relocated their library into one of the rooms, which

can still be used for meetings outside Library hours. There is a monthly Film Night (Flix in the Stix) and, during school holiday periods, there are special film showings for children. The Scouts, Cubs and Beavers groups also meet in the Hall.

For very many years, Lavenham never had a Village Hall. Although over the years many schemes were discussed, for one reason or another they did not proceed. The Lavenham Village Design Statement, completed in 2001, confirmed (yet again) the need for such a building. The Community Council decided to fulfil that need, and the hall was opened in May 2005.

Opening of the Village Hall by Elsie Hynard

On her left, Martin Weaver (Chairman, Community Council) and Marylyn Gurling (Chair, Parish Council)

The value of the project — at just over £1 million — was funded by grants from many sources including, amongst others, the Big Lottery Fund, County, District and Parish Councils, Defra and the Foundation for Sport and the Arts. The land on which the hall stands is leased from the Diocese at a peppercorn rent, and Lavenham Parochial Church Council agreed to sell their Church Rooms and contribute the proceeds in return for use of the hall for church functions. A loan of £100,000 was also taken out to prevent further delay in completing the project. The architects were Wincer Kievenaar and the hall won a Regional Architects Award for a community building project.

Contributions were received from Lavenham residents and benefactors, and special fund raising events were held in the village. A very dedicated group of volunteers came forward to form the Project, Fundraising, Marketing and Management Committees.

The lobby

The main hall

Looking towards the church from the Village Hall front entrance

The main hall set for a function

The lobby corridor

The Village Hall from the church tower

99

The Guildhall of Corpus Christi

www.nationaltrust.org.uk/lavenham

After the parish church, the Guildhall of Corpus Christi, in the Market Place, is probably Lavenham's best known building. Built about 1530, it is one of five guildhalls that once existed in Lavenham.

Today the Guildhall and its two adjoining buildings are the focus of much of the village life. Tourists and visitors are very welcome to view the fascinating museum with exhibitions about timber-framed buildings, local industry, farming

and the woollen cloth trade. There is also a unique dye plant garden. Owned by the National Trust, a Guildhall Committee is responsible for the

local use of the building, including management of the museum.

There are about 30,000 visitors a year to the Guildhall and annual turnover is in the region of a quarter of a million pounds. Visitor comment cards are 95% positive. Many comment on the fact that the building is very different to many other National Trust properties in that it is still a working building. About 60% of visitors are over 55 and some 10% foreign nationals.

The hall and its two adjoining buildings together form a section of an early Tudor street. The National Trust tea-room at one end is a rare example of a Tudor shop, goods being traded through the two arched windows, and the Guildhall itself demonstrates the skill of the late mediæval carpenters and wood carvers.

During Queen Mary's reign, in 1555, prisoners were housed in the Guildhall and from 1596 to the late 1600s it was the Town Hall, afterwards becoming a prison which closed in 1787. Later, it served as a workhouse, an almshouse and, in the 19th century, a wool store.

Sir Cuthbert Quilter Bart. MP bought the dilapidated building in 1887 and renovated and repaired it. During the Second World War the hall was variously a nursery school, British Restaurant and home for evacuees, as well as the

Jane Gosling

The Guildhall dye garden

Ready to burn witches in front of The Guildhall (actually, it was only for TV in 2000)

'Welcome Club' for US Air Force personnel from Lavenham Airfield.

In 1946 the Guildhall was presented to the Lavenham Preservation Committee by Sir William Eley Cuthbert Quilter, and in 1951 it was endowed and vested in the National Trust.

Jane Gosling

Jane, who became Manager of The Guildhall in 1998, is deeply involved in village life, being — literally — at the centre of things. She is widely admired throughout the village for her dedication and hard work.

With her 15 regularised and seasonal staff and volunteers, Jane quietly and efficiently organises the building and its many activities — including the monthly Parish Council meetings and many other village clubs and associations meetings.

Apart from supervising the museum and dye garden already mentioned there is the Ranson Room, gift shop and tea shop to be looked after. The Guildhall is also where a Roman Catholic Mass is held once a month, instilling a beautiful sense of continuity.

For someone who is a timber-framed enthusiast, says Jane (she had studied this from her early days), it is like being a child in a chocolate factory! She spoke with Prince Charles and the Duchess of Cornwall about the ecological value of timber-framed buildings during their visit to the Guildhall in 2005.

Apart from her Guildhall work Jane is Chairman of the Lavenham Society, a Director/Trustee of the Dyehouse Wood, on the committee of the Extra-Mural Association, Secretary of the Suffolk Historic Buildings Group and has been much involved with Jim Keohane and the Community Council on the 'Our Memories' project (two volumes to date).

She also played an important role in preparing Lavenham's Village Design Statement, one of the first in the country and now adopted as additional planning guidance. If you need to know anything about The Guildhall, timber framed buildings, and general history of Lavenham, Jane is one of the best informed I have ever met. She says that when she goes on holiday she is always ready to come back to Lavenham and would like to be remembered as having made a significant contribution to the village and, in particular, to the Guildhall.

Lavenham's 'other' Guildhalls

The Guildhall of Corpus Christi is not the only guildhall that Lavenham has enjoyed. There were at least four halls and the site of a fifth is not known.

The primary objects of the Lavenham gilds were religious — they were not trade associations. Membership was open to both men and women, from all classes of society. Regular feasts were held, often preceded by splendid processions to church and extensive outdoor pageants.

The gilds were dissolved at the Reformation.

The Hall of the Gild of Our Lady

Now part of The Swan Hotel, it was established in the 15th century as one of the five gild halls in Lavenham. Following the decline of the manufacture of woollen cloths it was converted to a Wool Hall towards the end of the 16th century.

It was used to store the great quantities of spun yarn that had now become the main source of employment, supplying the clothiers in Norwich, Hadleigh, Colchester, etc.

In the early 18th century the property was converted into three houses and a bakers shop. In 1911 the building was threatened with demolition and removal to Ascot. With strong local protest supported by The Society for the Protection of Ancient Buildings, the building was reinstated at the expense of the Duchess of Argyle, Princess Louise, who then gave it to the Railway Company for use as a convalescent home. In 1963 it was bought by Trust House Ltd., who brought it into The Swan Hotel.

The Hall of the Gild of St. Peter & St. Paul
(usually referred to as St. Peter's)

Demolished in 1896, this guildhall was in the High Street. After the dissolution of the guild in the 1540s it was used as a wool store and later to store coconut fibre bales until required for weaving in the Ropers mat factory at what is now Ropers Court.

The hall stood on the site of the present Post Office and next door to what is thought to have been the priest's house (St Paul's hall), which has undergone a very sympathetic restoration into a private dwelling. St Paul's hall, built about 1530, is believed to be the last remaining part of the original Guildhall.

It is thought to have been linked at the first floor, spanning across the lane (which now leads to the Royal British Legion Club) to the side of the building. At that time the lane gave access to the rear of the hall and to the former Guildhall courtyard.

St Paul's hall served four purposes — a shop, priest's quarters, cloth weaving workshop and kitchen. The front was rendered over during the period 1702–1714. A Victorian extension was aded in 1882, when the hall was purchased at auction for just £150!

The Gildhall of Holy Trinity, after remodelling in Georgian style.
courtesy Alec Betterton & David Dymond

St Paul's Hall

The Hall of the Gild of Holy Trinity

It stood at the top of Prentice Street, on a site which is now a local authority car park. Early photographs show it to have been a large three-storied building. It was demolished in 1879.

The Hall of the Gild of St Christopher

It is not known if this guild actually had a guild hall.

Further information about the Lavenham guildhalls

The excellent book *Lavenham — Industrial Town*, by Alec Betterton and David Dymond, printed by Lavenham Press and published in 1989 by Terence Dalton Limited, of Lavenham, (ISBN 0 86138 070 3) is highly recommended reading on the subject of the Lavenham Guildhalls.

Little Hall

www.littlehall.org.uk

Little Hall, in the corner of the Market Place, is open to the public (since 1978) as a museum and is also the headquarters of the Suffolk Preservation Society. The hall very recently had a new 'paint job'. The photo below shows it in its earlier colours (which most people seem to have preferred).

This late 14th century house (though mainly built in the c15th) was originally an open hall, used as a family home and workplace. In the next century a new brick chimney was added and a floor inserted, providing a completely new first floor room.

The left hand side of the house may be 14th century, while the right hand side was probably added (enlarged, improved and modernised) in the mid 16th century. In the 18th century the hall was divided into tenements, and was giving homes to six families. The building was again extensively altered by the Gayer-Anderson brothers, starting in the 1920s. Overhanging jetties were restored and a double door of mediæval type installed.

In 1975, Surrey County Council offered Little Hall to the Suffolk Building Preservation Trust, complete with the Gayer-Anderson collection of pictures and artefacts, in addition to the two cottages. Before selling the cottages, the Trust was able to restore Little Hall. It was opened to the public in 1978 and now operates as a museum.

Opening times (see website)

From Easter to the end of summertime on Wednesday, Thursday, Saturday and Sunday afternoons from 2.00 - 5.30 p.m., and Bank Holidays, 11.00 a.m. to 5.30 p.m. Admission charge — adults £2.50; children with the family free. Groups may be booked outside these hours at any mutually convenient time. School parties 50p each and accompanying staff free, adult groups £2/head. Please phone, write or fax at least one week ahead to arrange a booking, or phone David Harris on 01473 827365 between 6pm and 7pm.

After repainting, 2008

A 2008 view

The hall garden

The hall stands near the site of the original Lavenham Hall, possibly a manorial hall of the de Vere family, and was mentioned in the Domesday Book.

The present hall is at the centre of a scattering of farm buildings and overlooks a large pond, probably the fish pond of a small religious grange, ruins of which can still be seen on the lawn. The hall is a timbered building of several periods, the oldest dating from the 15th century, with some panelled rooms.

Extensive alterations and upgrades to the hall and grounds have recently been instituted by the current owners.

Standing at the end of Hall Road, Donald Insall described the road as "a relic of feudal Lavenham which was the way that once linked the heart of the

The little bridge at the bottom of the garden

town with the palace of the Earls of Oxford." Lingard Ranson described the hall as standing "on the site of the Saxon Grange, head house of the Manor of Over Hall, held by the Saxon, Ulwin, in the reign of Edward the Confessor and where the Hall Mote (local Court of Justice) was held.

The Domesday book mention is among the terrae of Alberici de Ver. When the de Veres held the manor the Hall became the Bailey House (where the bailiff probably lived) and a new Manor House was built near the top of Park Road. The de Veres sold the hall towards the end of the 16th century.

The hall some years ago

Lavenham Priory

www.lavenhampriory.co.uk

Lavenham Priory, which stands in three acres of grounds, is a "Grade 1 listed" half-timbered mediæval house dating from the 13th century. Once condemned, restoration was begun, over a four year period, by Alan and Gwenneth Casey of Lavenham in the 1980s and completed by the current owners, Tim and Gilli Pitt, over the first four years of their ownership.

When they purchased The Priory the part renovation needed finishing and the wing in which they live was completely rebuilt, gaining an important regional award for their work from The Suffolk Association of Architects. W.A. Deacon & Sons of Lavenham were the builders.

Bespoke furniture was made for the house by Jason Bryan, a 25 year old cabinet maker then living in Lavenham, over an eight month period. This included beds, tables, chairs, bookcases and a Welsh dresser. All were specifically designed to fit and complement the large rooms of The Priory.

Within the Priory Tim and Gilli organised a substantial number of upgrades after moving in, including electrical systems, hot water systems, bathrooms and in the grounds. They also opened two new guest bedrooms. The six bedchambers feature braced crown posts, Elizabethan wall paintings and oak floors, with four poster, lit bateau and polonaise beds. Private parking facilities are provided.

 Tim and Gilli now offer Luxury Bed & Breakfast accommodation at their home and have won the highest quality grading available of 5 Stars with Gold Award given by the English Tourism

The Great Hall

The Merchants Chamber

The Great Chamber

Council and the Automobile Association for bed and breakfast accommodation.

The house has also won three important national prizes: "the AA's Guest Accommodation of the Year award"; and two awards from the "Which? Hotel Guide." It is also described as one of the "very best places to stay in Great Britain and Ireland" in the Hardens Hotel Guide.

As many guests, (who include many honeymoon couples) will attest, staying at The Priory is a unique and unforgettable experience. They often comment on the amazing tranquillity and peace of the building. 30 to 40% of guests come from East Anglia (*including many from as near as within 10 miles away*) but people from every continent have visited.

Tim has for many years operated as a broker and consultant in sugar by-products, has been Chairman of the local tennis club three times and been involved in the Lavenham Carnival, raising money for the sports fields.

Tim and Gilli Pitt

Since arriving in the village he and Gilli have noticed few changes (with the exception of the new Village Hall), and rejoice — like so many of us — in the overall quality of the village and its embrace of many generations. As Tim says "the village feels like a proper working community."

The Priory Suite

The Priory was originally a hall house belonging to the Benedictine Priory of Earls Colne in Essex. Over the next three hundred years it passed through a series of major extensions and alterations. After being used in connection with the wool trade and owned by the Earls of Oxford, in the late 1500s it became the home of the Copingers, rectors of Lavenham.

Throughout the 18th and 19th centuries it was a working farm, owned by a succession of professional people and absentee landlords. Today it stands as a bridge between past and present, the structure remaining much as it was in Copinger's time, a fine example of the incomparable timber-framed houses of Lavenham.

The Painted Chamber

The Priory (cont.)

above and below — photos taken in the 1980s, before restoration

How the Priory developed

diagrams courtesy of Alan and Gwenneth Casey

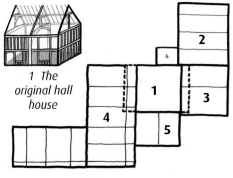

1 The original hall house

2 Kitchen and cross passage

3 Solar and hall extension

4 Five bay house

5 The last addition over the cellar

The Old Grammar School

Now a pair of modern homes, the Old Grammar School sits modestly in Barn Street next to a conversion of a factory into dwellings. I well remember going into that factory — and into the Old Grammar School — many years ago.

It is fair to say, I think, that the building is a mixture of styles and, like many old house in Lavenham, most of the really interesting bits are inside.

The best description of The Old Grammar School of which I am aware can be found in Volume 1, 1998, of The Journal of the Suffolk Historic Buildings Group — *Historic Buildings of Suffolk*.

Leigh Alston there describes it as "the finest and best preserved of all the great merchant's houses to survive from Lavenham's early-16th century heyday ... the building is one of the best of its type in the county." Leigh also notes that the artist John Constable and agricultural surveyor Arthur Young studied there. He continues "... a large and thoroughly ostentatious domestic house, it was built in two or possibly three phases, dating from about 1530 and comprises a continuous-jetty house..."

Lavenham Old Rectory

www.lavenhamoldrectory.co.uk

When Susie and Jonathan Wright first came to view the Old Rectory they were both stunned by the beautiful setting opposite the church of St Peter & St. Paul and the rolling Suffolk countryside. The house, dating from 1720, was in need of complete renovation, although most of the original features were still intact including the window shutters and even two original door keys!

After four years of extremely hard work The Old Rectory has finally been restored to its former glory and it opened to guests in August 2008. This stunning country house offers sumptuous accommodation in three individual and impressive en-suite bedrooms. Each room has been furnished to an extremely high standard and impeccably designed.

The Thomas Gainsborough Room has country decor and triple aspect views of the gardens and church. It enjoys a particularly large sitting area. The bathroom has an original Victorian shower bath. The John Constable Room, based on the Chinoiserie theme, with its elegant furnishings and stunning four poster bed is a superb reflection of the Georgian period. The de Vere Room is decorated in the Provençal style, with classically painted furniture and an impressive brass four poster bed with views over the formal gardens at the rear of the house.

Lavenham Old Rectory offers a very intimate and relaxing stay in a beautiful country house.

The breakfast room

Above — the three guest bedrooms

De Vere House

www.deverehouse.co.uk

De Vere House (also known as Oxford House and Oxford Cottages) is a grade 1 listed property and was one of three properties within the centre of Lavenham that were owned by the de Vere family from the 14th to 17th centuries.

In 2008 it was operating as luxury B&B accommodation, rated 5-star by 'Quality in Tourism' 2008 and with a Silver award from 'Visit Britain'. In 2009 it will offer luxury self-catering accommodation only.

It is said that the house has ghosts — friendly ones — including the ghost of the 13th Earl of Oxford's son who died in the Tower of London at the time of the disappearance of the Princes in the Tower, the ghost of Sir Frances Vere, the great soldier, who died in the Thirty Years War, and many others. Needless to say, all of their many manifestations have perfectly logical and scientific explanations.

Although the demolition of the house in the1920s was halted, part of the house was removed, auctioned in London and taken to Southampton. Most of the house was returned and restored. At the time the demolition was halted, over half of the house you see today had not been removed and remains in its original state.

The house stands over the Water Street culvert. During the 15th century the weavers in Lavenham had complained about the water system being used as a sewer and interfering with the washing of wool. This resulted in the culvert being covered in brick. Many of the houses along Water Street were then extended over the culvert. This can best be seen by looking west along Water Street towards the Priory and where it joins 66 Water Street. No 66 follows the original line of houses, whilst the Priory has been extended 15 ft forwards over the culvert.

Originally a hall house, de Vere House was extended just after the Battle of Bosworth (1485). The 15th century extension (in particular most of the internal and external beams and some of the internal and external brickwork) is pretty much as it was over 500 years ago.

The house contains the remains of one of the last garde-robes to be installed in this country; a rare and original medieval wall painting; and a magnificent front door-way, with its carved huntsmen (dating back to the early 15th century) and the heraldic symbols of John de Vere, the 13th earl of Oxford (boar, star, wool jack and scales).

It is reported that King Henry VII may have visited the house when visiting Lavenham in 1498, for a day's hunting, because many guests and retainers of the king and the 13th Earl of Oxford were housed there. The sister and youngest brother of Charles II and James II were held under house arrest in the house during 1651 (in the Commonwealth period), under the custody of Mary de Vere, the wife of Lord Fairfax.

Building close-ups

Calendars produced in 2005, '06 and '07 (to support the Village Hall project) by Mike Hodges showed close-up aspects of Lavenham. As he wrote, "first impressions of this pretty village are the classic 'chocolate box' views with which we are so familiar. However the elements that make up the big picture are very interesting in their own right."

(above) Some Lavenham chimneys, (below) some Lavenham house names, from pages in calendars produced by Mike Hodges and printed by The Lavenham Press, to support the Village Hall project

Samples of business signs in the High Street — sometimes a very emotive subject in Lavenham !

House roof repairs in Lavenham can sometimes be quite tricky !

Pargeting

at the corner of Bears Lane and Church Street

on Lavenham Priory in Water Street (above & below)

Pargeting applies to timber-framed houses whose plastered exteriors are decorated in relief or with scratch patterns (pargeted), and then washed with colour.

Keen visitors may have spotted a "Lion and Tree" in the pargeting of some of Lavenham's ancient houses. One is over the door of the Market Keeper's Cottage, once owned by the Gayer Anderson twins, the last private owners of Little Hall.

It is understood that the tree symbolises "home" in Egypt, and together with the lion were used by the brothers on copper dishes they had made out there, and again here, in Lavenham, on buildings in which they were involved in restoring, or advising. The motif appears on the walls of Little Hall, viewed from the garden.

on The Swan Hotel in Water Street

on Church Street

This splendid pargeted ceiling is in the resident's lounge of The Angel Hotel

Market Place and Market Cross

The Market Place is a wonderful sight — the centre of the village, with the famous Guildhall of Corpus Christi, Market Keeper's cottage, Little Hall, The Great House, The Angel Hotel, The Angel Gallery, Heeks grocers shop, Sparling & Faiers bakers shop, other retail outlets and a selection of lovely houses.

A plaque commemorating the 487th USAAF Bomb Group is attached to a wall facing the centre of the place and, in 2008, a plaque commemorating the 750th anniversary of the granting of the Market Charter was placed there too.

The Market Charter (Wendy Gibson, 2007)

The houses haunt
and close around
the Market Place. Getting
ever closer to
destiny, as knights
and gallows echo
an era when the
Market Charter was
granted, and life
was vibrant with
smells, noises and
fear. Still it
lingers but unobtrusably,
as Autumn colours
flourish, and oak beams
still stand to
amaze and awe.

The Market Place acts for most of the year as a car park, whether for visitors, shoppers or residents. Funding is available to improve this situation during 2009.

The Market Place was formed in the 13th century. The Toll House dates from around 1520 and was where tolls would have been collected from the semi-permanent stallholders.

The cross, bequeathed to the town by rich clothier William Jacob in his will of 1500, was modelled on a cross standing in Cambridge Market Place at the time (*it no longer survives*). The base of the cross is original though the shaft shows the date 1725.

The cross is Monument No.9 of the Babergh list of Scheduled Ancient Monuments, gridref TL 916 493.

The Market Cross

Listed buildings

I thought it would be interesting to see exactly where Lavenham's listed buildings are so I visited the Planning Department of Babergh District Council. I was surprised to learn that — apart from the scheduled ancient monuments of the Market Cross, and the Gasholder in Water Street — we also have three listed walls and two listed telephone kiosks. The details of listed buildings/walls/kiosks shown to me at Babergh were as follows:

BARN STREET

Grade I	2
Grade II*	1
Grade II	2

BEARS LANE

Grade II	3

BOLTON STREET

Grade II	13

(one of these is said to be the oldest house in Lavenham)

BRENT ELEIGH ROAD

Grade II	1

House in Bolton Street

House in Bolton Street

BRIDGE STREET ROAD

Grade II	1

BRIGHTS LANE

Grade II	1

BURY ROAD

Grade II	2

CHURCH STREET

Grade I	1
Grade II*	25
Grade II	36

THE COMMON

Grade II	1

FROGS HALL ROAD

Grade II	1

HALL ROAD

Grade II	6

HIGH STREET

Grade II*	9
Grade II	67

LADY STREET

Grade I	2
Grade II*	1
Grade II	8

MARKET LANE
    Grade II   5

MARKET PLACE
    Grade I   4
    Grade II*   3
    Grade II   22

PRENTICE STREET
    Grade II*   2
    Grade II   44

SHILLING STREET
    Grade I   2
    Grade II   23

SUDBURY ROAD
    Grade II   1

Houses in Water Street

WATER STREET
    Grade I   8
    Grade II*   2
    Grade II   48

House in Lady Street

Other buildings

A house in Barn Street

Arbons House, Water Street

The entrance to Bakers Mill

Houses in Prentice Street

Events

- Lavenham Carnival

- Lavenham Press 'Rare Breeds' car show

- French Markets

- Farmers' Markets

- The 1257 Market Charter celebrations

- Lavenham's Hidden Gardens

- Lavenham Sinfonia

- Lavenham Vintage Volkswagen Show

- Bunbury All Stars cricket match

- Lavenham Old Codgers

Lavenham Carnival

Lavenham Carnival is held each August Bank Holiday Monday, on the sports field, usually starting with a parade from the Market Place.

The 2008 Carnival theme was Food and Farming and buy locally, which struck a chord with the local rural and tourist interests. Friday evening saw a light-hearted quiz night, with proceeds in aid of Lavenham Church funds. On Saturday there was a family fun morning and the Ed Zachary band in the evening, both in the marquee. Sunday featured Songs of Praise with the Salvation Army Band in the evening, again in the marquee.

Monday 25th August was the big day. The procession sets the tone of Carnival day as much as the weather. It led from the Market Place to the playing fields, with spectators invited to dress as scarecrows, accompanied by the Glenn Morriston Pipe and Drum Band.

On the playing fields there were stalls, donkey rides, a fun fair and a tea and beer tent. Arena events included the Flying Fergies, the Raptor Trust, the Suffolk Trinity (animals), a geese and ducks demonstration and performances by the band.

The 2007 Carnival was, in the opinion of the Chairman of the Carnival Committee, one of the best in recent years. It featured a mediæval procession, with the Women's Institute winning first prize.

Carroll Reeve (the retiring Carnival Chairman wrote "The current series of carnivals were started in 1994, after an interval of 15 years. During that time themes have ranged from '50 Years of Peace' through 'Mardi Gras' to '1257 and All That.' Tales of mishaps, mostly behind the scenes, abound such as: the many occasions when the electrics failed (one year Adrian Pryke replaced the entire temporary supply in under two hours!). Another year, as the procession assembled and the Carnival Queen's transport was readied, it was discovered that there was no Carnival Queen! A mermaid was found floating by and Stacy

Scarecrows and the Flying Fergies in the Market Place — 2008

Photograph by Lavenham Photographic Studio

118

*The Glen Morriston Pipe and Drum Band lead
the 2008 Carnival procession*
Photograph by Lavenham Photographic Studio

David and Joan Deacon, 2008
Photograph by Lavenham Photographic Studio

Children's fancy dress contestants, 2008
Photograph by Lavenham Photographic Studio

Photos above — scenes from earlier Carnivals

Howlett was quickly installed as queen."

Over the years the Carnival, and other fund raising events organised by the Community Council, has raised a great deal of money, including upkeep of the recreation ground, rebuilding of the sports pavilion and the development of the Village Hall.

The 2008 Carnival raised the splendid sum of over £12,000.

*Market Charter Carnival procession, 2007.
Note the banners on the Guildhall frontage*

Lavenham Press 'Rare Breeds' car show

The Lavenham Press Rare Breeds car show is an integral part of the Carnival, and takes place on the cricket ground, between the church and sports pavilion.

Towards the end of the Carnival and Rare Breeds Day, on the August Bank Holiday Monday, there is a parade of cars around the main arena. The 2008 show was sponsored by Lavenham Press, the premier provider of services to car clubs.

Bryan Panton was the chief organiser of the Rare Breeds car show from 2001 to 2005 and, from 2006, Jane Hodges has taken over.

The Rare Breeds Show — a view from the Church tower, 2005.
photo courtesy Bryan Panton

The show grew from just over 100 cars to some 500 and has become a well known event on the classic car circuit.

Photographs by Lavenham Photographic Studio

Rare Breeds car show at the 2008 Lavenham Carnival
Photograph by Lavenham Photographic Studio

French Markets

French Markets — 2005, 2006, 2007 and 2008

The Market Place bustling as it might have done in the past, as BrunoMart brought French Markets — arranged by Lavenham Merchants' Guild — to the village

The French Markets in the Market Place in June bring a definite continental flavour to the village, with — as the photograph above shows — very colourful stands and stalls. The markets are arranged by Lavenham Merchants' Guild, in association with BrunoMart.

One particular feature of the French Markets held in Lavenham is that — as first suggested by Régis Crépy of The Great House — tables and chairs are set out in the Market Place so that visitors can sit and eat their purchases. In practice it has meant that a happy 'party' atmosphere has prevailed each time.

The cheese stall

Garlic — lots of it !

Party time !

Farmers' Markets

Lavenham Farmers' Markets are staged on the fourth Saturday of each month from 10.00 am to 1.00 pm. Farmers' Market trading was resurrected in Lavenham in April 2006 when the brand new, modern, light, airy and architecturally designed Village Hall opened its doors to Lavenham's first Farmers' Market.

To tie in with the '1257 Market Charter' celebrations (in 2007) the market ventured outdoors onto that same Market Place where our forefathers traded 750 years ago. For a while, in the summer months, the markets continued to run outdoors in the Market Place, but now have returned to take place permanently in the Village Hall.

Farmers' Markets evolved in the UK 10 years ago and are appearing in more and more towns and villages throughout the country. Each market has it's own character and is quite different from the others. All, however, have the Farmers' Market ethos in common, which is quite simply to give 'local' farmers, growers and producers, the opportunity to sell, in person, their own produce, direct to the public. This cuts out the middle man (and his profits), and gives the customer confidence that they are buying the freshest, most local produce available.

Market Managers are proud to say that all products for sale have been grown, reared, caught, brewed, pickled, baked,

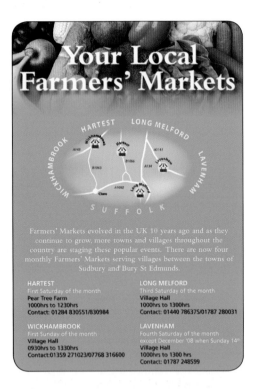

Your Local Farmers' Markets

Farmers' Markets evolved in the UK 10 years ago and as they continue to grow, more towns and villages throughout the country are staging these popular events. There are now four monthly Farmers' Markets serving villages between the towns of Sudbury and Bury St Edmunds.

HARTEST
First Saturday of the month
Pear Tree Farm
1000hrs to 1230hrs
Contact: 01284 830551/830984

LONG MELFORD
Third Saturday of the month
Village Hall
1000hrs to 1300hrs
Contact: 01440 786375/01787 280031

WICKHAMBROOK
First Sunday of the month
Village Hall
0930hrs to 1330hrs
Contact:01359 271023/07768 316600

LAVENHAM
Fourth Saturday of the month
except December '08 when Sunday 14th
Village Hall
1000hrs to 1300 hrs
Contact: 01787 248599

smoked or processed by the stallholder. To this end, by supporting your local Farmers' Market, you are supporting the local community, the local economy, and helping the environment by reducing food-miles.

The Farmers' Market Café is a place where customers can rest their feet and put down their shopping baskets to be served steaming cups of tea and coffee, melt-in-your-mouth home-made cakes, or hot sausage baps. The café becomes a real hub of social activity where producers and customers mingle, swap stories and swap goods; reminiscent of how local trading may have taken place in days gone by.

As well as food products, Farmers' Markets are open to local artisans wishing to sell their own arts and crafts; hand-made soaps, cushions, pottery and lavender products are all examples from some of the many talented individuals we have here on our doorstep.

The 1257 Market Charter celebrations

2007 was the 750th anniversary of the granting of Lavenham's Market Charter, on 15th September 1257, in the reign of King Henry III (1216—1272). The charter — to Hugh de Vere, Lord of the Manor — allowed the citizens of Lavenham to hold a Market on Tuesdays and a Fair on Monday, Tuesday and Wednesday of Whitsun week.

This momentous event in the history of Lavenham was, perhaps, more significant than is realised. Not only did it give the town (as we were then regarded) the right to hold regular fairs and markets, it provided the momentum for the woollen cloth produced here to be sold at markets all over the country and, less than a century later, to be famous in Europe too. It could, therefore, be reasonably argued that the great wealth generated here in the 15th and early 16th centuries, and the legacy of the wonderful buildings left by rich clothiers, stem directly from the granting of the charter.

Heraldic banners, shown opposite, (*sponsored by Lavenham Merchants' Guild, The National Trust and Lavenham Parish Council*) were designed and painted by Alison Englefield, resident artist at The Crooked House Gallery.

Charter celebratory activities included village characters charting the progress of Lavenham's wool trade, a village fete, Lavenham Market Charter Ale, mediæval meanders, the unveiling of the new village sign and the Carnival theme of "1257 and All That."

1. **Two lions** rampant, representing The Guildhall and the Guild of Corpus Christi.

2. The **boar and star**, both symbols of the de Vere family. The pattern behind represents ermine, symbolising wealth.
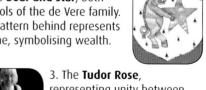

3. The **Tudor Rose**, representing unity between the Houses of York & Lancaster. Wild roses abound in Lavenham hedgerows.

4. **Crossed keys and sword**, the symbol of St. Peter and of St. Paul. Assorted birds from the stained glass in the church.

5. The **sheep and implements**, celebrating the wool industry.

A commemorative plaque was unveiled in the Market Place by Lord Tollemache KStJ JP, The Lord Lieutenant of Suffolk and an opening address was given by Mrs Gurling, Chairman, Lavenham Parish Council. In attendance were representatives of the Churches, Suffolk County Council, Babergh District Council, Lavenham Parish Council, Lavenham Community Council, Lavenham Merchants' Guild, Lavenham Guildhall NT, Lavenham Society and the Suffolk Preservation Society.

Lord Tollemache KStJ JP, Lord Lieutenant of Suffolk, unveils the plaque to commemorate the granting of the charter

Lavenham's Hidden Gardens

Each June, some of Lavenham's best kept secrets are revealed to visitors for about four hours. The Hidden Gardens (*with their Tudor Rose logo*) are a 'must-see' for residents and visitors alike, and thousands of pounds are raised for charity in this way. A programme and sticker are sold from various outlets (*including each participating garden*) though children go free, and admission to each garden is then by sticker.

The gardens that are open vary from year to year. Money raised from the sale of programmes goes to Lavenham Community Council and the proceeds are used to maintain and improve the village and its amenities for present and future generations.

Inn 2008 there was a free Gardens Bus (*operated by LAMBS*), stopping at well indicated points around the village. Several of the gardens offer teas and cakes and some have a plant stall — the revenue from these activities being shared between the Community Council, NSPCC, church organ fund and the Hospice.

The organisers of this great day in 2008 included Gaye Hodges and Ray & Barbara Peevor, plus — of course — all those kind enough to give up their peace and privacy for the day. Rob Holmes printed the programmes.

The Hidden Gardens event idea originated with Marjorie Newman and was masterminded by Gwenneth Casey (then chairman of the Community Council), first opening in 1990. The purpose was to raise funds for the Community Council, specifically for maintenance of the Sports Grounds. Thanks to Gaye Hodges and her committee in 2008, £2,300 was raised for Community Council funds.

Lavenham Sinfonia

www.lavenham-sinfonia.co.uk

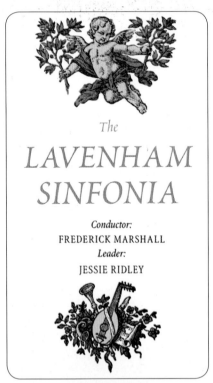

The

LAVENHAM SINFONIA

Conductor:
FREDERICK MARSHALL
Leader:
JESSIE RIDLEY

sponsored by
The Great House

Church, or other fine churches in the area.

The handpicked members come from all over East Anglia; many have been professional musicians, several music teachers and some of their best students. The Sinfonia has played all the Beethoven and Brahms symphonies, much Mozart, Haydn, Mahler, Wagner, also Baroque music and — where possible — the best of contemporary music.

Jeremy Hughes — new conductor

Those wishing to support the Lavenham Sinfonia may become a friend for £25 per annum and obtain priority booking. The Sinfonia's Chairman is Richard Toft and the Treasurer Lionel Baker. A former President was the distinguished music critic, Alan Blyth.

Jessie Ridley (Leader) and Frederick Marshall (who has been Conductor since the Sinfonia was founded in 1979) started the Sinfonia as a small string orchestra and quickly expanded it into a full symphony orchestra. Most of the concerts, usually four a year, are in Lavenham

Lavenham Vintage Volkswagen Show

Saturday 28th June 2008 saw the first Lavenham Vintage Volkswagen Show.

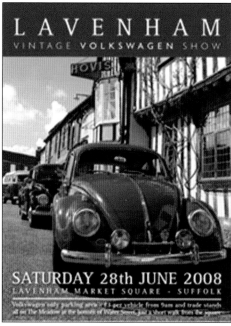

The show differed from most VW shows by featuring only stock, un-modified pre-1967 vintage Volkswagens. This was a new style of vintage VW gathering, never before seen in England. Apart from the main display in the Market Place, there were additional displays in other areas, including a large parking and trade stand area in the meadow at the bottom of Water Street.

Big crowds gathered to view this unique show and it was quite clear that the VW owners were having a great day.

Bunbury All Stars cricket match

www.bunburys.co.uk
www.bunburycricket.com

When you see Mark Ramprakash (Middlesex, Surrey and England) hitting sixes out of the ground and Eamon Boland with a stick, straw hat and white coat as an umpire you know there's something unusual happening.

When you add to that a seven-piece steel band from St Kitts and Nevis, an enormous white marquee and several inflatable children's play areas you know something very unusual is happening.

That was the mixture — and much more — on Sunday 21st September 2008 when Lavenham Cricket Club, with Mark Ramprakash (who has scored 100 centuries) as star guest, played the world's number one celebrity cricket team, the Bunbury All Stars in aid of The Anthony Nolan Trust, Chase (Ben Hollioake Fund) and Born Free — Mark's chosen charities for his testimonial year.

Players gathering before the match started

Lavenham Cricket Club and The Bunbury All Stars teams
(Mark Ramprakash second from left, kneeling)

Lavenham cricket ground has seldom looked so interesting and it was refreshing to see so many young children there with their parents, enjoying the unfolding spectacle, getting autographs from notable cricket players and taking advantage of all the entertainment laid on for them by the sponsors.

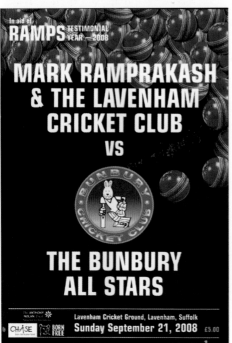
Cover of the match programme

The marquee and Player/VIP lunch tables

Holly Bellingham and her husband Simon (who are also committed to Ipswich Town Football Club), sponsored the game and have a large beamed house here in Lavenham. Simon, apart from his superb support for the match, was there to promote Sumaridge Estate Wines from South Africa. Holly was sponsor for both the 2007 and 2008 Bunbury games. She is Chairman of both Marketform Group Ltd and Marketform Ltd as well as Vice Chairman of Marketform Managing Agency Ltd. Marketform is one of the world's leading suppliers of specialist liability insurance, with over 25 years of experience delivering flexible solutions tailor-made to address their clients' specific areas of exposure.

The football pitch comes in handy !

Formed in 1987 by Dr. David English MBE (cricket's most famous charity fundraiser), Bunbury Cricket Club has raised over £11 million for charity. The Bunbury's are a maverick team which fields a host of stars from the worlds of sport and show business. They are relentless in their quest to raise much needed funds for the disadvantaged whilst showcasing the talents of their famous players in order to provide fun and entertainment for all the family.

Ben Bellward, LCC Chairman, said what an honour and privilege it was for

Simon Turner discusses Sumaridge Estate Wines with a potential buyer

Lavenham Cricket Club to stage the match on such an opportunity to give tribute to Mark Ramprakash and to support his chosen charities. He also thanked all the players for their hard work and commitment.

Oh, and just in case you were wondering, the final score was Lavenham 140 for 12 from 27.1 overs (Mark Ramprakash top scorer with 70, Bunbury bowling David English 3 wickets for 36 runs, Stephen Crook 2 for 3) and Bunbury All Stars 141 for 6 from 17.4 overs (Owais Shah — current England international — top scorer with 40, Lavenham bowling James Andrews 3 wickets for 6 runs, Andrew Young 1 for 12).

Steel band entertainment

Bouncy entertainment for the children

Lavenham Old Codgers

Lavenham Old Codgers was formed in 2004. It is a group of friends who get together once a year and organise a small vintage Rally in aid of local charities.

In 2008 the Old Codgers joined with the John Smith Organ Grinders Society to organise the event for local good causes, including support for DebRA (which provides support and funds research into Epidermolysis Bullosa). The event took place on a field off Frogs Hall Road (beware of koalas !). There was also a display of vintage cars.

In 2007, in the best weekend of the summer and a great collection of vintage cars, the Lavenham woodland project had a stand and Lavenham First Responders did a display. The Parish Council and the Church had a stall each. The proceeds went to the Lavenham Village Sign Appeal, the Lavenham Woodland project and The Lavenham First Responders.

In 2006 the Old Codgers filled the field with exhibits. Nine gypsy caravans assembled, the most caravans in one place that year, a great sight. Some

regulars turned up not having told the organisers that they were getting married and coming to Lavenham to the event especially for their honeymoon. The van was decorated with ribbons and balloons. The proceeds that year were £1,100, which went to the Church.

In 2005, for the first time, some village organisations joined in. The weather was terrible, unfortunately, so on the Saturday night it was decided to have a Christmas Party. Being a hardy lot, the organisers and others sat in their party tents in fleeces and holding umbrellas, pretending it was December. They had a terrific night, with roast Turkey, stuffing and Christmas Pudding, and sang carols around a tree with fairy lights. During the day the school and the church were represented, and there was a display of vintage cars, plus a raffle and games stalls. At the end of the day the Old Codgers had raised £500 for the school.

In 2004 — the first year — there was a musical extravaganza with barrel organs, gypsy caravans and a few other bygones and they raised £400 for PAT dogs (Pets as Therapy). Don King, a group member who is greatly involved with the organisation, and his dog Ellie, were selected to do a lap of honour at Crufts.

People

Preparing the People section of this book has been the most challenging. Whatever the outcome someone, almost inevitably, will wonder why he, she or they were not included.

No one has been left out on purpose. To include all those perhaps worthy of mention would make this section a giant tome in itself and would not be practical.

So I have had, of necessity, to make choices — a selection of people who are in Lavenham today and of interest. They are not the only ones but, for this edition at least, are included.

Some people are also mentioned elsewhere, perhaps in the Business section or even in the Buildings section.

In addition, I've included a brief mention of the de Veres, the Springs and some other well known persons no longer with us but who are remembered.

If you feel miffed about my selection then I'm sorry. It wasn't personal.

- John & Val Barry
- Klair Bauly
- Alan Blyth
- Sue Hamilton Blyth
- Eamon Boland, Caroline Eves & Annie Eves-Boland
- Michael Burn (see The Swan Hotel)
- Clare Calder-Marshall & Alison Englefield (see The Crooked House Gallery)
- Alan & Gwenneth Casey
- Harold & Jill Chrystal (see also Agriculture & Farming)
- William & Gay Clegg
- Régis & Martine Crépy (see also The Great House)
- Cyril & Evelyn Curtis
- Terence Dalton (see The Lavenham Press)
- David & Joan Deacon
- Lynda Dobbin-Turner
- Paul Evans (and Lavenham Contemporary Gallery)
- Alan Fayers (see Agriculture & Farming)
- Jan Foster (see Lavenham Primary School)
- Leonie Frieda
- Philip & Wendy Gibson (see also Angel Gallery)
- Jane Gosling (see The Guildhall)
- John & Marylyn Gurling
- Dougie & Annabel Hawkes (see The Rather English Co.)
- Nigel & Beverley Hensby (see The Chapter House)
- Mike & Gaye Hodges (see also Lavenham Photographic Ltd)
- Stephen Hogger (see The Church)
- Robert Holmes
- Ben, Simon & Stacey Howlett (see Howlett of Lavenham)
- Eileen Huffey
- Elsie Hynard
- Christopher & Patricia Jay (see Lavenham Pharmacy & Perfumery)
- Jim and Carol Keohane (and Blaize Cottages)
- David Lane (see Agriculture & Farming)
- Matthew Manning
- Amanda Mansell
- Frederick Marshall (see Lavenham Sinfonia)

- Marjorie Newman
- Elizabeth Norman
- Bryan Panton (see First Responders)
- Alex Paul (and Suffolk Tourism)
- Tim Partridge (see Agriculture & Farming)
- John Pawsey (see Agriculture & Farming)
- Jeremy Pembroke (S.C.C.)
- Tim and Gilli Pitt (see Lavenham Priory)
- Martin Ransome (see Police)
- Tony & Eve Ranzetta
- Carroll & Barbara Reeve
- Patricia Rockall (B.D.C.)
- Sir Clive Rose GCMG
- Robert Rush (see Agriculture & Farming)
- Yvonne Skargon
- Desmond & Frances Skinner
- Nellie Smith
- Lizzi Stevens
- Richard Ward (see Suffolk Preservation Society)
- Martin and Vickie Weaver
- Tim West (see also Sworders Estate Agents)
- Roy and Anne Whitworth
- Derek & Maureen Wilding
- Jonathan & Susie Wright (see Lavenham Old Rectory)
- Tim Yeo MP

- Lavenham's Royal visitors

- The de Veres and Earls of Oxford
- Edward de Vere was Shakespeare ?
- The Spring family

- Reginald Brill
- John Constable
- Henry & Ambrose Copinger
- Roy Turner Durrant
- The Gayer-Anderson twins
- William Gurnall
- Ivan Howlett
- Kenneth Merrylees
- John Millar-Watt
- Sir Alfred James Munnings
- Taylors of Lavenham and Ongar
- The Winthrop family

John & Val Barry

John and Val punting in Cambridge

Val has recently retired from a management post in local government administration and John retired last year (2007) from running the Angel Hotel in partnership with Roy and Anne Whitworth. John and Val now live near the centre of the village in a building converted from a barn.

They have both taken the opportunity to resume their academic studies after a lengthy gap, and are taking forward their interests through the University of Cambridge Institute of Continuing Education. Val is studying History of Art and John studying Local History. John is also involved in the Guildhall museum.

John has just completed an Advanced Diploma in Local History, with a dissertation entitled *Lavenham: Industrial Town to Tourist Village: Economic and Social Change in the Twentieth Century*. The study investigates why the population declined, textile manufacture ended after 600 years, and tourism developed. It looks at the conflict between the urge to preserve mediæval and Tudor houses and the need to provide the local population with jobs and decent housing.

It goes on to ask what influence national trends have had on Lavenham's local history.

Klair Bauly

Sitting at the Guildhall loom, showing me how it works and should be threaded, it is just as if she only stopped work yesterday. Klair, who spent many years of her life here in Lavenham, trained in art and design at West Surrey College (part of Reading University) and, shortly after her arrival in the village, was asked to help get that loom working again.

Purchasing a house in Prentice Street she started a business — weaving, selling and exhibiting fabric and cushions, with silk her favourite material. She rented a show cabinet in the Swan Hotel which brought good business.

Klair featured in a TV programme as a weaver, filmed in the Guildhall, in the early 1980s and produced Lavenham broadcloth, some of which is still on show in the Guildhall museum.

She moved to the Market Place in the early 90s, needing more space for her business 'Silk Shades', which had expanded ten-fold, later moving it into Water Street. Advertisements in Vogue and Bride magazines brought many orders and selling fabric became very successful.

Although she sold her business in the late 90s, Klair retains her enthusiasm for and interest in weaving and, particularly, Lavenham broadcloth. Seeing her at work on the loom was a privilege.

Alan Blyth

Alan was a distinguished and internationally respected critic of vocal music (and for many years music critic of *The Daily Telegraph*), with an encyclopaedic knowledge of the singers of what he regarded as the 'golden decades' of the 1940s, 50s and 60s. Throughout his life he was a great supporter of young singers, but regretted the modern tendency to overlook the importance of good diction in singing.

When Alan moved to live in Lavenham full time in 1992, having had a weekend

cottage here since 1979, his work no longer focused primarily on live performances. Rather, in his semi-retirement, most of his time was spent reviewing recordings, writing notes for CDs and DVDs, and obituaries for several national newspapers and music journals.

Drawing on his extensive portfolio of music contacts, he started a series of music evenings in Lavenham, which ran for over a decade. Guests were invited to spend the evening talking about their lives in music, and listening to relevant recordings chosen from Alan's vast music library. The rollcall included many notable names from the music fraternity, such as Sir Charles Mackerras, Dame Janet Baker and Sir Thomas Allen.

During the course of his career, Alan wrote many books on singers, conductors and composers as well as reference books on recordings of opera on CD and DVD. His last book was *Heddle Nash, The Recorded Legacy*, published in 2007.

For many years Alan was Chairman of The Guildhall and enthusiastically opened his garden as part of The Hidden Gardens scheme. He contributed to appeals to maintain the fabric of the church, seeing it as part of the 'Englishness' of the village which he so loved. He died in 2007.

Sue Hamilton Blyth

Sue Hamilton, who lives near the centre of the village, is author and editor of many publications on Buddhism and other Indian religions. Her most recent book was *Indian Philosophy — a very short introduction,* published by OUP in 2001.

She began university in her 30s, having no previous academic experience, at a small college in West Sussex, where the only degree that appealed to her was in Religious Studies. Initially she had hoped a BA would enable her to take a TEFL course, but instead she went on to take two graduate degrees at Oxford: an MPhil in Classical Indian Religions and a Doctorate in Buddhism.

These led to a locum lecturer's job in Indian religions at King's College, London, where two years later she was given a permanent position. By the time she took early retirement in 2003, when she married Alan Blyth and moved full time to Lavenham, she had been promoted to Reader in Buddhism.

Sue had been friends of Alan and his first wife Ursula (who died in 2000) for many years before she and Alan married. The contrast between Lavenham and living and working in central London was, she says, something of a culture shock. Whereas Londoners thrive on anonymity and constant activity, here in Lavenham people have time for each other. Over the years Sue has grown to love the pace of life and friendliness of Lavenham and particularly enjoys being able to spend time gardening. She now would not want to return to London.

Sue and Alan in Austria

Eamon Boland, Caroline Eves & Annie Eves-Boland

Eamon the Actor, Caroline the theatre director and Annie the theatre production manager. The stage and TV runs in the family. Eamon Boland and Caroline Eves have lived in Lavenham since 1985, determined to be a part of the village, not just weekenders.

Eamon, a renowned stage and TV actor has recently been appearing at the National Theatre in Simon Stephens acclaimed new play, "Harper Regan" and will soon feature, again, in ITV's "The Bill". He has worked extensively in the theatre over the past forty years, notably for the National Theatre, the RSC, The Royal Court Theatre, The Bush Theatre, The Royal Exchange Theatre in Manchester and of course the West End, appearing in several productions ranging from Shakespeare to Ibsen, including several World premiers.

Eamon's TV career has been long and varied. Perhaps his best known parts have been in Fox, Casualty, The Chief, Singles, Crossfire, The Bare Necessities, All the King's Men and Early Doors. Not an extensive film career but one film he was proud to have had a major role in was "Business as Usual" starring with Glenda Jackson and the late John Thaw.

Eamon originally trained as a teacher of History and holds an Honours Degree in the arts. However the call of the stage was too strong and he reluctantly, at first, departed the teaching profession for the hazardous life of the stage and screen; a decision that leaves him now with no regrets. He intends to continue acting right to the end and is in almost constant demand for parts. He generally prefers theatre to TV, never counts lines and is now in the fortunate position of being able to pick and choose as befits his talents.

Caroline has been a freelance and resident theatre director working in theatres throughout the UK, Europe and the USA. She has been a founding director of several companies as well as directing new plays on the fringe at Edinburgh and on national tours. Most notably, she was co-director of Joan Littlewood's famed Theatre Workshop. Her productions have ranged from revues in prisons to classic plays in the West End of London. In the States she has directed Medea outside LA, and The Importance of Being Earnest in Alaska with many Shakespeare productions between these places. She has lectured, taught and directed at most of the major drama schools especially LAMDA and RADA.

Daughter Annie, as noted in *Lavenham Life* for August 2008, was just 18 when she thought it would be a good idea to revive the Lavenham Carnival tradition. She plugged away at it for over two years, with many others, and eventually a new Sports Pavilion became the fruit of their efforts. The 2008 Carnival was the fifteenth since she worked so hard to restart the event. Having trained at LAMDA Annie became an assistant production manager of the National Theatre and is now The Head of Production at the Sydney Theatre Company in Australia where she runs four theatre spaces as well as touring shows to Europe and the USA: achievements of which her parents are extremely proud.

Being active members of this wonderful village has been a source of great joy to Eamon, Caroline and Annie.

Alan & Gwenneth Casey

Alan and Gwenneth are now retired, but they have played an important part in Lavenham as it is today.

They moved here in 1979, to restore a derelict cottage in Prentice Street and shortly afterwards bought the derelict Lavenham Priory at auction — a great leap into the unknown at the time but which resulted in the beautiful building we all see today.

That restoration was a very daunting task and, surprisingly, the subject of quite some adverse local comment at the time, but after four years hard work the house became habitable. "It required someone with courage, money, ability and enthusiasm."

Alan and Gwenneth feel that it helped to raise the standards of what could be done to bring Lavenham houses and buildings back to life.

A grant was obtained from the Historic Buildings Council to assist in the work and, as a 'quid pro quo', they had to open to the public for 30 days a year. Later they opened much more than that and ran a shop and tearoom in the building as well.

Alan and son Bruce later transformed the Coach House in Lady Street. Apart from house restoration, Alan and Gwenneth operated a specialist insurance business until their retirement.

While Alan was concentrating on restoration work, Gwenneth was President of Lavenham W.I. on two occasions, is now involved with The Elderflowers ladies group, and started Tai Chi lessons at the Village Hall.

Alan and Gwenneth founded the Lavenham Publicity Group in the early 1980s. They designed and produced thousands of leaflets which they distributed at EETB shows all over East Anglia. They also got advertising in the cross North Sea ferries to publicise Lavenham.

On leaving The Priory they lived in, and cared for, Shilling Grange, until recently.

Gwenneth has undertaken a great deal of local historical research since coming to Lavenham and, when chairing the Community Council for five years, started the Open Gardens project.

Alan and Gwenneth have concerns about the traffic through Lavenham and, like others, wish something could be done about it. They realise, however, the financial implications. One wish is that Market Lane could be closed and both Market Lane and the Market Place be properly paved. They like the good transport links, good shops and excellent eating facilities. They also, again like many others, wish that more affordable 'local' housing could be provided.

Harold & Jill Chrystal

Although now retired and having, sadly, suffered a number of medical reverses of late, Harold is extremely well known both for his very successful farming activities and, latterly, his tireless work as the senior Church Warden.

He is taking a back seat from farming now, leaving it mainly to son Richard and son-in-law Kevin to operate. Now run by just two persons, compared with 13 in 1948, the size of fields has changed considerably. Harold says he improved the look of the countryside locally by removing hedges, so that the rolling Suffolk countryside could be better seen. Quite incidentally, it also much improved the productivity of the farm!

Harold's interest in the church arose from a visit to see the new organ there. Churchwarden for many years, he would often visit the church two or three times a day, including at evening concerts and events and is looking forward to resuming his full duties there, because he enjoys it so much.

Harold and Jill met at The Swan, where he saw this good looking girl who was working there. Harold came to Lavenham in 1948, he and Jill married in 1960, and have been at their farm ever since. A goose acts as a watchdog there, and is capable of giving visitors a very punishing welcome. Harold would like to be remembered as 'a person who enjoyed life and lived it to the full. As for Lavenham, Harold says it is, to him, an old village that has grown up.

William & Gay Clegg

www.2bedfordrow.co.uk
www.gayhutchings.com

William Clegg QC moved to Lavenham in 2001 and he and Gay Hutchings married in June 2008. They find Lavenham to be very self-contained and friendly and they like being able to buy almost anything by merely walking to the shops.

Bill's work is based in London, where he is Head of Chambers at 2, Bedford Row, one of the country's leading sets of barrister's chambers. Bill specialises in white collar fraud, regulatory work, health and safety as well as general criminal law. Perhaps one of the best known cases in which Bill has been instructed was the defence of Barry George, who was found not guilty of the murder of Jill Dando, the well known television presenter. Bill first acted for Barry George in his second appeal when the original conviction was quashed because of doubts over the forensic evidence.

Gay Hutchings met Bill in Colchester. She is a highly talented architectural and stained glass painter and printmaker. As her website indicates "her work is largely representational, the aim being to combine reality with imagination in a way which produces a certain ambiguity of interpretation in the eye of the beholder."

Gay, who studied Fine Art Stained Glass at the Central School of Art in London, was previously a French and German interpreter at the Munich Olympic Games, having also worked for the International Olympic Committee.

Cyril & Evelyn Curtis

Cyril and Evelyn have lived in Lavenham since 1993, having moved here from Frinton, buying their house before it was even built. Cyril, who for many years ran the Church bookstall, is now mainly

retired, though still involved with the Churches & Cathedrals Shops Association and is a Trustee of the Papworth Hospital Trust in Cambridge.

Evelyn is still heavily involved in journalism. She has published four cookery books, detailed opposite, and is a regular contributor to the Suffolk Free Press, Bath Chronicle, Somerset Guardian and Somerset Magazine.

Cyril spent 11 very successful years running the bookstall (prior to its new format) and achieved sales of £340,000 for the church during that time. His former extensive retail experience paid big dividends there.

Evelyn was editor of the village magazine for six years and helped Cyril run the church bookstall. In 2006 she started the 21st Ladies Luncheon Club (*see details in the clubs and associations section*). She gets her writing inspiration from living in Suffolk.

Cyril and Evelyn with Church bookstall volunteers on the occasion of Cyril's retirement in 2008 from managing the gift shop

www.evelyncurtis.co.uk

Lavenham Church Cookbook

Published 1999 and reprinted 2003, it was designed and printed by Lavenham Press. ISBN 0-9539806-2-6. It has made over £4,000 to date for church funds.

My kind of people, my kind of cooking

Published 2000, designed and printed by Lavenham Press. ISBN 0-9539806-0-X. Includes contributions from a number of well known Lavenham people.

Step into my Kitchen throughout the Year

Published 2001, designed and printed by Lavenham Press.

ISBN 0-9539806-1-8.

Another Step into my Kitchen

Published 2006, designed and printed by Lavenham Press.

ISBN 0-9539806-3-4.

Evelyn

Cyril

Régis & Martine Crépy

For an excellent example of the Entente Cordiale in action it is difficult to think of better 'ambassadors extraordinaire' than Régis and Martine who, apart from their very busy work schedule, do a great deal for the village in many ways. Both French, Régis was born in Lille and Martine in Tarn. They met at the University of Lausanne, in Switzerland, the finest hotel and catering university in the world.

After working in Switzerland and France, running luxurious establishments, they headed to England to learn English, starting in London, then Hertford and arriving in Lavenham in May 1985 just in time for their daughter's first steps. It was that year when they converted The Great House into a restaurant, with five bedrooms being opened in 1986.

Régis and Martine loved the village at first sight and the warmth of The Great House just confirmed their decision to start their new venture! They have had tremendous support from all their customers over the past 20 years, most of whom have become friends. Their trade is at the centre of their family life either for a birthday, a wedding anniversary, celebrating a graduation or just something to eat!

The Great House has been a strong supporter of Lavenham Sinfonia for many years. In addition, the Crepy's are involved with different charities on a regular basis. In addition to The Great House, the Crépy empire includes two other fine restaurants — Il Punto The Brasserie, at Neptune Quay, Ipswich, and Maison Bleue in Bury St Edmunds.

David & Joan Deacon

David and Joan live near the centre of the village. David, who has been based in Lavenham all his life, is still working and taking part in many village activities. His office is in the new complex off Norman Way, where he combines managing funeral services with consultancy to the building firm started by his father.

He served on Lavenham Parish Council for no less than thirty years, and as Chairman for about 12 to 13. Getting the social housing up Bears Lane was one of his favourite achievements. With other councillors he became involved in many meetings to discuss reorganising the Market Place layout. The Parish Council view was over-ridden by planning officers from Babergh District Council and the current poor marking is the result. During his time on the Council they were very active in arranging various visits by members of the US 487 Bomb Group to the village and airfield.

Soon after leaving school and having served a short apprenticeship in plumbing, he served two years National Service in the Royal Horse Artillery, mostly based in Germany (near the infamous Belsen camp) at the height of the Cold War. He later intended to go and work in the Middle East but the business of the family firm kept him at Lavenham.

The most significant change he has seen is the demise of agricultural workers, whose numbers peaked at about 100 on Parish farms. Industry has also changed considerably, as have transport and shops. Housing has been another massive difference in his time here. He would like to see more local employment, with rewarding jobs, which would improve the social fabric of the village.

Paul Evans

www.paulevans-arrist.com
gallery@lavenhamcontemporary.fsnet.co.uk

Paul Evans is one of the leading landscape painters working today. In addition to showing his work with a selection of top galleries, Paul also has his own gallery — Lavenham Contemporary — which gives him the valuable opportunity to meet and discuss his work with interested collectors.

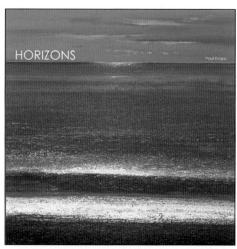

Cover of Horizons by Paul Evans, published 2005, printed by Lavenham Press, published by Terence Dalton Ltd

The gallery is run jointly with his colleague, Lizzi Stevens (see later in this section). They encourage numerous people to visit Lavenham to see Paul's work, who then go on to enjoy the many other attractions the village has to offer.

Paul lives with his wife Lesley at Milden, just outside Lavenham. Originally from Sussex, he studied Printmaking and Illustration for four years at Eastbourne College of Art and Design, and has been fortunate to make his living solely from his painting since graduating in 1976. He then started to show his work at the Ralph Lewis Gallery in Brighton's Lanes, immediately selling everything that he could produce.

Since then Paul has held over 50 solo exhibitions and been involved in numerous group shows, usually attended by large numbers of collectors, and quite often selling out within hours of the opening. He is now widely known for his highly individual style, inspired by East Anglia's landscape and coast, Sussex Downland, the Kent Weald and Cornwall's rugged coast and moorland.

His painting explores only a few locations in detail through all times of the year, to convey a deep sense of place in the finished piece. His early work was mostly in watercolour and ink, and he now uses mainly water based mixed media, often employing unorthodox techniques such as flicking, spraying and dribbling the paint.

Lavenham Contemporary Gallery

Paul paints every day, often starting as early as 5 o'clock in the morning, especially if he later spends some time in the gallery. He can usually be found in his gallery at weekends. Paul's first gallery in Lavenham was in Water Street, and when the Crooked House came on the market the gallery relocated, and quickly attracted as many as 40,000 visitors a year.

Then, after about ten years, and working with much larger canvasses (needing more hanging space), he bought what had been the old Wildlife Gallery building, and launched Lavenham Contemporary. The Crooked House was

Cover of Travels by Paul Evans, published 2006, printed by Lavenham Press

Cover of Coasts by Paul Evans, published 2006, printed by Lavenham Press, published by Terence Dalton Ltd

sold to his friends Alison Englefield and Clare Calder-Marshall, known from their gallery in Cornwall, who have continued a gallery in the Crooked House in their own individual style.

There have been two books published about Paul's work -— Horizons and Coasts. In Horizons there is a question and answer session with writer Laura Scamponi, in which his life, work and inspirations are fully explored. Recommended reading!

In 2005 Paul was filmed for Anglia Television painting on Aldeburgh beach, and the resulting watercolour has been

used both as the cover for Coasts, and also as a Limited Edition Print included with the book. Coasts follows Paul's fascination with his favourite parts of the British Coastline and investigates the draw it has always held for artists and creative people. A very few copies of both books are still available either in the gallery, or by post from the Publisher, Terence Dalton Ltd., part of the Lavenham Press.

Paul is currently working on another book, about Churches, a recurring theme in his painting. After this he has plans for future book projects on the Suffolk Coast, and then Sussex, which will lead to a series on other counties in England.

Leonie Frieda

www.leoniefrieda.com

Leonie had rushed back for our first meeting from a day escorting HRH Prince Michael of Kent. She acts as part-time lady-in-waiting to Princess Michael who, unfortunately, was unable to attend the event — the opening of the radiography wing of the Veterinary School of Cambridge University teaching hospital.

Leonie with HRH Prince Michael

Currently living in a fascinating pink, beamed cottage near the centre of the village, Leonie is now writing a book on '*The Deadly Sisterhood — Princesses of the Italian Renaissance*'.

Leonie's office is a true 'command central', with three computers, a well-arranged table with carefully annotated research documents and numerous tidily arranged files. She tends to write from about 10am to 4pm each day, other duties permitting.

Her first book, published in 2004, for which she has become very well known, is a biography — *Catherine de Medici, Renaissance Queen*. It was described as a No.1 biography best-seller by *The Independent*, No. 10 non-fiction best-seller by *The Sunday Times* and No. 4 in *BBC History Magazine*'s "Top Ten History Books."

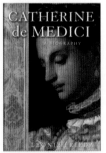

Cover of Catherine de Medici, Renaissance Queen

Published in the USA in 2005, the book received great acclaim in the USA and Canada. Research for the book took her to Paris, Florence, Rome and the chateaux of the Loire region.

Leonie, Swedish by birth, was educated in Britain, Germany and France and speaks five languages. She modelled for a while, having been 'discovered' by Yves St Laurent while visiting the Rive Gauche store in Paris, became an interpreter and lived in the Middle East.

When younger she was a very keen tennis player, and played against Sue Barker on several occasions. Her friendship with Bjorn Borg began in 1972 (the year he won Junior Wimbledon), thanks to Ile Nastase insisting that, as Borg spoke no English, Leonie should wish him a happy birthday in Swedish.

Leonie was formerly married to Nigel Frieda (brother of celebrity hair stylist John Frieda) and has two children. She and Nigel together built up and co-owned Matrix, 17 recording

studios (the largest independent group in the world) used by The Rolling Stones and Oasis. Top of the Pops was recorded there and, at one time, Madonna was a client.

Why Lavenham? Her sister, Anna Ponton, lives nearby in Thorpe Morieux and suggested it would be an ideal and peaceful place to continue her writing. Having only passed through Lavenham before she is fascinated with it and, like others, including myself, regards the village as a fine example of what England used to be like or, as she puts it, "an extraordinary walk back into the past and the best of today. The past with compassion."

At St Tropez, summer 2007

Philip & Wendy Gibson

Having lived in Suffolk for many years, Philip and Wendy came to Lavenham in 1995, where they own and manage the Angel Gallery and the Angel Gallery B&B in the Market Place.

Wendy, who has a Masters Degree, spent many years in the professional theatre, acting and directing plays. Latterly she lectured in schools and colleges, including Suffolk College. She is active in many aspects of village life and is an established published poet.

Philip is also District Councillor for Lavenham, Vice-Chairman of the Parish Council, committee member of Lavenham Merchants' Guild and actively involved with the Lavenham Society, Lavenham Woodland Project and the Guildhall. With a previous career as a Land Agent, mainly in Suffolk, he has considerable experience in planning, environmental and agricultural issues.

He has served on several national and county countryside committees, including locally the Dedham Vale and Stour Valley Project and the Suffolk Farming and Advisory Group.

Philip is helping to address the current challenges facing Lavenham, amongst which are concern for the commercial viability of the village, affordable housing, planning matters, revising the layout of the Market Place and access provision for the disabled.

In their spare time, both Philip and Wendy enjoy Scottish Dancing.

The Market Place (Wendy Gibson, 2006)
Sun on the
Guildhall.
A sight to
lighten the
heaviest heart,
and recall the centuries
of toil and travail
which created the
imposing façade.
Linking past and
present in an
explosion of light
to force away
darkness and
fear of the
unknown.

The Wish (Wendy Gibson, 2000)
The day with its golden wash
Drifted across the mountains
Of horror, linking together both
The prison of day and the
Blessed freedom of the night
Spent in silent dreams,
The dream of a nether world
In which death and destruction have no place.

143

John & Marylyn Gurling

John and Marylyn live close to the village centre. John was born in Lavenham, in a house in the High Street, and Marylyn first came here in the 1960s. The Gurling family came to Lavenham in 1630 from Stradbroke, where they had lived since the 1400s.

Actively engaged in village matters in so many ways, John & Lyn organised production and distribution of a Millennium Medal, in conjunction with Lavenham Parish Council, to all Lavenham children (up to the age of 18) in 2000.

John is a mine of information about the village and featured, with others, in the first edition of *Our Memories*, published in 2006. He keeps a delightful garden, has a fascinating library of items

about the village and collects 17th century Suffolk tokens (which were issued as small change), one of them to his ancestor John Girling who kept The Swan in 1667. He also has a photograph of Miss World 1964, Ann Sydney, in the Market Place in 1965 after the opening of the Wool Hall.

He remembers playing football in the street and rarely having to move out of the way for traffic, Green Willows as a meadow with a tennis court and some chickens, and charity houses that had no bathroom, an outside toilet and a curtained off bedroom.

Marylyn Gurling is another person to whom the adage 'if you want something done, ask a busy person' truly applies. In addition to her many hours as Chairman of the Parish Council she supports Lavenham Merchants' Guild and works long part time hours in a local business. Instrumental in starting Lavenham First Responders, she is also a Governor of Lavenham School, Link Adviser for Age Concern, Chairman of LAMBS and Treasurer of the Lavenham Exhibition and Museum Trust.

Lyn holds a Parish Surgery every week in the Village Hall, dealing with

matters often outside the Parish Council remit. She also gets numerous telephone calls from residents about non-parish items. Lyn is working hard with the Parish and District Councils to try and realise more affordable (i.e. 'never-to-be-sold') housing. A project is afoot to improve and expand sheltered housing facilities, and Lyn would like to see a care home (and a charity shop).

The biggest changes John and Lyn have seen in Lavenham have been the improved appearance of houses, some of which were in a fairly parlous state following World War II (though not as a result of bombing, of course). They have also noticed the marked improvement in street appearance (wires and posts being removed) and the build-up of traffic through the village.

They have also noted the large change in social mix and the changed expectations amongst residents — particularly in terms of housing requirements. Standards have widened considerably between the less and better off — differences were far less marked when John and Lyn first met. Indeed, Lyn recalls thinking she had stepped back into another age when she first came to the village.

Both John and Lyn feel that Lavenham is a village that has everything to offer, with so many facilities, the magnificent church, its bus services, lovely views, tourists in reasonable numbers, working shops and excellent eating establishments.

Mike & Gaye Hodges

Gaye is chairperson of the Cambridge Extra Mural group in Lavenham, which has about 25 regular participants in the classes, sometimes up to 100 for well known tutors. She's also chairperson of Lavenham's Hidden Gardens, organised annually with Ray and Barbara Peevor and Diana Snelling.

For Lavenham Carnival, Gaye organises publicity, food outlets, the tea tent and, with Jill Jones, the family fun morning. She's a team member of the Woodland Project and is also on the Guildhall Local Committee and Museum sub-committee, including the remaking of various exhibitions.

When not busy with all these activities she is a sidesperson and occasional guide in church and enjoys Scottish Country Dancing at the Village Hall.

Gaye would like to see the Railway Walk improved, more social housing, a care home for older persons, better street lighting and youth club upgrades.

Husband Mike is busy with Lavenham Photographic Studio and other associated businesses in Merchants Row and is deeply involved in village activities, including the Woodland Project, Lavenham Merchants' Guild and the production of the 'Our Memories' book project. The studio business is reflected elsewhere in this book.

Robert Holmes

Rob is probably best known for his work as Production Manager of *Lavenham Life*, the village magazine. To produce this he has his computer linked to a very powerful Canon iR5870Ci A3/A4 laser printer/copier and has a stapler/folder machine. Other work includes parish magazines for Cockfield and Brettenham, plus programmes for Lavenham Sinfonia, Hidden Gardens, Choir concerts, Over 60s, the Carnival and funeral service sheets.

Born in March 1953, he has lived all his life in Lavenham. He has been confined to a wheelchair since December 1971, when he was involved in a serious car crash on the Bury Road, near Bradfield. He worked at Holloways (the former factory on Lower Road), after his accident, until 1986, printing labels for cosmetics. He then took computer courses at Suffolk College and has been involved in computing and printing ever since.

The biggest changes he has seen are in the traffic, particularly car parking, and he says that Lavenham has been 'tidied up' since his boyhood. He has also been involved with the Salvation Army in Lavenham all his life, being Deputy Songster Leader (assistant choir leader) and former cornet player in the band and Singing Company Leader (junior choir leader).

Eileen Huffey

Like many other older residents in the village, Eileen is a mine of information and reminiscences. She also has a wonderful collection of photos going back many years. She has lived in Lavenham all her life, since the early 1920s, in the same house but on different streets. That came about when the Station Road houses were renumbered as part of the High Street, largely at Eileen's insistence with Babergh District Council.

She ran a hairdressing business for many years, later as a freelance for the housebound and elderly, helped in several local businesses and nursed a friend with cancer for a time. She is, or has been, a member of Lavenham Women's Institute, the Keep Fit group, Garden Club, Bird Club, Over 60s Club and was a founder member of the Theatre Group and the Friends of Lavenham Church. She was a Trustee of the Lavenham Charities and helped at the church bookstall.

Eileen has particularly welcomed the many newcomers, noticed the large increase in traffic and the number of shops in Lavenham that have opened and closed during her lifetime. Eileen thinks Lavenham is a great place, with so many facilities, a good bus service, excellent shops and wouldn't want to live anywhere else.

Elsie Hynard

What with her secretarial work with Lavenham Royal British Legion and opening Village Halls, Elsie is a busy person. It's as Secretary to the Women's Section of the Legion that involves her most but she is also involved in other aspects of the branch and club.

Elsie has been Secretary at the Legion since 1946, on and off, and looks forward to the day (as does this author) when the Women's Section combines with the men to create just a Royal British Legion. It is, she feels, an event that is due to come soon, despite reservations from some of the male members.

The club has gone through a lot of changes recently, including staff changes, and Elsie works hard to ensure things run smoothly. She is pleased to report that the financial situation is also improving. With Sue Fayers she is involved in the Poppy Day collections, which provides funds for assistance with stairlifts, electric wheelchairs, domestic items and care in convalescent homes.

Having lived in Lavenham all her life, Elsie went to Lavenham School (where she contributed no less than 2/6d to a Village Hall — a concept that eventually took many years to come to fruition) and left at age 14. She spent World War II in the WAAF, working with aircraft. After being demobbed in 1946 she worked at a number of jobs, including corset making, home help, work at Perseverance House for two teachers, metal stamping at Stockos in Barn Street and rug binding with the Lavenham Rug Company, which was then based where Lavenham Co-op currently operates.

Elsie (right) in car with relations

Jim & Carol Keohane

Blaize Cottages — Church Street

www.blaizecottages.com

Luxury, 5 star, Grade II listed, 16th century self catering cottages with vaulted ceilings and log fires. Tourism award winners in every year since opening.

Jim and Carol are a busy couple who have made a big contribution to Lavenham today — not least their involvement, with others, in the new Village Hall. If you ask them, Jim would wish to be remembered as "he didn't waste time'.

Like the author, they're incomers, arriving in 2000, when Jim was semi-retired, having been involved at a high level in the energy industry and having previously lived in Nottingham. They now run Blaize Cottages (two units) as a five star self-catering business.

Jim was on the Village Hall management committee for several years and put a lot of time in there. He also still works in a senior consultancy role in the aviation industry, including briefing of MPs (who come in very differing shades of intelligence, apparently).

Changes they've noticed in the village since they arrived include more traffic, differences at both The Swan and The Angel, a rapid turnover of some shops and parking in the Market Place

Blaize Barn

The barn comfortably sleeps four persons. Associated with Blaize House for many years, the barn's most famous claim to fame is its use as a brothel in World War II (one of three, I'm told)!

Wool Cottage

Sleeps two. Named because of the strong links Lavenham has with the wool cloth trade and, indeed, historically part of Blaize House.

A lovely garden

Matthew Manning

www.matthewmanning.com

Matthew Manning, who moved to Lavenham fairly recently is, as his website describes, a world-famous healer who lectures and demonstrates his techniques all over the world. He has been involved in more scientific research and testing than any other healer in the world and has addressed the Royal Society of Medicine and spoken to MPs in the Houses of Parliament about his healing work.

Regularly featured in the media, he devotes himself to healing and is the author of *One Foot in the Stars*, his autobiography, *No Faith Required*, *The Link* and *The Healing Journey*.

Sir David Frost said "Matthew's abilities are literally beyond belief" and Karel Sikora, Professor of Cancer Medicine at Imperial College and Consultant Oncologist at Hammersmith Hospital, said "Matthew Manning has a remarkable track record of working at the interface between body and soul. His knowledge is outstanding in both breadth and detail."

The Guardian wrote that "Matthew Manning offers positive approaches — from techniques to control stress and bring relaxation to those which build and foster positive self-image. He sets no limits to where it can lead."

Amanda Mansell

If it's the 1st or 7th chakra, or anything in between, then Amanda Mansell can tell you all about it. Indeed, you can read about it in detail in her book, *Attention, Seekers* (a serious book, written humorously), published in 2007.

Amanda, formerly a nurse, midwife and school matron, shares her home with her partner, four whippets,  two cats and some chickens, and has lived in her current home in Lavenham since 1997. She has planted a wild flower meadow behind her home, a fruit orchard and old English hedgerows.

It was her early interest in reflexology that led to her interest in chakras, combined with her need to resolve her pain problem (she suffered atrocious ill health for years). She also trained as an iridologist at Cambridge, but because of illness has only been able to practice iridology part-time at home.

Attention, Seekers is a 480 page publication with alphabetical musings on chakras, colour, bores, bullies, health, life, love, politics, spirituality, dogs, cats, chickens and anything else that amuses, infuriates or fascinates her. Her beloved whippets are always there too, ready to listen gravely.

She feels (*like this author*) that politicians are deaf to the wishes of the voters and Europe has nothing less than federal intentions. The changes she has  noticed in Lavenham are the move of the library, the loss of young families, and general social cohesion.

Marjorie Newman

Marjorie is over 80 and enjoying village life to the full — like so many older people in Lavenham. She finds that friends and family take up much of her time, but she still manages to do many other things. "One thing I have learnt is that in Lavenham, age means nothing."

Along with others she's trying to prove it. She currently helps in the running of the recently opened new church gift shop and the bookstall, which bring in very useful money for the church. She was involved with the kneeler project and is also one of the welcomers at the church which, she says, is teaching her more and more about that beautiful building.

She is on the Guildhall Local Committee, organises the Guildhall flower rota and was first President of the new Carpet Bowls Club. She enjoys opening her home as a venue for village events — such as occasional strawberry teas, the annual party of the Friendship Club and other sundry gatherings.

Marjorie is active each year, with several other ladies from the village, in presenting the event so dear to her heart — Donkey Day. This is a real Lavenham and District effort each year, which all donkey lovers enjoy and support generously. It takes over almost the complete house and raises money for Marjorie's favourite charity. In 2008, with a large team of willing volunteers, she raised over £1,100.

Donkey day takes place in the garden, if fine, or otherwise in the house. There are the usual stalls, lots of bargains, tombola and coffee and biscuits. Gifts and cards are also on sale.

Marjorie's interest in donkeys started after she contacted a donkey sanctuary in Devon which she had recently visited. Some donkeys there had come from good homes but many had been cruelly treated all their lives, knowing nothing but harshness.

A teacher at Lavenham Primary School for over 30 years, she was founder and later chairman of Lavenham Tennis Club and also a regular member of Amateur Dramatic shows in the Primary School. She and her husband Derek (who died in 2004) operated the butchers shop in the High Street for 38 years.

Marjorie was secretary and treasurer of Lavenham Womens' Institute and was its President from 1962—65. She was heavily involved in fund raising for the playing field, was for many years an active member of the Community Council and is a past Chairman and President of Lavenham Tennis Club.

Marjorie's main sport these days is golf — she plays at Newton Green. She has two children and four grandchildren.

Watch out ! He's behind you !

Elizabeth Norman

photo courtesy Lavenham Photographic

You may not know her but almost every person in Lavenham, like millions all over the UK, will know her voice. You hear her frequently as the smooth, dulcet tones of BT Answer 1571, BT Call Minder and BT's messaging service.

Elizabeth comes from a strong theatrical background and is still involved, after many years in the theatre, in voice-over work and talks to groups about life on the stage.

Elizabeth first had a weekend retreat in Lavenham as far back as 1977, moved here permanently in 1980, and had houses in the High Street and Water Street before moving to her present home. The changes she has noticed most since coming here — apart from the continuing property renovation — are the loss of the local 'bobby', removal of play equipment on 'health and safety' grounds, the increase in traffic and the arrival of the new Village Hall.

In Lavenham, she presented a very popular performance of "Anne of Cleves" during an Arts Festival organised by Lavenham Merchants' Guild (and again later) giving a dry, funny, sideways look at how 'The Flanders Mare' was determined to keep her head on her neck.

Elizabeth entered the theatrical profession in 1968 after a two year course in Theatre Design and Stage Management at Croydon College of Art. After a brief spell as assistant stage manager she then worked continuously and successfully as an actress in repertory, the West End (Gisela "Abelard and Heloise", The Wyndham's Theatre and Davina "Otherwise Engaged", directed by Harold Pinter at the Comedy Theatre), in television and as a voice over artist. She also became known as "The British Caledonian Girl", when she featured in the award winning TV advertisement.

Other TV work included The Dick Emery Show, "Rough Justice", "Target", "Don't Forget to Write", 'Dr. Who" and "The Rough with the Smooth." Commercials have included Courtelle Clothes, Milton II, Motherware, Crackerwheat and Sholley Trolley. Over the last twenty years she has mostly been locally and community based, ranging from performing, teaching and voice overs. Elizabeth has performed in productions in a prison, been involved with a dance performance by communities all over England to celebrate the opening of the Royal Festival Hall and was involved with Dance East in a promotional DVD for their new Dance House.

Elizabeth playing 'Anne of Cleves'

photo courtesy Lavenham Photographic

Alex Paul

Partnership (STP). He has been working in the tourism industry for over 20 years. His experiences range from international student/youth travel, online accommodation provision, to sales/marketing of high end special interest programmes in the international marketplace.

A lex Paul and his family moved to Lavenham in Easter 2008. He told me "My wife and I had been coming to East Anglia for many years for holidays and short breaks. We've always loved the unique and authentic feel of Suffolk, the big skies, fantastic food and wonderful heritage. Once we had made the decision that we wanted to leave London with our young family we explored all our favourite places in search of a home.

Lavenham just offered us exactly what we wanted in terms of size, the welcome we got from everyone in the village, the primary school is fantastic and there can't be anywhere as beautiful or unique to live. Now to match the perfect home, I have the perfect job in supporting the tourism industry in Suffolk and my wife Justine now helps organise the Lavenham Farmers' Markets and Arts & Craft Fair."

For the past four years he has worked for VisitBritain, initially developing marketing partnerships with UK industry and then as Director of Trade & Business Relations for North America, based out of Chicago, USA. He returned to VisitBritain's HQ in London last year to set up a new initiative called eventBritain which was focussed on delivering more events for Britain on the back of the London 2012 games. He is really excited about his new role with STP and looks forward to working with Lavenham Merchants' Guild and others to make Suffolk the first and best choice of destination for the visitor.

Suffolk Tourism
www.visit-suffolk.org.uk

Alex is the new Tourism Manager at the Suffolk Tourism

The Visit Suffolk website opening page

Tony & Eve Ranzetta

Note: During the writing of this book, very sadly, Eve tragically died. There was a magnificent Requiem Mass for her in Lavenham Church. After consultation Tony felt the article should proceed.

From their lovely home on the outskirts of the village, near the only ford, Deacon Tony and his wife Eve played a strong part in village life. They moved here in 1996, from Brentwood, to be nearer their son and daughter-in-law, already having visited and taken part in activities within the village on quite a number of occasions.

A medley of styles and periods, the oldest dating back to 1485, there have been several additions and alterations to the family home since that time. Several older local residents remember visiting when it operated as a Bed & Breakfast.

In the twelve years since they arrived they felt warmth and comradeship between the various groups in the village although, strangely, the Village Hall seemed, to them, to have moved the centre of gravity of the village further away from the actual centre. They liked the design of the Village Hall and felt it plays an important part in village life.

Tony's involvement with the village includes pastoral work for the Catholic community (*probably around 80 strong at the time of writing*), active participation in the Clergy Fraternal Group (CofE, RC and Salvation Army) which is growing in strength, work as a Village Hall trustee and the editorial committee of *Lavenham Life*. He feels that the magazine is a healthy and useful addition to the village. He also notes a thirst for unity amongst Christians in the village and runs a Bible Group monthly at home.

The ford on Frogs Hall Road

Eve used to be on the Guildhall Committee, was Manager of the Little Hall Committee and used to be a governor at Lavenham School. She studied and had extensive in-depth knowledge of the de Vere family and was writing a book about John de Vere, 13th Earl of Oxford, with additional plans to write a book about Lavenham in the 17th century.

Tony would like to see additional parking towards their end of the village in order to spread out the business hub. Car parking on the roads, particularly in the centre of the village, means that it is actually safer to walk and cross the road, because cars and lorries are automatically slowed down most of the time. Like others, he's noticed that many of the cars parked on the Market Place and streets belong to residents who have garages or more than one vehicle.

Tony and Eve Ranzetta at a function

Carroll & Barbara Reeve

Carroll and Barbara had only been here a year before they found themselves helping with the Carnival Rare Breeds Car Show and tea tent. In 1999 Carroll volunteered to chair the Carnival committee (half the previous committee having resigned) and remained Chairman until 2008. The Committee — part of the Lavenham Community Council — has helped raised over £200,000 for the village from the Carnival, together with the Hidden Gardens, Annual Street Fayre and other ad hoc fund raisers.

The rebuilt Pavilion on the Recreation Ground was largely funded from this and likewise the early stages development of the Village Hall. The 2008 Carnival theme was Food and Farming and buy locally. Many people commented they they liked the 'country feel.'

The 2007 Carnival, celebrating the 1257 granting of the village's market charter was, no doubt, financially the most successful in recent years.

Apart from the Carnival (with its six strong organising group), Carroll has been, or is, involved with the Cambridge Extra-Mural Committee, the new Pavilion at the Recreation Ground, the Lavenham Society, planning, grant raising and development of the Village Hall (6 years in all) and the Village Design Statement. They all bear his clear imprint. The Village Design Statement, mentioned later in this book, was based on hard work by a small group and should perhaps, in his opinion, be used more by both the Parish and District Councils in their deliberations on where Lavenham is going. Many of the initiatives he's been involved with have been driven by the move by successive governments to push down services and unless a community has the infrastructure such services cannot be delivered.

Carroll and his wife Barbara moved to Lavenham in 1996 from a small-holding in Finchingfield, Essex. As frequent

Carroll & Barbara Reeve at the 1257 celebrations in 2007
photo courtesy of Lavenham Photographic

visitors to Lavenham, before their move here, they had little idea of the village's attractions as a resident — friendly, great range of clubs and societies and so on.

Changes they have noticed since coming include the development of the Village Hall and its undoubted success by all the uses it is put to. They don't wish to see the village preserved in aspic and believe that rational changes for the future should include increased affordable housing (especially three-bedroom houses, not built in ghettoes), building on brownfield sites and perhaps a park and ride system, including leaving the car at home and ride, to prevent residents and retail staff using the Market Place or other streets as permanent parking places.

A concept Carroll is interested in is the Transition Initiative (see http://transitiontowns.org for further information). This involves:

- exploring and following pathways of practical action that will reduce our carbon emissions and dependence on fossil fuels
- building a town's (or village's) resilience, that is its ability to withstand shocks from outside, through being more self-reliant in areas such as food, energy, health care, jobs and economics.

Sir Clive Rose GCMG

Over a considerable number of years, Sir Clive Rose has been involved in many aspects of village life, always in a quiet but very effective manner.

Currently, apart from his author's activities (*A Fanfare for Lavenham*, 2007; *Lavenham Remembers*, 2006 (ed); *Alice Owen — Tudor Lady*, 2006; *The Unending Quest*, 1996; *The Soviet Propaganda Network*, 1988 and *Campaigns against Western Defence*, 1985/6), he is one of the Community Centre Trustees.

He is extensively involved in the plans for a Coat of Arms for Lavenham and for a Literary Weekend in 2009. He is also Vice-Patron of the Suffolk Preservation Society, whose headquarters is in Little Hall.

Sir Clive Rose, with his wife Elisabeth, moved to Lavenham in 1978. His choice of house was, apparently, written up in *The Times*. His ancestors lived in West Suffolk from the 15th to 19th centuries.

Previously in Lavenham, Sir Clive was Community Emergency Adviser. He also sat on the Parochial Church Council for 18 years, the Guildhall Committee for 18 years and was President of the Scouts and Guides in the 1980s.

The changes he has seen in Lavenham since arriving thirty years ago include a more open, flourishing village,

newcomers welcomed — particularly if they get involved in village activities — the loss of local police, the formation of the Lavenham Society and, after years of attempts, the opening of the Village Hall.

He was born 15 September 1921, and was educated at Marlborough College, and Christ Church, Oxford (MA). In 1946 he married Elisabeth Lewis, who died in 2006. They had two sons and three daughters. One son, with his wife, has recently come to live in Lavenham.

During World War II, Sir Clive served as a Major in the Rifle Brigade, (1941-46), in Europe, (1944-45), India, (1945) and Iraq, (1945-46).

His diplomatic career began in 1948, and included service in the Foreign Office, Madras, Bonn, Montevideo, Paris, Washington, and as Head of the British Delegation to negotiations with the Russians on force reductions in Central Europe (1973—76), Vienna; Deputy Secretary in the Cabinet Office (1976—79) as UK Permanent Representative on the North Atlantic Council (1979—82).

Yvonne Skargon

Yvonne Skargon, who has lived in Lavenham some 28 years, is a wood engraver and book illustrator. Watercolours, drawings and engravings, often on botanical and culinary themes, have been commissioned by many leading English publishers and she is

a frequent contributor to *Hortus*, the quarterly gardening journal.

Her work will be familiar to readers of Jane Grigson's books on food and cooking and, in 1991, the author was privileged to be at the launch, at Little Hall, of Yvonne's Royal Mail commemorative issue of Roses postage stamps which she designed and engraved. They are beautiful examples of the illustrator's art.

She exhibits with the Society of Wood Engravers, of which she is a long-standing Member, and in a number of commercial galleries here and abroad which specialise in wood engraving. Examples of her work are in the collections of the Victoria & Albert Museum and the Hunt Institute for Botanical Documentation, Carnegie Mellon University, Pittsburgh. For many years she worked in London as a typographer and book designer and for five years she taught wood engraving at the Royal College of Art.

Her book *The Importance of Being Oscar*, in which she brought together Oscar Wilde and her cat Oscar, has reprinted many times since its publication in 1988 and has been published in American, Dutch, Scandinavian and Japanese editions. *Lily and Hodge and Dr. Johnson* makes a conjunction between Johnson's

From *A Garden of My Own*

words and the two kittens who succeeded Oscar.

Her other books include *A Garden of My Own* which contains wood engravings based on her Lavenham garden, *A Concatenation* — an anthology of cat writings and engravings, and *Watermarks* — engravings with writings by a wide range of authors on watery themes.

The *Oscar* and *Lily and Hodge* books have been issued together in a special edition, with the original blocks finely printed from the wood. A selection of engravings from throughout her career, *Yvonne Skargon, The Engraver's Cut*, was published in 2004.

Yvonne Skargon's Picture Book offers a delightful pocket-size celebration of her work. Calendars for 2005, 2006 and 2008 were issued in small editions, and a further calendar is scheduled for 2009.

'Anybody can be good in the country'
The portrait of Dorian Gray

From *The Importance of Being Oscar*

Desmond & Frances Skinner

Desmond and Frances have lived in Laveham since 1986. They have taken part in many village activities, including raising money for the St Nicholas Hospice. Desmond even built a tombola machine for those events.

They both feel that Lavenham retains the village atmosphere yet with all the facilities of a small town and have never regretted coming here. Frances was a WI member and the first member of Alan Blyth's music circle and Desmond, who was on the Parochial Church Council for a while, has given many talks to village organisations on his hotelier experiences, saying "Laughter is the best medicine."

Many of us remember the excellent shows that Desmond and Frances (*the Othello and Desdemona winners of a Shakespeare competition in the Toynbee Hall in 1946*) arranged in the old Church Rooms, with Desmond as compere and Frances as one of the star acts.

They celebrated their Diamond Wedding in 2008. Luckily for those privileged to be invited, including the author, their Sapphire, Golden, Emerald and Diamond Wedding anniversaries have all been held at The Great House.

Desmond and Frances at their Emerald wedding celebration at The Great House

Nellie Smith

Nellie has lived in Lavenham most of her life and was 102 on 22 October 2008. She has lived in her current home (*which was one of eight in a sea of mud when she moved in*) for some 50 years. She remains very bright and talkative, with a phenomenal memory for names, events and places.

Most of her working life she has been a cook, including stints at the old Woolhall when it was a railway convalescent centre, Lavenham Hall, Little Hall (*when Reginald Brill was there*) and The Angel (*up until the time the Whitworths and Barrys took over*).

She moved to Lavenham with her parents just before World War II and, after a number of brief jobs joined the WAAF, at Ipswich. Her service time she remembers as some of her happiest days. She recalls the Americans being in Lavenham in 1944/45, but says she only ever talked to one of them!

The changes she has noticed most are people's clothing and the increased number of houses, especially those in Harwood Place, Meadow Close and Spring Street. Although she wasn't too keen on the village at first, having moved here

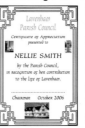

from London (*a very, very different London from the one we know today*), she has come to love the village, knows almost everybody and wouldn't want to live anywhere else.

Lizzi Stevens

Lizzi is a partner in Lavenham Contemporary, the very successful High Street gallery. Her mother is a born-and-bred Lavenham person and Lizzi now lives nearby, having been based in and around Lavenham since 1991.

She started her first Suffolk gallery (having previously been involved with the Alfriston Gallery in East Sussex) in partnership with Paul Evans in Water Street that year, followed by a very successful 10 years as co-owner of the Crooked House Gallery before it's subsequent sale to Clare Calder-Marshall and Alison Englefield.

Lizzi also finds times to produce her own artworks. An early interest in theatre, fairy tales and magic is clearly reflected in much of her work today. She works in collage, with some watercolour for the finer details, building up layers of different papers, sequins, leaves, flowers and fabric — plus any found objects that will fit along with the theme of the image. She describes this as a wonderful excuse to rummage in haberdashery shops, antique markets and art shops. Her work is reproduced as prints by Rosenstiel's, and Christmas cards by Greetings UK. Even without her close family links, Lizzi believes that Lavenham is the perfect place for an art gallery - working in harmony with the draw of the old houses, the church, the Guildhall and Little Hall. Like Paul, her working partner, she does a good deal to promote the village.

Martin & Vickie Weaver

Since Martin's arrival in Lavenham with his wife Vickie, in 1998, he has played a very prominent part in village activities.

This includes bell-ringing at the Parish Church, being a playing member and former Chairman of Lavenham Tennis Club and his current role as a very active Chairman of the Community Council — where he was much involved (with many others) in helping to ensure the Sports Pavilion was built and getting the Village Hall up and running.

He has also (in conjunction with Carroll Reeve and a large team of volunteers) been instrumental in organising the very popular annual Lavenham Carnival.

The Community Council raises considerable funds from Carnival activities, with a record £14,000 in 2007 and £11,000 in 2008. These funds go towards paying for social and recreational facilities in the village.

Martin retired as Director and Shareholder of a construction business in Yorkshire to come to Lavenham, having

visited the village on several occasions and having relatives nearby.

Martin and Vickie originally lived at Hill Green but have now moved right into the centre of the village. What attracts them is the rural location, the nice village atmosphere, the convenient position for visiting London and East Anglia, all the shops and not too many tourists (though acknowledging, of course, that without them Lavenham would not be quite the same).

Roy & Anne Whitworth

'An enclave of peacefulness and tranquillity' is Roy and Anne's description of Lavenham. They don't see the need for much change and feel it a privilege to continue living here since their retirement from The Angel in 2007.

Many of us will remember the Angel Hotel under their aegis. It was their first venture into the pub trade and they ran it in partnership with John Barry for nearly 18 years. Identified as an opportunity for its position, they soon found it to be the centre of a great social scene and far from the kind of rural 'semi-retirement' that they originally had in mind.

There were highlights too numerous to mention at The Angel (including the award of the Good Pub Guide's 'National Pub of the Year' in 1997) Also, a few disasters, like a double booking for wedding parties soon after they took over. Weddings were never so popular after that!

Roy and Anne are now finding life a bit quieter, looking after the garden and spending more time with family and friends. Roy continues to be involved locally with Lavenham Merchants' Guild as Treasurer and is also working on the Guild's new Lavenham website at

www.discoverlavenham.co.uk

Derek & Maureen Wilding

Maureen Wilding has been the Salvation Army historian for Lavenham since 1986 and her husband Derek (who has lived in Lavenham all his life) is the bandmaster. The Army history files are voluminous and extremely detailed and would certainly merit further attention in another volume, rather than this one. Both are very involved with the Salvation Army. They spend many hours organising army events and regular activities, with other army supporters and are usually in the thick of the action.

Derek served in the Royal Air Force for three years and worked for W H Smith then Magson's of York as a sales representative before retirement. Maureen worked at Boots in Bury St Edmunds, which is where she and Derek met. They married in 1962.

Their home near the centre of the village was built on a plot of land for a price that today would hardly buy a tent. It seems like it has been an extremely sound investment, even with the housing market in freefall as it is in 2008.

Lavenham's Royal visitors

Lavenham has enjoyed visits from several Royal persons, including:

2005 — HRH the Prince of Wales and The Duchess of Cornwall

Prince Charles (who is President of the National Trust) and Camilla visited Lavenham on 22nd July 2005 to visit The Guildhall and Little Hall. Amongst the welcoming crowds were a dancing troupe from Kenya, who just happened to be staying in the village at the time.

In the picture below, Jane Gosling, curator at The Guildhall is seen talking with Prince Charles. The Duchess, in pink, is facing the camera.

At Little Hall the couple wished to see the garden and graciously extended an invitation to the gardeners to visit

Highgrove in 2006. They also tried their hands at pargeting, toured the museum section and signed a calligraphic memorial.

As might be expected, there was a heavy police presence in Lavenham that day, indeed most of us have never seen so many police officers, of various types and ranks, in the village together.

Motorcycle police outriders await The Prince of Wales and The Duchess of Cornwall

The schoolchildren made a collage of the day

1996 — HRH The Prince of Wales

Prince Charles, heir to the throne, visited Lavenham church on 24th May 1996. The Prince is the 21st holder of the title in 700 years. Leaving the armed forces in 1976, he set about his royal duties, including some 500 public engagements in Britain and overseas each year.

1928 — HM Queen Mary

Queen Mary visited Lavenham church on the 8th of November 1928. Amongst other things she accepted an album of photographs of the town, taken by Francis Lingard Ranson of Lavenham.

1578 — HM Queen Elizabeth I (?)

It was in 1578 that Queen Elizabeth the First made a royal progress through the counties of Norfolk and Suffolk, the year that Sir William Spring was High Sheriff of Suffolk. The grandson of "the rich clothier", Sir William's duty was to receive and accompany the Queen during her progress through the county. During the Queen's progress it is said that she paid Sir William the honour of a visit (*see Canon Scott's book*).

There is some dispute as to whether she actually visited Lavenham. The visit is not recorded in the 'official' record and modern historians cast doubt on the story.

1275 — HM King Edward I

Edward the First (1239—1307) passed through Lavenham in 1275. He was the eldest son of King Henry III and succeeded his father in 1272. Edward held regular parliaments.

Lavenham remembers

It is tempting to add, in any book about Lavenham, reference to the famous people of the past who have lived here and whom we all remember. However, this book is about Lavenham at the beginning of the 21st century so only a passing reference will be appropriate.

There are, in my opinion, two main exceptions — the de Vere family and the Spring family, because both are still much in evidence today in the buildings we see. I have, therefore, included an entry about the de Veres, about the possible Shakespeare connection (contentious, I know, but fascinating), and the Springs.

These two families are also mentioned in the Church entry in the Buildings section, where a timeline shows how their lives intermeshed with the monarchs of the time and the building of the Church.

In addition, I've also included brief mentions of just some of the famous people who have lived here and who are remembered. Again, my choice.

The de Veres and Earls of Oxford

The de Vere family is represented in Lavenham today by the magnificent church and also by the persistent rumours that Edward de Vere, the 17th Earl of Oxford and Lord of the Manor of Lavenham, was the real William Shakespeare.

The church connection is undeniable, the marks are everywhere. De Vere House still stands in Water Street, Lavenham. The Shakespeare connection is more debatable but is, a very interesting story and books have been written about it.

The de Veres are reputed to be descended from the days of Caesar, but certainly from Alfonsus de Veer of Zealand, who married Countess Katherine of Flanders, daughter of Arnold II. Their son, Alberic (Aubrey) de Vere, came to England and held land under Edward the Confessor. He took sides with William the Conqueror in 1066 and, following the Norman conquest, the two Lavenham manors of Overhall and Netherhall were given to him and he married Beatrix, the Conqueror's sister. Their son, Aubrey II, who was created Great Chamberlain of England in 1133, died in 1141.

Aubrey de Vere, 1st Earl of Oxford (c.1130—1194)

Grandson Aubrey III (who was by tenure the third Baron of Kensington and Count of Guisnes through his marriage) was confirmed in office as the 2nd Lord Great Chamberlain. He was created the first Earl of Oxford by Empress Matilda (Henry's wife), confirmed by Henry II himself with an additional charter in 1156. Aubrey was another crusader/veteran, sometimes known as "Aubrey

the Grim", perhaps because of his height and stern appearance, though there is confusion between "Albericus Aper" (Aubrey the Wild Boar/Vere) and "Albericus Afer" (Aubrey the Grim).

Aubrey's first marriage was to Euphemia Cantilupe, his second to Lucia Abrincis, by whom he had six children. He died in 1194 and was succeeded by 19 earls until the title became extinct in 1703. Lavenham Hall stands near the site of the original mediæval home (mentioned in the Domesday Book) of the de Vere family.

Aubrey de Vere, 2nd Earl (c.1163—1214)

Aubrey was the first son of the 1st Earl and was also the 3rd Lord Great Chamberlain. He was a Privy Councillor, fought alongside Richard Lionheart in Normandy, and later commanded King John's forces in Ireland.

Robert de Vere, 3rd Earl (c.1170—1221)

Robert was the second son of the 1st Earl and 4th Lord Chamberlain of England. He was one of the barons who drew up the Magna Carta (at Bury St Edmunds). King John visited his castle in Castle Hedingham on two occasions

He married Isabel de Bolebec (1176—c.1245), daughter of Hugh de Bolebec, and had two sons. Robert took part as a crusader in the holy wars. Having fallen out of favour with King John, he was returned to favour by King Henry III.

Sir Hugh de Vere, 4th Earl (c.1210—1263)

Hugh was first son of the third Earl and 5th Great Chamberlain. He participated in the crusade of 1248—1254. He was knighted in the reign of King Henry III and was granted the 1st Lavenham Market

Charter by Henry in 1257. He married Hawise Quincy, daughter of the Earl of Winchester in 1223 and had six children. He founded several hospitals and almshouses and built the steeple of Earls Colne church.

Sir Robert de Vere, 5th Earl (1240—1296)

Eldest son of Hugh, the 4th Earl. He became the 6th Great Chamberlain and was a follower of Simon de Montfort, Earl of Leicester, who knighted him on the field of battle in 1264.

Robert made his peace with King Henry III after his return to the throne and later served King Edward I in battle. He married Alice de Sandford and had at least five children

Robert de Vere, 6th Earl (1257—1331)

Eldest son of the 5th Earl and 7th Great Chamberlain. Took part in the wars against Scotland by King Edward I and later with Kings Edward II and III. He officiated at the coronation of Queen Isabella, wife of King Edward II in 1308. He married Margaret Mortimer, daughter of the Earl of March. His only son, Thomas, pre-deceased him and he died without heir. He is buried at Bures, near Hedingham and Lavenham.

John de Vere, 7th Earl (1313—1360)

John was the son of Sir Alphonsus, second son of the 5th Earl and a nephew of the 6th Earl. He became known as one of the most famous of the "Fighting Earls of Oxford", becoming one of Edward III's greatest generals. He fought at Crecy and the siege of Calais and later with the Black Prince at Poitiers. He was killed during the siege of Rheims in 1360 and his corpse was buried at Colne Priory.

Sir Thomas de Vere, 8th Earl (c.1336—1371)

Son of the 7th Earl, he was another "Fighting Vere" who served under King Edward III. He married Maud de Ufford, daughter of the Chief Justice of Ireland and had three children.

Vero nihil verius

De vere

Robert de Vere, 9th Earl (1362—1392)

Robert was only nine years old when he succeeded his father. Nevertheless, he was allowed to act as Lord Great Chamberlain at the coronation of King Richard II (who was himself only 10). From boyhood till his death, he was the closest friend of his cousin King Richard II. He was with him at the quelling of Wat Tyler's Peasants Revolt. Richard created Robert as Marquess of Dublin and Duke of Ireland. Robert, aged 16, married Philippa de Coucy (daughter of the Earl of Bedford and Isabel, daughter of Edward III), divorcing her in 1387. His second marriage was to Agnes Lancerone. In trouble with other aristocrats, and being impeached by Parliament, he fled to France, never to return alive to England. He died childless.

Aubrey de Vere, 10th Earl (c.1338—1400)

Aubrey was Robert's uncle and the son of John de Vere, 7th Earl of Oxford and Maud de Badlesmere. He was also Constable of Wallingford Castle.

Richard de Vere, 11th Earl (1386–1417)

A commander for Henry V at the Battle of Agincourt.

John de Vere, 12th Earl (1406–1462)

A staunch Lancastrian, beheaded with his eldest son by King Edward IV, married the heiress of the barony of Plaiz.

John de Vere, 13th Earl (1443–1513)

Second son of the 12th Earl, he led Henry Richmond's (King Henry VII) army to victory over Richard III at the battle of Bosworth in 1485. John was godfather to Prince Henry (King Henry VIII) in 1491. He was known as King Henry's most trusted general, but did not escape the King's fine of 15,000 marks for having too many liveried servants at a banquet at Hedingham Castle. Associated with Thomas Spring III in the building of Lavenham Parish Church.

John de Vere, 14th Earl (1499–1526)

This John was a nephew of the 13th Earl.

(The male line deviated several times to nephews, uncles and grandsons, but didn't end until the 20th Earl. Several Veres exist from the female line, notably the Irish Veres [originally Vere-Hunt] and the current wife [2006] of Lord Tollemache claims descent from a female Vere)

Sir Robert de Vere, 15th Earl (1490–1540)

A descendant of the eleventh Earl, Richard and a Knight of the Garter. His second son Aubrey married Margaret, niece of Thomas Spring the Rich Clothier, of Lavenham. Robert was patron of the Lavenham Gild of Corpus Christi and granted its charter in 1529. His effigy, depicted in plate armour, is carved on a corner post of Lavenham Guildhall.

John de Vere, 16th Earl (1512–1562)

Granted the charters of the Gilds of St Peter and of Holy Trinity in Lavenham. He was alive during the rebuilding of the church. John officiated as Lord Chamberlain of England at Mary Tudor's coronation. He also officiated as Lord Great Chamberlain of England at Elizabeth's coronation, having accompanied Princess Elizabeth from Hatfield to London where she was proclaimed Queen. Sponsored a dramatic troupe, the Earl of Oxford's men.

Edward de Vere, 17th Earl (1550–1604)

Only son of the 16th Earl (and his wife Margery, née Golding) and the last Earl to hold the Manors of Lavenham. Also known as Viscount Bolbec. He had his own company of actors, became the lessee of Blackfriars Theatre, and his band of actors appeared before the Queen. Edward is thought by many to be the 'real' Shakespeare.

Henry de Vere, 18th Earl (1593–1625)

Son of the 17th Earl by his second wife. Married Lady Diana Cecil. Fought and died in Flanders. He was the last de Vere Lord Great Chamberlain.

Robert de Vere, 19th Earl (1575–1632)

A second cousin of the 18th Earl. He served as a Captain in the Dutch Army.

Aubrey de Vere, 20th Earl (1627–1703)

Only son of the 19th Earl. He was described by Lord Macaulay as "the noblest subject in England." He restored the family fortunes by marrying Anne Bayning, a great heiress, in 1647. His daughter Diana married the first Duke of St Albans.

[Note: Birth and death dates vary from source to source and sometimes there are considerable variations]

Edward de Vere, 17th Earl of Oxford, was Shakespeare?

www.deveresociety.co.uk

Edward was the last Earl of Oxford to hold the position of Lord of the Manor of Lavenham and this adds to the interest in him, possibly, being 'Shakespeare'.

Most readers will be aware of the enormous controversy surrounding any suggestion that a non-Stratfordian wrote "Shakespeare". There are, of course, very strong arguments put forward by the Stratfordians, who pour scorn on the Oxford theory. However — at the very least — the subject makes compelling reading and a vigorous talking point.

A book published in 2006, entitled *Shakespeare by another name. The Life of Edward de Vere, Earl of Oxford, the Man who was Shakespeare*, by Mark Anderson makes compelling reading. There are many other books on the

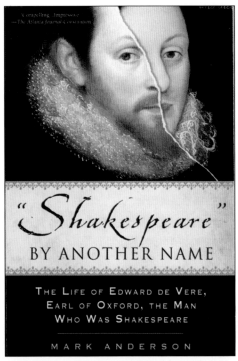

by Mark Anderson, published by Gotham Books in 2006, ISBN 1-592-40215-1, foreword by Sir Derek Jacobi

subject, including *Shakespeare, Who was He? The Oxford Challenge to the Bard of Avon*, by Richard F. Whalen.

Michael Shermer, writing in *Scientific American* in September 2002, lists numerous reasons why he thinks that de Vere was the author. Included in his points are the encoded message by Ben Jonson on the Shakespeare monument at Stratford naming Edward as the man behind the name, documentary proof that the monument was subsequently altered and replaced, and a temple built by the Countess of Pembroke in memory of Shakespeare's (i.e. de Vere's) visit to her estate on the Wiltshire Avon in 1603.

Parallels between Edward's life and the plays are numerous, consistent, complex and intimate. Edward took over the players of the Earl of Warwick in March 1580. When outraged law students from the Inns of Court rioted at the

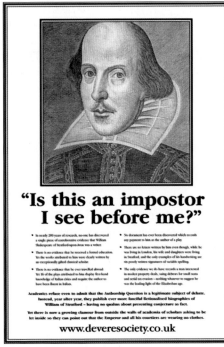

The DVS poster campaign aims to raise the profile of the Shakespeare Authorship Question in the public's mind by questioning the Stratfordian claims to authorship

theatre, Oxford's men replied with such spirit that three of them landed in jail. Lord Burghley then came to Edward's aid by recommending his company to the Vice-Chancellor of Cambridge University. Among his servants at the time were two playwrights. Oxford's company amalgamated with the Earl of Worcester's men in 1602.

Edward de Vere succeeded to the hereditary title of Lord Great Chamberlain of England. He was an active patron of several acting companies and numerous writers. He was himself known as a poet and a leading, anonymous, writer of comedies, which were performed at Court. Many literary works were dedicated to him. Poems under his name were published between 1576 and 1592, the year that saw the publication by "William Shakespeare" of Venus & Adonis.

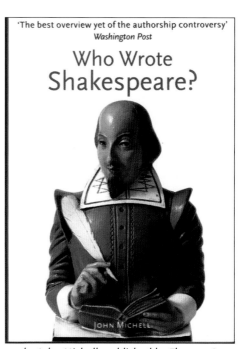

'The best overview yet of the authorship controversy'
Washington Post

Who Wrote Shakespeare?

by John Michell, published by Thames & Hudson Ltd in 1996, ISBN 0-500-28113-0

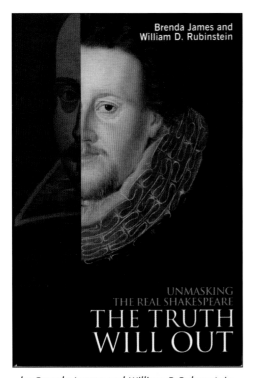

Brenda James and William D. Rubinstein

UNMASKING THE REAL SHAKESPEARE

THE TRUTH WILL OUT

by Brenda James and William D Rubenstein, published by Pearson Education Limited, ISBN 978-1-4058-4086-6, foreword by Mark Rylance

People who favour the Oxfordian theory include, amongst many others: Mr. Justice Harry A. Blackmun (US Supreme Court Justice); Mr. Justice John Paul Stevens (US Supreme Court Justice); Orson Welles; Mark Twain; Charles Dickens; Henry James; Ralph Waldo Emerson; Sir John Gielgud; Sigmund Freud; Walt Whitman; Mr. Justice Lewis F. Powell (US Supreme Court Justice); Charles de Gaulle, US Ambassador Paul Nitze, Daphne du Maurier, Enoch Powell, Brian Hicks (former Education Officer who has made a study of the Shakespeare authorship problem), Sir Derek Jacobi (Claudius in Kenneth Branagh's Hamlet and who has performed in 31 Shakespeare plays) and Mark Rylance (Artistic Director of The Globe Theatre in London).

Perhaps the only certain thing about all this is that nobody, repeat nobody, knows for certain who the real Shakespeare was. A massive industry has failed, after years of research, to unearth conclusive evidence of the solution.

The Spring family

If it isn't the mark of the de Veres you see all round the village it is the Spring mark — whether on a boss in the canopy above the rood screen in church, in a frieze running around the ceiling of the Spring chantry, or elsewhere.

Lavenham's prosperity, the basis of much of what we see today, was based on the prosperity of the decade which saw Thomas Spring III's death, together with the building of the church, the Guildhall of Corpus Christi and many fine houses. Like the de Veres, the Springs left their mark on our village so it is proper to mention it here.

Non mihi sed patriae

Spring

Thomas Spring III

(son of Thomas Spring II and known as the "Rich Clothier") (1456—1523)

This Thomas may have been rather over-zealous in making money, which led him to apply for and obtain a general pardon from King Henry VII in 1508.

Thomas Spring III's General Pardon

The King "Pardons, permits and releases Thomas Spring of Lavenham of all murders, felonies, accessory murders or felonies, rebellions, contempt, etc., also of all usurious contracts, usurious bargains, corrupt covenants, etc., of illicit sales of cloth, wool, linen, and for non-payment of foreign merchants, for all false deception and offences in making cloth, in stretching out the length, or the breadth of it, and all deception in the selling of woollen Cloth."

Thomas III owned tenements and land in Cambridge, Essex, Suffolk and Norfolk. In Lavenham it is said that he owned at least five large houses and four crofts, one of which had connections with the Lord of the Manor, the Earl of Oxford. Being so wealthy meant he was a target for the then tax man, and this was noted in a poem written by the then Poet Laureate.

His daughter Margaret (Bridget?) (from his first wife Alice Appleton of Little Waldingfield) in her second marriage, married Aubrey de Vere, second son of John de Vere, 15th Earl of Oxford. From this marriage sprang the 19th and 20th Earls of Oxford.

His first son, who became Sir Robert Spring was knighted sometime after June 1544 and before his death on 12 August 1547. His son Robert, the second husband of Agnes Eden, was buried at Lavenham in 1549. Robert bought the manor of Pakenham Hall in 1546, having previously acquired the manor of Icklingham.

In his will Thomas III left money to each parish in which he owned property or land to say masses for the repose of his soul — this may have amounted to some 130 parish churches.

The will, proved at London in 1523, is quoted in full — with the original spelling and capitalisation — in *Lavenham, Industrial Town*, by Alex Betterton and David Dymond.

Thomas Spring II

(died 1486)

This Thomas was a clothier. He had the Lavenham church vestry built and was buried there. A memorial brass (illustrated right) records the fact. He united with the 13th Earl of Oxford to build a new church,

Spring family merchant mark

lived to see the foundations of the new tower laid in 1486 and in his will left 300 marks towards the church tower. His wife was called Margaret and she was her husband's executrix.

Thomas's will, proved at London in 1486, is quoted (translated from Latin) in full in *Lavenham, Industrial Town*, by Alex Betterton and David Dymond.

Thomas Spring I

(died 1440)

Thomas Spring I first came to Lavenham in 1425 from Houghton le Spring, County Durham. He was clothier who came to Lavenham at a time of great expansion and was able to inject money and expertise to organise the 'cottage' workers, making the marketing more efficient and creating a prosperous business as Merchant/ Clothier. His wife is thought to have been called Agnes. He left money in his will for the repair of Lavenham church.

The will, proved at Cockfield in 1440, is quoted (transcribed from Latin) in full in *Lavenham, Industrial Town*, by Alex Betterton and David Dymond.

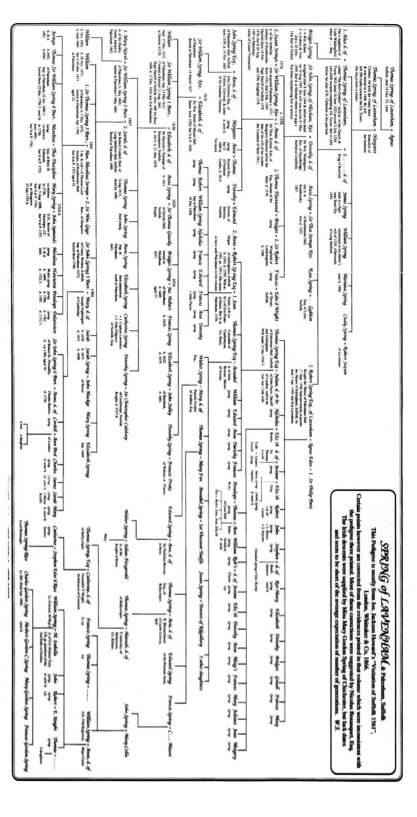

A family tree of the Springs of Lavenham, prepared by the author in 1991 from information supplied at the time. It is known that there may be some inconsistencies, as these were brought to the attention of the then Rector at the time by descendants of the family

Reginald Brill

Mr Brill with 'Timmie'
photo from local Lavenham source

Following his retirement in 1964, Reginald Brill spent ten happy years as Warden of Lavenham's Little Hall. He was a regular exhibitor at the Phoenix Gallery, Lavenham, and was lucky enough to have a large retrospective exhibition with them in 1974. He published two books, *Modern Painting*, 1946 and *Art as a Career*, 1962, both bearing a strong educational angle. He continued nurturing art students until his untimely death.

Reginald, was Principal, Kingston School of Art from 1934 to 1962. He won a scholarship to The Slade in 1921, where he studied under the famous Henry Tonks for three years. Leaving The Slade School he found patronage in Lincolnshire, painting murals for Christopher Hatton-Turner for two years. He married Rosalie, a painter, and in 1927 won the much coveted Prix de Rome in decorative painting. He took up residence at the British School of Rome for two years and during 1930 spent three months painting in Egypt as a guest of the Egyptian Government.

Whilst staying in Cairo he met Colonel T.G. Gayer-Anderson and his twin brother.

John Constable

John Constable, the world-famous artist, was educated partially at Lavenham Grammar School in Barn Street. Born 11 June 1776 (in East Bergholt, of a wealthy merchant and his wife who owned Flatford Mill and, later, Dedham Mill), he died 31 March 1837 and was buried in Highgate Cemetery

Constable was an English Romantic painter. In 1799 he persuaded his father to let him pursue art and Golding even gave him a small allowance. John is known principally for his landscape paintings of the area surrounding his home — the area of Dedham Vale is now known as "Constable Country".

His most famous paintings include Dedham Vale of 1802 and The Hay Wain of 1821. Although his paintings are now among the most popular and valuable in British art, he was never financially successful. He sold more paintings in France than in his native England — only 20 in England during his lifetime but in France more than 20 in just a few years.

He was not elected to the Royal Academy until he was 52, just eight years before his death. Constable refused all invitations to travel internationally to promote his work, and wrote, "I would rather be a poor man [in England] than a rich man abroad."

John married Maria Bicknell in 1816 and they had seven children. Maria died of tuberculosis in 1828 and Constable cared for his children alone for the rest of his life. In 1835 his last lecture to the students of the RA was cheered enthusiastically. He died on the night of the 31st March, apparently of indigestion.

Henry & Ambrose Copinger

www.copinger.org.uk

Lavenham enjoys fine outdoor sports facilities — a cricket pitch, football pitch, three floodlit tennis courts with an 'astroturf' surface and one other court, complemented by a new pavilion opened in 2003. The field where these facilities lie, west of the Church, is considered by some as part of Copinger's Piece. Why? Because Dr. Henry Copinger, rector of Lavenham for forty five years, once owned the land.

The famous wealth and hospitality of the Copinger family led to the proverbial expression used in Suffolk in the past as "living like the Copingers". Apart from Henry, other Copingers were parsons of Lavenham for many years.

Henry Copinger (1550—1622) was interred in the Chancel of the Church of Sts. Peter & Paul and is now remembered by the magnificent marble and alabaster monument erected to his memory on the North wall of the Chancel.

Ambrose Copinger was born in Lavenham, and baptised on 29 December 1583. He married Judith the only daughter of Roger Kedington or Kerington, by whom he had two sons and two daughters. He was a Doctor of Divinity. On 23rd December, 1622, he was presented to the living of his native place, his father having died on the 21st of that month. His successor at Lavenham (Mr. Gurnall) was presented in December, 1644.

The Copinger monument in the church, on the wall to the north of the altar

Roy Turner Durrant

(reference: Modern British Artists)

A prolific painter and poet, Durrant *(first cousin of the Gurling family of Lavenham)* was born on 4th October 1925 and brought up in Lavenham. He began drawing aged 5 and exhibited his first painting in Bury St Edmunds at the age of 12. From 1948 to 1952 he studied at the Camberwell School of Art, then in its post-war hey-day.

Durrant had his first one-man show in Lavenham Guildhall in the late 1940s and continued to exhibit regularly at the Royal Academy, Beaux Arts, Loggia Gallery and Belgrave Gallery, London annually throughout his life, including over 38 one-man shows. He was a fellow of the 'Free Painters & Sculptors Society' and a member of the 'New English Art Club'.

He lived in Chelsea during the 1950s, where he met and married Jean Lyell in 1959, before moving to Cambridge. He continued to develop his early figurative style, abstracting and simplifying,, drawing on a strong natural sense of design and draughtsmanship to push the boundaries of his paintings.

Durrant's work is held in many private and public collections, including The Imperial War Museum, Bradford City Art Gallery and Balliol College, Oxford. He exhibited widely during his lifetime in many solo and group shows, including the annual Royal Academy exhibition.

In 1960 he exhibited at the Phoenix Gallery in Lavenham (with Roland Suddaby and Aubrey Blake). He died in Cambridge in 1998.

Sunset Note, Suffolk (1954)

by Roy Turner Durrant

The Gayer-Anderson twins

The Gayer-Anderson twins were responsible for the restoration of Lavenham's Little Hall in the 1920s and also for the formation of the Lavenham Preservation Committee.

A photograph of the Gayer-Anderson twins at Edfu on the River Nile, perhaps taken in the early 1920s

courtesy Little Hall

The collection in Little Hall consists mainly of furniture, paintings, sculptures, porcelain and artefacts with which the Gayer-Anderson brothers equipped and adorned Little Hall in the 1930s. In addition there are several paintings by Colonel Gayer-Anderson of relations and friends and drawings and sketches given by an artist who stayed in Little Hall when it was a hostel for art students.

The Gayer Anderson twins were descended (through many generations) from Sir John Gayer, "a merchant of the Levant" who was Lord Mayor of London in 1647. It was he who instituted "The Lion's Sermon" in gratitude to God for his escape from one of those beasts when he was travelling across the deserts of Arabia. The Lion's Sermon has been preached yearly (it is believed without a single break) on the 15th October at St Catherine Cree's church in Leadenhall Street in the City of London.

In 1935 Major R. G. Gayer-Anderson Pasha's home (dating to 1632) and contents were converted into a museum. He had been a long-term resident of Cairo.

William Gurnall

William Gurnall was the author of a book called *'The Christian in Complete Armour'* which was, until recently, on sale at Lavenham Church gift shop. William, about whom not a great deal is known, was a puritan divine of the seventeenth century, who wrote the well known book described above and was

the minister of Lavenham for thirty five years.

He was born in Lynn (now King's Lynn) in Norfolk in 1616, the son of parents who held a prominent position in the town and was educated at Cambridge. It has been conjectured that little is known about William because of his conduct in the year 1662, on the passing of the Act of Uniformity. He did not secede from the Church of England. He was not one of the two thousand ministers who gave up their preferment on St. Bartholomew's Day and became non-conformists. He retained his position and continued as Rector of Lavenham.

An early study about William Gurnall was a small volume, published in 1830 (see Part 7) by a writer named Mr. M'Keon who was an inhabitant of Lavenham and an antiquarian of considerable research.

Following his university education at Emmanuel College in Cambridge Gurnall became BA in 1635 and MA in 1639. The next five years are shrouded in mystery until William reappears as rector of Lavenham in December 1644, when he was just twenty-eight years old. His entrance into the ministry is also obscure — and it is possible that he never initially received episcopal orders at all.

Ivan Howlett

Reproduced from *Lavenham Life* (by permission):

Ivan Howlett (1942-2008)

Ivan, who died on 9th July 2008, was born and brought up in Lavenham. Growing up he helped his father by doing the butcher's round and he sang in Lavenham Church choir. He travelled to his school in Bury St Edmunds by train from Lavenham.

After university and teacher training he switched to a career in media and became founding Managing Editor of BBC Radio Suffolk. He also contributed articles to many newspapers and magazines.

Besides being talented and successful, he was also a charming man, always finding time to talk to people. One of his specialities was in giving very amusing and informative talks, either about Suffolk (when he would tell anecdotes in a broad Suffolk accent) or about his experiences in broadcasting, or both.

He was described in *The East Anglian* as a 'Champion of Suffolk", a title fully justified by his work and achievements in and on behalf of Suffolk. For many, too, he was "Champion of Lavenham", to which he retained a life-long devotion.

Ivan was a regular participant in as many of Lavenham's events as his busy life allowed. He was a Life Member of the Friends of Lavenham Church and was a member of the Friends of Lavenham Sinfonia, of which he had been elected Chairman in 2008.

In August 2008 he secured wide publicity for the 750th anniversary of Lavenham's Royal Market Charter, by a full account in *The East Anglian Daily Times*.

Kenneth Merrylees

Colonel Merrylees lived for many years in Church Street, Lavenham until his death in 1994. I met him on several occasions and was privileged once to see him at work, doing what he is best known for — 'dowsing.' On the sports field he accurately indicated all drainage systems, using his magic dowsing rods.

The Colonel worked as a bomb disposal expert during World War II, particularly using his dowsing skills to find delayed-action fused bombs under the surface. His skill extended to inventions for defusing them safely and some of his methods and devices are still in use.

He was born in Tasmania in 1896, was educated in the UK at Charterhouse and Woolwich, and became an officer in the Royal Engineers in 1915. Serving in France, he was wounded in 1917, leading a night raid. Having recovered he was posted to Italy, where he was wounded again.

In World War II he served in France, Egypt, Syria, Turkey and India. After the war he served in Pakistan. When he retired to Lavenham, his superb reconstruction and conversion of cottages earned a Civic Trust National Award.

He was Chairman of the British Society of Dowsers and also a talented water-colourist and etcher. He was much in demand as a lecturer and appeared on television.

He married, in 1938, Nina Shepstone (whose father had arranged the annexation of Transvaal). She died in 1980 and in 1988 he married secondly, Diana Stedman.

Particular thanks to the Telegraph Group Limited for permission to quote brief extracts from The Daily Telegraph Book of Military Obituaries (ISBN 1 804943 27 6).

John Millar-Watt

On 2nd June 1972, the *Bury Free Press* ran an article about Lavenham. Amongst the feature there appeared this one: "Creator of Pop, the *Daily Sketch*'s famous cartoon character, is one of many artists who made Lavenham their home. Cartoonist John Millar Watt, who first introduced Pop to the British public in 1921, lived in Lavenham, on "active retirement" with his artist daughter Mary for many years. [She had portraits accepted for the Royal Society of Portrait Painters' exhibitions in London.]

During the First World War John, fighting with the Essex Regiment in Italy and France, cheered up his comrades by caricaturing the officers. By the time the next World War broke out his cartoon character, Pop, appearing daily in the national press, was considered such a morale booster that he was asked not to join the Forces but to carry on cartooning.

So Mr Millar Watt served in the Home Guard and Pop went off to war instead. His military escapades in the *Daily Sketch* and *Sunday Graphic* helped bring a daily touch of brightness to the war years. John Millar Watt's cartooning career began when he answered an advertisment in The Times for a cartoonist. In 1921 Pop arrived on the scene, and landed him with a job for 25 years."

John Millar-Watt was born in 1895 and died in 1975.

Sir Alfred James Munnings

It was a visit to Lavenham Horse Fair that sparked off Sir Alfred's lifelong fascination with painting horses and stimulated his first major composition, A Suffolk Horse Fair (1901; Dedham, Essex, Munnings A. Mus.).

From his book *An Artist's Life* (Bungay, 1950) comes the following extract.

"Lavenham Horse Fair. What a sight! This famous fair of heavy draught-horses eclipsed anything of its kind I had ever seen. The Swan was then unaltered, and not the swell place it is to-day. I got a room there in spite of its being packed with a breed of men long since gone: men with fat jowls, wearing wide-brimmed bowlers or half high hats, who came from London to buy heavy horses for London work — for railway companies' vans, brewers' drays and a host of other trades.

.... The day started with rashers of Suffolk-cured bacon — a pleasant detail to remember. The Grays called for me soon after, and I saw scenes which started me off painting horse fairs. We went from inn-yard to inn-yard, where straw lay strewn on the ground, and those well-fed, clean-shaven, purple-faced men already were seeing horses trotted up and down in the yards, in the main street, in the lesser streets, on a green and up near the great church with its tall tower.

.... Magnificent! a sight for the gods! Gone are such scenes; gone are the horses."

Munnings (1878—1959) was elected President of the Royal Academy in 1944 and was knighted in the same year. He judged entries in the George V Jubilee celebrations, which were held on Lavenham's Home Field.

Taylors of Lavenham and Ongar

The Rev. Isaac Taylor was a famous engraver, who came to Lavenham in 1786 and lived in Shilling Grange in Shilling Street, which he rented for £6 a year. It was possibly for health reasons that the family had left London and moved to Lavenham.

The Rev. Taylor and his wife Ann Martin arrived in Lavenham with two daughters — Ann had been born in Islington in 1782 and Jane in Holborn in 1783. There was also a son born in Holborn in 1785 who died at the age of 9 months.

In June 1789 the mother Ann took the two young girls to London to see a procession of George III and the following day they attended a ball in India House.

After renting Shilling Grange the family moved to Arundel House, next door, in summer 1793, further down Shilling Street, which house they actually owned, where six more children were born.

Shilling Grange, Shilling Street

Who renovated Shilling Grange?

In 1920 it was derelict. The then owner (?) offered it to the Society for the Protection of Ancient Buildings. They then appealed in Country Life for somebody to restore it, saying it would probably cost about £1,500—£2,000. Percy Green, a London architect, bought the property and reconditioned the whole structure, restoring only the south portion to its original appearance.

This was the year the then French king died. There were riots in many places, including Lavenham, and the mob pitted part of their fury against the 'Meetingers' (the Dissenters) — *yet another religious based war*! With flags flying and drums beating the mob vowed to burn Mr Taylor's house over his head. The Rev. Clarke, who had returned to live in Shilling Grange, managed to stop them doing that because, as he said, "the noise would have inconvenienced my ill wife!"

The family could not afford to send their children to school so Anne and Jane's early education was entirely at home — reading, the needle and the catechism — taught by their mother.

The Star

Twinkle, twinkle, little star,
How I wonder what you are!
Up above the world so high,
Like a diamond in the sky.

When the blazing sun is gone,
When he nothing shines upon,
Then you show your little light,
Twinkle, twinkle, all the night.

Then the traveller in the dark,
Thanks you for your tiny spark:
He could not see which way to go,
If you did not twinkle so.

In the dark blue sky you keep,
And often through my curtains peep,
For you never shut your eye,
Till the sun is in the sky.

As your bright and tiny spark,
Lights the traveller in the dark,
Though I know not what you are,
Twinkle, twinkle, little star.

JANE

Arundel House in 2006. Jane Taylor's Cottage was to the right, through the gate

Together with her elder sister Ann, Jane wrote poems and hymns for children. Ann and Jane kept detailed diaries and, at age 15, Ann wrote her first poem.

In Lavenham Rev. Taylor's Presbyterian beliefs made him unpopular and there not being enough to support and maintain his lifestyle he decided to look elsewhere for somewhere he could support his family. Thus he moved to Colchester and took up a ministry at the Chapel in Bucklersbury Lane (now known as St Helens Lane). It was the youngest daughter Jane who wrote the well-known rhyme "Twinkle, Twinkle, Little Star", whilst living in Colchester.

In 1803 the sisters were invited to submit poems, with other contributors, for the first volume of 'Original Poems for Infant Minds', for which they were paid £5. There were three subsequent volumes.

In 1806 they wrote for a new publication, 'Rhymes of the Nursery' and were paid £20. This was the first publication of the well-known 'Twinkle, Twinkle, Little Star'.

On 11 September 1811 the family moved to Ongar. Ann was 28 — she married (becoming Mrs Gilbert) and moved to Nottingham, where she died aged 84. Jane died aged 42.

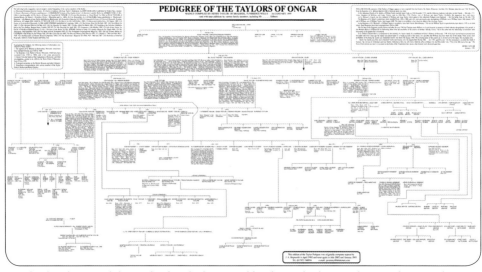
The family tree of the Taylor family (prepared by the author) is on show in the Lavenham Guildhall museum

The Winthrop family

Adam Winthrop (1) came to live in Lavenham from the village of Groton, not far away in Suffolk, while Joan, his wife, was a Lavenham girl. Adam was a clothier and lived in Barn Street, in what was at one time the Old Grammar School. After Adam (1) died, Joan married John Ponder, another well-to-do Lavenham clothier.

Adam (2) was baptised in Lavenham Church, by the Rev. Thomas Appleton, in 1498. Members of other Lavenham clothier families — the Springs, Risbys and Ponders — may have been present. He was apprenticed to The Fullers Company of London from 1515 to 1526 and became a Freeman of London. The Fullers Company merged with others to become The Clothmakers Company and Adam was elected Master in 1551. He was also granted the manor of Groton by King Edward VI.

Adam (2), who came to own a ship called the "Mary Flower", had six children by his second wife Agnes Sharpe, the fifth of whom, yet another Adam (3), was born in 1548. That Adam, by his second wife Anne, had four children, the second of whom, John — born in 1588 — married four times. His fourth wife was one Martha, whom John married in America, where he had emigrated with the Pilgrim Fathers. John became the first Governor of the State of Massachusetts.

Seventeenth century England did not have freedom of religion. It was at the age of forty-two that John decided to move away from the country to a place where he could worship God freely and raise his children in an environment of faith. In 1629 John heard about a new venture called the Massachusetts Bay Company. John was recognised as a man of tremendous ability and was elected Governor of the company. John sold all his possessions and, on 7th April 1630, set out in four ships with four hundred people across the stormy Atlantic.

The rest, as they say, is history.

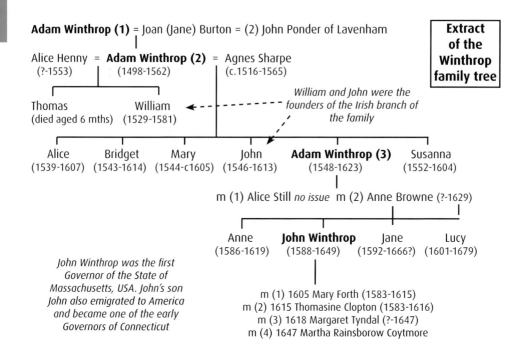

Adam Winthrop (1) = Joan (Jane) Burton = (2) John Ponder of Lavenham

Extract of the Winthrop family tree

Alice Henny = **Adam Winthrop (2)** = Agnes Sharpe
(?-1553)   (1498-1562)   (c.1516-1565)

Thomas   William
(died aged 6 mths)   (1529-1581)

William and John were the founders of the Irish branch of the family

Alice   Bridget   Mary   John   **Adam Winthrop (3)**   Susanna
(1539-1607)   (1543-1614)   (1544-c1605)   (1546-1613)   (1548-1623)   (1552-1604)

m (1) Alice Still *no issue* m (2) Anne Browne (?-1629)

Anne   **John Winthrop**   Jane   Lucy
(1586-1619)   (1588-1649)   (1592-1666?)   (1601-1679)

John Winthrop was the first Governor of the State of Massachusetts, USA. John's son John also emigrated to America and became one of the early Governors of Connecticut

m (1) 1605 Mary Forth (1583-1615)
m (2) 1615 Thomasine Clopton (1583-1616)
m (3) 1618 Margaret Tyndal (?-1647)
m (4) 1647 Martha Rainsborow Coytmore

Other items of interest

- Lavenham Airfield
- Lavenham on film
- Lavenham's pillboxes
- The Lavenham Waltz
- *Lavenham Life* parish magazine
- Lavenham gasworks
- Lavenham's water standpipes
- Lavenham services
- Dyehouse Field wood
- Local walks
- The River Brett
- Agriculture and farming
- Washmere Green and bull-baiting
- Lavenham railway station
- The youth view of Lavenham
- Places to visit nearby
- Lavenham, Manitoba, Canada
- Other publications about Lavenham

Lavenham Airfield

The Control Tower as it is now

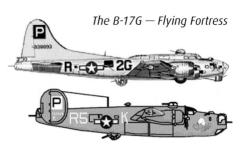

The B-17G — Flying Fortress

The B-24H/J — Liberator

Lavenham Airfield — a very important factor locally in World War II — lies west of the Lavenham-Bury Road, near Smithwood Green and east of the Sudbury-Bury Road, close to Alpheton.

The airfield has mainly reverted to farmland, though the Control Tower is well preserved and in use as an office, and some buildings and tracks survive. Although not generally open to the public, visits can be arranged through Lavenham Tourist Information Centre.

In Lavenham Market Place there is a bronze plaque commemorating the presence of the USAAF 487th Bomb Group (Heavy) in the area and there is an illuminated Roll of Honour in Lavenham Parish Church (*prepared by the author*), honouring all those American servicemen based at Lavenham in WWII who gave their lives on our behalf.

In The Swan Hotel there is a section of wall that has been preserved on which many World War II American pilots signed their name.

Lavenham Tourist Information Centre has a permanent display of photographs, etc., sent by veterans when stationed here, on show to the public.

For the images above I am indebted to Paul Webber, with whom I was in regular contact regarding amendments to the Roll of Honour in the Church.

The B17 is 43-38893 of the 836th Squadron (2G:R). It survived the war and returned to the USA. The B-24 is shown dressed up as 42-52618 "Chief Wapello" The original B24s that deployed to Lavenham were painted olive drab, with neutral grey undersurfaces. The demarcation between olive drab and neutral grey on the fuselage was either a straight line or a wavy line, depending on the manufacturer (source: Tom Brittan). The squadron code was painted aft of the gun position and the radio call letter was painted forward of the waist gun position.

An overhead aerial shot in 1944

photo courtesy of Ivo de Jong

The badge of 487 Bombardment Group (Heavy) of the American 8th Air Force — the "Gentlemen from Hell"

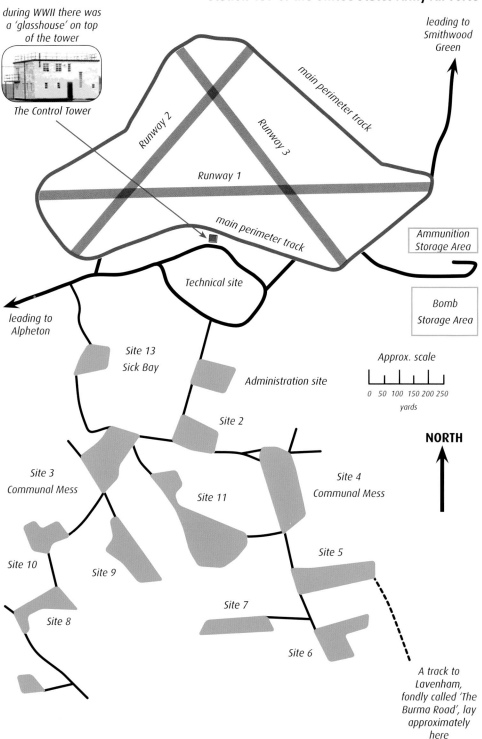

Outline sketch map of Lavenham Airfield
— Station 137 of the United States Army Air Force

during WWII there was a 'glasshouse' on top of the tower

The Control Tower

leading to Smithwood Green

Runway 2

Runway 3

Runway 1

main perimeter track

main perimeter track

Technical site

leading to Alpheton

Ammunition Storage Area

Bomb Storage Area

Site 13 Sick Bay

Administration site

Approx. scale

0   50 100 150 200 250
yards

Site 2

NORTH

Site 3 Communal Mess

Site 11

Site 4 Communal Mess

Site 10

Site 9

Site 5

Site 8

Site 7

Site 6

A track to Lavenham, fondly called 'The Burma Road', lay approximately here

Lavenham Airfield began life in 1943, when the war against Germany was very critical. John Laing & Son construction company, on the gently rolling farmland between Lavenham and Alpheton, built what was to become a standard USAAF bomber airfield, with three runways, two of which were 1,400 yards long and the main runway 2,000 yards. With fifty hard standings and two large hangars, there were three and half miles of perimeter track.

The airfield was handed over to the USAAF on 21 March 1944 and the 487th Bomb Group (Heavy) — one of forty such groups — moved in on 5th April. For the first three months the group operated Liberator aircraft (B-24H/Js), generally flying with three squadrons of 12 aircraft each. They then converted to Flying Fortresses (B-17G), initially flying in two 20 plane formations, then reverting to 12 or 13 plane squadrons and finally in four nine plane squadrons. The crew numbered ten: pilot, co-pilot, navigator, bombardier, engineer, radio operator and four gunners. The payload consisted of 6,000 lbs of bombs and the aircraft were armed with 13 machine guns.

The group's wartime record was particularly distinguished: they flew over 185 combat missions over Germany and the occupied countries, flying 5,242 effective sorties and dropping 141,416 tons of bombs. As Lieutenant General

The Roll of Honour commemorating the 233 US Army Air Force personnel based at Lavenham who gave their lives for service to the country is in the Parish Church

Martin USAF said "the group led the Third Division and was second in Eighth Air Force in percentage of bombs in 1,000 feet of the M.P.I. during the period from September 1944 through February 1945."

Brigadier-General F.W. Castle USAAF was one of the group's officers and was the highest ranking 8th Air Force officer to be awarded, posthumously, the Congressional Medal of Honor. He was killed during a raid when flying over Belgium on 24th December 1944, in the lead aircraft of the 487th Group, leading the Eighth Air Force on its largest mission (760) of the war.

Pittsley Crew
photo courtesy Ivo de Jong

Note: Ivo de Jong has been an avid Eighth Air Force enthusiast and researcher for more than 20 years. He is a Colonel in the Royal Netherlands Army. His superb book *The History of the 487th Bomb Group (H)*, ISBN 1-59652-018-3, published by Turner Publishing, is highly recommended.

Station 137 from the air
photo courtesy Ivo de Jong

Lavenham on film

A number of films and TV series have been shot partly in and around Lavenham.

The former Ideal Cinema, Water Street

Lovejoy, starring Ian McShane as a "divvie" in the antiques business, ran for several TV series in the early 1990s and Lavenham (*including The Angel and The Great House*) featured in several episodes. The cast stayed at The Swan and breakfasted regularly at The Angel.

In 1986 Horace Ove directed the story of a culture clash in cricket, **Playing Away**, where the teams thrash out their differences at Snedington (Lavenham). It showed on television. Most scenes were filmed during the day, with one in the evening. The cast booked all the rooms at The Angel for a week.

A couple of the actors were members of The Magic Circle and entertained the landlords and regulars. Some Lavenham local people got bit parts in the film.

In 1982 a half-hour film entitled **Spun Gold** was produced by Anglia TV all about Lavenham, featuring local people.

The 1975 film **Barry Lyndon**, directed by Stanley Kubrick, used Lavenham Guildhall for inn scenes. It was a screenplay adaptation of a Thackeray novel depicting the rise and fall of a sensitive rogue in the British aristocracy.

Pier Paolo Pasolini's **The Canterbury Tales** (1972), had Lavenham substituting for mediæval London in some scenes.

Sharon Tate's last film, **The 13 Chairs** (1970), featured Lavenham interiors and exteriors. It was a comedy about a madcap search throughout Europe for 13 chairs, in which a fortune in jewels was hidden.

John Lennon and Yoko Ono, in **Apotheosis 2** (1969), were filmed peeking out from under huge black capes as they took off in a hot air balloon from the Market Place.

Perhaps the best known, described as the English cinema's best ever horror film, was **The Witchfinder General** (1968), starring Vincent Price. The burning of a witch on the Market Place was one of several scenes filmed in Lavenham.

Other film and TV shoots which have featured Lavenham include **Children of the New Forest**, **Good Friday 1663**, **Highway** (*with Harry Secombe*), **Holly Joe** and various TV ads.

Two Cinemas

Lavenham used to have two cinemas. One was in Water Street, called The Ideal. It is now staff accommodation for the Swan Hotel. The other was in the High Street, owned by one Percy King, which has now become the Wildlife Art Gallery.

entrance to former cinema, High Street

Lavenham's pillboxes

www.pillboxesuk.co.uk

Lavenham still has a number of 'pillboxes' standing, as a reminder of some dark days in World War II. There were standard plans for some 12 types of standard pillbox, though local variations were allowed, as well as some purpose built ones.

At the old railway bridge across Bridge Street Road. This pillbox, apparently a type FW3/28A. has almost disappeared under the growth of shrubs and trees

A type FW3/27 pillbox, close to the edge of Bridge Street Road, looking south. Another pillbox of the same type lies in the middle of the field, slightly further to the southwest

As the pictures show, some pillboxes in the vicinity of Lavenham remain in quite good condition. Mostly they lie north of the line of the old railway. The Defence of Britain database lists most of the locations, with an ID number and the type of pillbox.

It was in June 1940 that the War Office Directorate of Fortifications and Works, Branch FW3, started hastily to arrange the building of a network of defences all over the British Isles to prevent an anticipated German invasion. Amongst these defences, the most common were the squat concrete forts (pillboxes) that were sited at strategic points including road junctions and canals. Although the invasion threat diminished after 1941 the possibility of German commando raids remained a constant fear. It is estimated that less than 6,000 of the total of 28,000 pillboxes that were built still survive. As the Defence of Britain database says "They remain as permanent monuments and a silent tribute to the courage and tenacity of the British people during the dark days of 1940 when Britain stood alone against Nazi Germany."

Pillboxes — Images of an Unfought Battle, by Ian J. Saunders, ISBN 1411626516, published by Lulu Press Incorporated, 2005, is interesting.

On Park Road, looking northeast. Note the other pillbox to the right, in the distance. The nearest unit is apparently a type FW3/22 and the further one type FW3/27

From the Lavenham Walk (St Edmund Way) — the old railway line — looking north, this pillbox, type FW3/22, can be seen

The Lavenham Waltz

Very few people today have heard of the Lavenham Waltz, let alone seen a copy or heard it. I know of three recordings extant — one instrumental, one on organ and one vocal.

The Lavenham Waltz was published in 1910 by Alfred Ives of Bury St Edmunds. Composed by Whittingham W J Roper of Lavenham, the score cost two shillings. The score starts dreamily (in 3/4 time naturally) in C major. Later sections are in G major, Ab major and Eb major.

In 1994, words to accompany the waltz were written, by Marjorie Newman of Lavenham, for the quincentennial of Lavenham Guildhall.

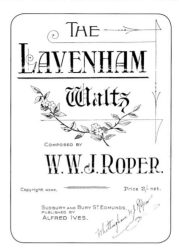

Chorus (all)

Come to Lav'n'am, this time of year.
For, here in Lav'n'am, waltztime's near.
So why not take your partners, join in the fun
Music playing, to welcome everyone.
So let us come to Lav'n'am, dancing for all
Here on the market, beside the old Guildhall.

Verse 1 *(male solo)*

Come now lads, bring your girls,
Join in the dance, let us see the twirls.
Musicians play, for you, for me,
Hear that music sweetly play.
Come all you dancers, get ready to dance
To the Lavenham Waltz tonight.

repeat Chorus *(all)*

Verse 2 *(male solo)*

Come, come to the dance
Sway to the music and hold your lass tightly,
Come, give her a glance, See how she steps over the cobblestones lightly.
See, stars in the sky that are shining for you and for me tonight
Telling all of us here to dance away the night.

repeat Chorus *(all)*

Coda

Moonlight fades fast, see yonder sky,
(male solo)
Dawn is now breaking, daylight's nigh.
(girls)
So let us take our partners, bid them farewell,
Waltztime's over, for daylight breaks the spell,
(all)
So we say, farewell Lav'n'am,
Waltztime is o'er.
Here on the market, tranquillity once more.

Lavenham Life parish magazine

Lavenham has an excellent monthly parish magazine, entitled *Lavenham Life*. This is jointly published by Lavenham's Christian churches and there is a local editor, production manager and business manager. A management committee meets from time to time to consider the direction of the magazine and to review policy and layout. Normally, the magazine sells for 50 pence, from a number of outlets within the village.

The magazine content starts each month with messages from the Rector, an officer of the Salvation Army and the Roman Catholic Deacon. Also included are comprehensive listings of church, army and catholic community services and events. Also included is a Village Hall diary, a diary of village events and dates, notes from clubs and organisations and a detailed report on Parish Council meetings, together with occasional articles on a variety of subjects.

The magazine is supported principally by its advertising income and of late has run in surplus sufficiently to permit an annual free issue, usually at Christmas.

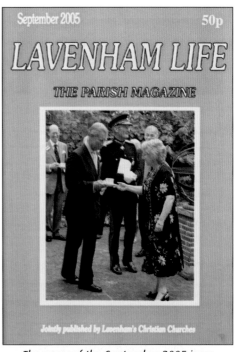

The cover of the September 2005 issue
HRH The Prince of Wales with Jane Gosling

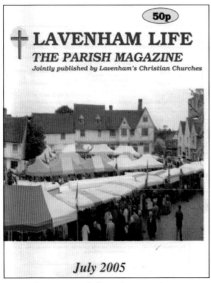

The cover of the July 2005 issue

The cover of the December 2007 issue

Lavenham gasworks

The 'listed' gasholder (an ancient monument, no less) at the bottom of Water Street

*The cover of the January 2008 issue
'Behold a new day is dawning'*

The cover of the July 2008 issue

At the bottom of Water Street, there still stands a rather forlorn and deserted reminder of how our lights were supplied in the late 1800s and early 1900s. It is not open to the public but can be viewed from the footpath nearby.

Lavenham Gas & Coke Works was apparently opened in 1863, though Transco plc archives have the date 1872. We still have a 'listed' iron gas-holder (Monument No. 220 on Babergh list of Scheduled Ancient Monuments — gridref TL 918 491).

The gasworks, when built, cost about £1,400. The retort house in use in the 1920s produced non-poisonous gas, there being — allegedly — no carbon monoxide; the gases consisted of methane and the higher hydrocarbons. Gas was expensive and also made a dark deposit on the ceilings of houses. Most gas lamps had a pilot jet and users can remember entering a darkened room groping for the chain hanging from the lamp bracket to pull to allow the pilot to light the main burner.

Mr Fred Wilson, who for years worked with the gas company and lived in Water Street, reported that in its latter days the gas composition was 60% hydrogen, 20% methane and 20% carbon monoxide.

Lavenham's water standpipes

To this day, water standpipes exist in Lavenham streets, as a reminder of the way water was provided in the not too distant past. They currently belong to the Parish Council. As we turn on our household taps today we easily forget how many still alive in the village got their water years ago.

Ten standpipes remain, at:

1 Brent Eleigh Road/Lolls footpath
2 Bridge Street Road
3 Church Street — near bus stop
4 Hall Road — High Street end
5 Hall Road — near fishpond gate
6 High Street/Norman Way
7 High Street — pinnacle
8 Prentice Street — lower end
9 Prentice Street — upper end
10 Pump Court

2. Bridge Street Road standpipe, at corner with Church Road

They are in various states of repair. David Deacon (*who for some 30 years was a member of the Parish Council*)

1. Brent Eleigh Road/Lolls footpath standpipe

started a project in 2003 to try to get them restored, not as working items but as things of interest and as an integral part of the village's rich history. Lack of support from Anglian Water and other engineering firms meant the project being put on hold. It would be splendid if somehow this relatively inexpensive project could be resurrected, which would improve the look of all these items and preserve them for posterity.

The standpipes were placed and became operational in 1936/1937,

under the auspices of the then Cosford Rural District Council, Lavenham being represented by Councillors W. Turner and B.W. Death.

The scheme was officially inaugurated by The Right Hon. The Earl of Stradbroke, Lord Lieutenant of Suffolk, on 5th February 1937. The new water undertakings were intended to serve the parish of Lavenham, as well as Bildeston, Boxford, Brettenham, Edwardstone (part) and Nedging with Naughton

The house at the Lavenham Headworks site was erected by Messrs

---

COSFORD RURAL DISTRICT COUNCIL

Thomas A. Harwood, Esq., J.P. - Chairman

OFFICIAL INAUGURATION
of
NEW WATER UNDERTAKINGS

TO SERVE THE PARISHES
of
BILDESTON   BOXFORD   BRETTENHAM
EDWARDSTONE (part)   LAVENHAM
NEDGING-WITH-NAUGHTON

by

The Right Hon. The EARL of STRADBROKE,
K.C.M.G., C.B., C.V.O., C.B.E., V.D., T.D., D.L., J.P.,
Lord Lieutenant of Suffolk

5th FEBRUARY, 1937

The cover of the inauguration programme for the new water undertakings, 1937

3. Church Street — Bus stop standpipe

4. Hall Road standpipe — High Street end

9. Prentice Street standpipe, upper end

10. Pump Court standpipe

5. Hall Road standpipe — near fishpond gate

6. Lavenham Walk standpipe — High Street/Norman Way

7. High Street standpipe, on the pinnacle

8. Prentice Street standpipe, lower end

Deacon. The water was derived from two boreholes, of 400 and 409 feet depth respectively.

In the 1920s and early 1930s, a resident in the large Georgian house opposite The Swan recalls "drinking water had to be carried in pails from a water spout on the south side of Water Street near the present printing works. In summer this supply had a habit of drying up and then water had to be brought in pails from Potlands, north of the church tower. One tended to carry two pails, with a wooden square separator between.

Our washing water was obtained from the pond in our garden which fed the stream which passes under Water Street in a culvert. This water was passed through a sand filter bed to a well and was manually pumped up to a tank in the attic."

Around 1937 an artesian well was bored by Green Willows (where Artesian Place now stands) but the water was very chalky and was later disused as a supply source. Initially this supplied houses and the stand-pipes in the streets.

Note: I am most grateful to David Deacon for providing much of the background information for this article of the book.

Lavenham services

When we turn on the light switch, gas tap or water tap we do not generally — if you're like me — question where it comes from. We complain quickly enough, though, if there are stoppages or breakdowns. Similarly, we often don't think too much about our rubbish collection, except insofar as remembering which bin to put out once a fortnight and fretting if caught behind the waste lorry on the road.

As for sewage, it's a subject most of us prefer to forget but we would be cross if it wasn't dealt with properly.

Electricity

www.edfenergy.com

Our electricity reaches us through a complex network, shown in the following diagram (taken from EDF Electric Journey).

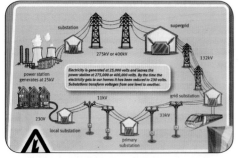

Having reached the village at 230 volts, the question most often asked is "why does my power go off when my neighbour's power stays on?" Low voltage distribution usually uses four wires — three live called phases and one neutral. Each live wire, but not the neutral, is protected by a fuse in the substation. Domestic customers get electricity from one of the three phases and, in a village like Lavenham, this can be in a rather random fashion. If one fuse blows, one third of customers lose power. If two fuses blow, two thirds of customers lose power, and so on.

More automatic and remote controlled switches are being installed all the time on the high voltage network. This aims to restore power as quickly as possible. These ideas are being extended — where possible — to rural areas, that often have long lengths of overhead supply lines.

Gas

www.britishgas.co.uk

It is understood that the gas supply for Lavenham is from the Sudbury base.

A National Grid van in the High Street

The National Grid main pipeline from Bacton runs round the edge of Lavenham but does not supply the village direct.

Water and sewage

www.anglianwater.co.uk

Anglian Water (AW) is one of the leading providers of water and waste water services in the UK, serving the needs of around six million industrial, commercial and domestic customers.

In Lavenham our water comes from an underground borehole in the Bury St Edmunds area. It is then pumped through treatment plants and storage reservoirs to Bradfield St Clare water tower, thence via gravity to Lavenham water tower, whose capacity is 509 cubic metres. Gravity, again, then takes our water into the village, via a 200mm plastic main, which feeds into the local network.

Lavenham's water tower at Hill Green. Note the multiple radio and mobile phone antennae attached

The works were modernised as recently as 2007. After treatment, the cleaned water is discharged back into the River Brett.

Rubbish collection

www.babergh-south-suffolk.gov.uk

Babergh District Council contract out this function in Lavenham. Like many councils, they operate a fortnightly collection for households, with varying arrangements for trade waste. There are a plethora of coloured plastic wheelie bins in current use — black (for non-recyclable material), blue (recyclable), brown (garden waste), green (superceded by black), and purple (trade waste).

Domestic recyclable waste collection

Overall, AW supply some1,200 million litres of water a day, through over 130 treatment works. Drinking water standards, very good in our region, can be viewed at www.dwi.gov.uk.

In the same way that we often don't know much about how our water gets to us (I certainly didn't until I asked questions), we tend not to worry too much about sewage, as long as it disappears satisfactorily.

Anglian Water are responsible for the large sewers, normally under the road or pavement and householders are responsible for rainwater and waste water from their property to the point of connection to the AW sewer. Of course, in Lavenham we have a very ancient system of sewers.

Lavenham Sewage Treatment Works is hidden behind trees just off the Brent Eleigh Road.

Recycling centre in the main car park

Telephone

Listed phone boxes — Church Street (left), High Street (right)

The K6 phone box was designed in 1935 by Sir Giles Gilbert Scott and cast in iron by various contractors. The Church Street box was listed in 1993 and the High Street box in 1987.

BT Openreach was launched in January 2006 — a new business responsible for the nationwide local BT network

BT van, with BT Openworld logo, outside the Lavenham telephone exchange on the Brent Eleigh road

Mail

Royal Mail van. Based in Sudbury, they deliver and collect our mail daily (except Sunday)

We will all have noticed, probably, that our mail deliveries arrive later than they did some years ago, sometimes even in the afternoon. The main sorting office for Lavenham is in Chelmsford, Essex, with a large delivery office in Sudbury.

Royal Mail have more than 33,000 commercial delivery vehicles, of a wide variety of types.

In October 2008 the local postman said he was now starting work at 6am instead of 3am. The letter he delivered at 11.30am on a Saturday in Lavenham had a Chelmsford stamp for 01.44am that same morning, for example.

We are lucky here in Lavenham that our Post Office survives, despite government attempts to close as many branches as possible. In my opinion a Post Office is a vital part of a village like ours and it would be tragic if it had to close.

Letter box at Tenterpiece

Dyehouse Field Wood

A recent project is the start of a small wood, just off the Bury Road (on the left leaving Lavenham), under the aegis of Lavenham Woodland Project Ltd.

The object of the project is to establish and secure the future of a woodland that will bring pleasure and benefit to villagers and visitors. The site is adjacent to the

Railway Walk and was planted by an army of volunteers in November 2005.

Working parties meet on Wednesday and Saturday afternoons to manage and enjoy the site, doing what is appropriate to the time of year, to ensure that the woodland develops. Volunteers are welcome and training and guidance are provided as necessary.

While the woodland will be predominantly oak and ash, as are most of the ancient woodlands in Suffolk, a large variety of other native species has been planted.

Dyehouse Field Wood was the site of a party in 2007 to celebrate Lavenham's Market Charter and, to add to the occasion, Eamon Boland read and acted part of Sir Clive Rose's epic verse history of the village.

Looking after a woodland is not plain sailing. It has had possible hawthorn virus problems and the dreaded ragwort. Cuts are arranged several times during each growing season, until the open field on which the ragwort

Getting the children involved

thrives becomes a woodland. The plant, as befits a British native, is persistent!

The project team, all volunteers, have seen how quickly open arable turns into a woodland. As a result of visits to other projects they have radically revised their perceptions and their management plan. They are thinking differently about the best width of rides in maturing woodland and how hedges might be managed.

Snowdrops and other spring flowers have been planted in the older woodland, where someone has erected bird boxes and hibernation devices.

It seems that the idea of a wood for the village is taking hold.

The wood in June 2008

Local walks

Lavenham is surrounded by lovely countryside — well worth a visit. The village lies within a gently undulating landscape of high visual quality, providing remarkable views into and out of the village.

There is an excellent and extensive network of footpaths and the Railway Walk is a County Wildlife site.

Designated Special Landscape Areas lie to the east and north-west. Ordnance Survey maps reference 165 and 196 show rights of way in the area, and both are available from the Tourist Information Centre in Lady Street.

Wilfrid George's *Footpath Map of Lavenham* is also very useful, as are the walks leaflets published by Suffolk County Council and Clive Brown's publication — *Walking Close to the Middle Ages near Lavenham*.

The Lavenham Circular Walk

A three and a half mile circular walk which starts at Lavenham Parish Church and then sets out into pleasant

countryside, in places running along the disused railway, through quiet pastureland and returning beside Lavenham Hall.

The Long Melford Walk

A four mile walk along the disused railway track and farm track to Long Melford.

In Lavenham walks

Within Lavenham the walks on offer include the Wool Walk, the Mediæval Meander and the Pub Perambulation. All these can be booked at the Tourist Information Centre in Lady Street.

Riders at Clay Hill Road bridge

The River Brett

Lavenham Brook is a tributary of the River Brett which runs through Lavenham, skirting Lower Road and running under the bridge at the bottom of Clay Hill before paralleling First Meadow on its way to Brent Eleigh.

The river rises near Stanningfield and has tributaries at Kettlebaston Brook (old River Brett), Bildeston and Kersey. It flows into the River Stour. The gauging station near Cockfield monitors the flow of water.

There are surveys of voles and newts. Priorities for upkeep are changing to reflect areas where flooding occurs, such as where the river goes under the bridge at Clay Hill Road, near The Common. Look at the EA website for flood mapping. The normal Ordnance Survey maps give more information about the river.

From the papers: "In August 2007 soap powder from a tank at a disused

Looking upstream from the bridge over the river. Notice the sloping kingfisher perch to the left of the photo, at the water's edge

Looking downstream from the bridge over the river. Herons have been seen here

Lavenham industrial site in Suffolk was washed into Lavenham Brook causing the deaths of a large number of fish. Thieves broke into the site to steal the tank and emptied its contents — soap powder to make liquid soap — onto the ground before taking the tank away. Unfortunately some of the powder ended up in surface water drains leading to the River Brett.

The River Brett was affected for about 2-3km and along this stretch stone loach, sticklebacks and minnows were wiped out. The estimate for the numbers killed is between 100 to 1,000.

By the time the water reached Lavenham Sewage Treatment Works the pollution was very much diluted and there were no fish deaths further downstream."

Agriculture and farming

In Lavenham today, agriculture and farming play an important part, though perhaps a less significant role than years ago, certainly in terms of numbers employed. There are eight major farms around the village and I spoke with several of the farmers about their working experiences in agriculture today.

Apart from weather, one emotive subject surrounding farming today is subsidies. Production subsidies and set-aside have largely disappeared, replaced with the Single Farm Payment. This voluntary scheme is not production related but could be considered as an incentive to environmental factors. The scheme is due to end in 2012 and an alternative EU scheme seems very likely.

Product marketing is currently subject to enormous price volatility, wheat being a prime example, having varied between £70 to £200 a ton during the past three years. All the farms sell through agents.

The Department for the Environment, Food and Rural Affairs (DEFRA) is a subject close to all farmers hearts and those around Lavenham are no exception. A regular comment from the farmers I spoke to is the lack of farming expertise amongst DEFRA staff and the

very considerable amount of paperwork required. DEFRA inspections to ensure compliance with complex EU rules take place on a random basis and can last over a week, while all the relevant checks are made, including fields and records.

Bridge Farm (155 acres)

Alan Fayers is a tenanted smallholder, growing wheat, barley, beans and oilseed rape, on land leased from Suffolk County Council. He runs the farm single handed but has also diversified into pet and animal feeds, making the operation much more commercially viable.

Brights (Hall & Slough) Farms (550 acres)

Ken and Robert Rush have recently purchased Brights Farm. Robert, at the time of writing, is refurbishing the modern farmhouse there. Robert and Amanda hope to make the farm a haven for wildlife and have entered EU-financed schemes to benefit the farm. For example, they have planted about a mile and a half of blackthorn, hawthorn, field maple, dog rose, crab apple and dogwood hedges.

Crops include winter wheat, spring and winter barley, spring and winter beans, oilseed rape and sugar beet. Robert said that 2008 had been very high yielding though very difficult to harvest. He has three permanent staff (two in Lavenham), four lorry drivers and some seasonal staff (usually students). He mostly owns his own machinery

Hill Farm, Lavenham (615 acres)

Harold Chrystal (now largely retired) and his son and son-in-law run the farm. 308 of their acres are within the Lavenham parish boundary (and, of those, 45 belong to the Lavenham Charity, whose income is the rent payable by Hill Farm). Crops include oats, wheat, barley, oilseed rape and sugar beet, though these are likely to be phased out soon as uneconomic. The farm has won many awards over the years.

Field vista from Hill Green area

Lodge Farm (1,700 acres)

John Pawsey is an organic farmer, having made the switch from conventional farming in 1999. He has three permanent staff. His crops include wheat, oats, beans and triticale. He sees the advantages as potential greater income and he enjoys the method.

John also lets out several small business premises on his land and has a very positive outlook about the next 10 years for farming and agriculture.

Nether Hall Farm (250 acres)

David Lane works the farm single-handed, most of the time. He currently grows wheat, oats, beans and barley. David has been in farming all his life.

Park Farm (500 acres)

Tim Partridge runs an arable farm, with some livestock, mostly single-handed though with occasional help from the family. From time to time he contracts out heavy work. His crops include wheat, oilseed rape, grass and spring barley. He has been an owner occupier for some years and considers farming to be a lifestyle as well as a commercial project.

Farming in East Anglia

As the NFU said recently "This region (Bedfordshire, Cambridgeshire, Essex,

Hertfordshire, Norfolk and Suffolk) has one of the most agricultural landscapes in the world. The region is best known for its cereal crops, with farmers growing more than a quarter of England's wheat and barley. Out of a total farmed area of 1.4 million hectares, almost a third of that land was used for wheat in 2007."

On the footpath to Preston St Mary, Lavenham church tower in the distance

UK farming

UK farming contributed £5.8 billion to the economy in 2007 (as measured by Gross Value Added at basic prices). It uses around three quarters of the country's land area and employs over half a million

people. One of DEFRA's major tasks is to help the industry to operate as efficiently as possible. They administer support policies agreed in Brussels which provide around £3 billion to UK agriculture.

Allotments

There are some very keen gardeners in the village who grow their own in the allotments behind Ropers Court.

A local farmhouse

Allottments behind Ropers Court

Washmere Green and bull-baiting

www.bulldoginformation.com

If you go into the Market Place or to Washmere Green, on the outskirts of Lavenham, today you would never recognise them as places where the last bull baiting in England took place.

In 1843 (*November 5th always being the date*) it was announced that a bull would be baited on the Market Place, the old and original ground. This apparent defiance of the authorities drew a large company of visitors and alert members, who found on their arrival the bull tethered by a rope to the ring, quietly feeding on hay which constituted the "bait". In a subsequent issue of the Bury and Norwich Post appeared a letter with the following editorial note:

"It is lamentable to find this town in so benighted a state at the present day, amidst all the appliances for the light of the Gospel and the principles of common humanity. Advantage might be taken of the Act of the last Sessions to appoint an efficient police force, but we are more disposed to look to the influence of moral restraint than to the strong arm of the law, putting down these brutal and brutalising practices."

The Bury and Norwich Post of 14th May 1901 published an article which read: "In view of the recent death of Abraham Hughes of Lavenham, who was present at the bull baiting at Washmere Green in this parish in 1842, the last bull bait in England and was fined 10s (50p) for assisting thereat, we thought it might be interesting to republish the account of the prosecution which appeared in the Bury Post on November 23rd 1842 and give the full details below. In all twelve persons were fined, some of them heavily and several went to prison in default of payment. By way of "righting a wrong", we suppose, the penalties and costs — amounting to £43 — were presented to Lavenham school."

"William Mattham landlord of Lavenham Black Lion, Noah Must a horse dealer of Sudbury, John Chinney, Martin Stearn and William Gurling, all butchers of Lavenham, Isaac Scarfe, Fred Stock, William Snell and William Duce all of Lavenham were summoned to answer a charge by Henry Thomas, secretary of the Society for the prevention of cruelty to animals, charging them with on November 5th at Washmere Green, Lavenham, that they did use a certain ground for bull baiting.

John Smith said he went to Washmere Green at 12 o'clock on November 5th where a great many people were assembled. At between 3 and 4 a bull was brought from the direction of Lavenham and several persons fixed a rope to its horns, they then led it to a stake fixed in the ground where a collar was put round its neck and the rope taken from its horns, then by noise and other means the bull was irritated to make it wild, Carter being the most active in this, he also collected money from the spectators.

Stearn had a dog which he set on the bull which it bit and several times, the dog was tossed in the air and severely injured. Gurling, Chinney and Ransom had dogs which they also set on the bull, Mattham was on horseback and appeared to direct the proceedings. The bull was baited for about half an hour and was torn about the face and nose, several of the dogs were much injured and bled a great deal. There were about 200 people present during the baiting with great uproar and filthy language being used.

Mattham, Must, Ransom, Chinney and Carter were fined £5 each. Gurling 20s. (£1). Hughes, Snell, Stock, Scarfe and Duce were fined 10s. (50p). Mattham, Must, Stearn, Gurling and Duce paid their fines, the rest were committed to prison for 2 months hard labour, the prosecution gave the fines to Lavenham National school."

197

Lavenham railway station

photo courtesy of Lavenham Press

As mentioned at the front of this book, my first arrival in Lavenham (*to see my parents at The Swan*) was by train. The railway line from Long Melford to Bury St Edmunds was opened by the Great Eastern Railway (GER) in August 1865. It had intermediate stations at Bury Eastgate, Whelnetham, Cockfield and Lavenham.

The railway played a vital part in the local Lavenham economy, bringing in raw materials for the horsehair and coconut matting industries and shipping out both finished products and agricultural produce such as sugar beet for processing in nearby Bury St Edmunds.

In the 1920s road competition set in. At the peak there were five or six trains a day between Long Melford and Bury, some of them coming from Marks Tey or Colchester. After World War II passenger services reduced dramatically and the line was closed to passengers in April 1961 and to freight traffic in April 1965.

The picture above shows Lavenham railway station in the early years of the 20th century. The church tower can be seen top left.

The Guildhall of Corpus Christi has a small but interesting exhibition charting the history of the railway and illustrating its contribution to the economy of Lavenham.

During the period prior to the First World War, the line through Lavenham saw some of its best traffic. The war brought little reduction in traffic but by the 1920s the familiar pattern of road competition was setting in although rail traffic continued quite healthily for some years; some economies were made.

After WWI the economic decline of the area deepened as did the population in many towns and villages in the area, together with traffic on the line.

When the Second World War came the situation changed dramatically; passenger services were reduced although freight services remained active. Changes came when British Railways announced a modernisation programme; from January 1st 1959, steam was scrapped and replaced by multiple diesel units.

Although passenger traffic showed some improvement it was not enough to overcome the increasing losses being incurred. Passenger traffic became very light and the line closed.

The Great Eastern Railway was formed on 7th August 1862 from the Eastern Counties, Eastern Union, East Anglian, East Suffolk & Norfolk railway companies, with their subsidiary companies. It survived until 1923, when the UK railway companies regrouped under a major amalgamation.

The GER dealt mainly with three types of customer: commuters, agriculturalists and holiday travellers. Lavenham's commercial traffic was not among these types.

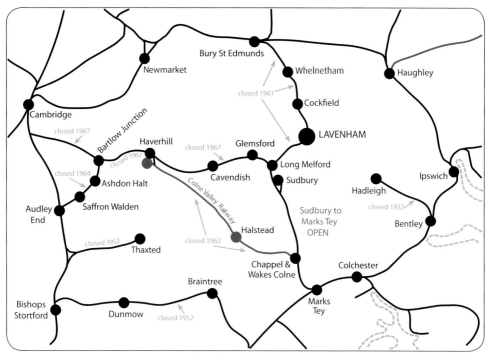

A sketch map of railways around Lavenham — many of which are long since closed, including the one through Lavenham itself. Not all stations are indicated on this sketch. The Eastern Counties Railway (1838—1862) became the Great Eastern Railway (1862—1923) which merged with the Colne Valley and Halstead Railway (1860—1923) to become the LNER — London North Eastern Railway (1923—1948) which then became British Railways.

Lavenham station c. 1950s
photo by kind permission of Blom Aerofilms Ltd

There is an excellent website run by The Great Eastern Railway Society, giving details of the railway, the Society publications, a journal and how to join the Society:

www.gersociety.org.uk

Very interesting information can also be seen on the Disused Stations Site Record at:

www.subbrit.org.uk/sb-sites/stations/l/ lavenham

The railway bridge today

A factory standing where the railway ran

The youth view of Lavenham

It seemed to me to be interesting to get the views of younger people about Lavenham at the start of the 21st century. Obviously, a young person is likely to have quite a different point of view about our village than the older residents.

The School, Youth Club and Salvation Army were very helpful in returning simple and anonymous questionnaires to me and I'm grateful for their help.

The questions asked were:

- How old are you?
- How many years have you lived in Lavenham?
- To which clubs and groups within Lavenham do you belong?
- What do you think about Lavenham today?
- What additional facilities would you like to see for young people in Lavenham?
- Is there anything else you would like to say about Lavenham?

32 replies were received, with answers summarised here (some spellings corrected). I suspect the voice of parents was echoed in some of the replies. Not all respondents answered all questions.

How old are you?

Ranged from 6 to 14 years old.

How many years have you lived in Lavenham?

Ranged from 1 to 14 years.

To which clubs and groups within Lavenham do you belong?

Beavers (4), Cubs (7), Football Club (1), Youth Club (19), None (7).

What do you think about Lavenham today?

1—A nice little village with lots of friendly people, nice houses and an interesting history. 2—A nice village that gets lots of tourists but not many things for young people. 3—Too many tourists and a lot of litter. 4—It's old/cosy. Never go. 5—It's noisy at weekends when the tourists are around. 6—Really nice, you can fit in easily. 7—Boring. 8—Excellent and cool. 9—Fine. 10—Fantastic and pretty well fabulous. 11—Exciting. 12—Nice, pretty, OK. 13—Pretty. 14—Quite pretty. 15—OK. 16—Good. 17—It's brilliant. 18—Good. 19—Nice place. 20—It is the best place for living. 21—It's brilliant. 22—It's a nice place to live. 23—Fantastic.

What additional facilities would you like to see for young people in Lavenham?

1—A tennis court open to the public (not just the tennis club). 2—A swimming pool. 3—A better skatepark. 4—A bigger park with more things, not just swings/slide. 5—More trees to climb. 6—More clubs/netball or sports clubs (like to hear about them/publicity). 7—Dance club. 8—BMX park, basketball nets/court, a mushroom seat and a climbing wall. 9—A neater park. 10—Ice cream park. 11—A gym. 12—Bigger playground. 13—Ice cream van. 14—A bigger park. 15—Doughnut park. 16—None. 17—Toy shop. 18—Nothing. 19—More toy shops and new things at the park.

Is there anything else you would like to say about Lavenham?

1—Need more bins. 2—Too many tourists. 3—It's generally a nice place. Zebra crossings would help. 4. The school is great and the old houses are cool. 5—School is a big place. 6—School is 'supercallafragilisticadocious' a lot. 7—I love living in Lavenham. 8—The school is nice. 9—The school is great. 10—School's excellent. 11—It's very peaceful. 12—It's cool. 13—It is very clean.

Places to visit nearby

Lavenham makes an ideal centre for touring this part of East Anglia. It is surrounded by many picturesque villages and beautiful mediæval buildings and churches. Excellent museums are nearby and there are good transport links by road. Stansted Airport is about one hour away, as is Harwich International Port.

Photos of Bury St Edmunds, Ipswich, Kentwell Hall, Newmarket and Sudbury courtesy Suffolk Tourism Partnership

Bildeston *(6 miles)*

Like Lavenham, Bildeston owed its wealth and prosperity to the mediæval woollen cloth industry. It is a thriving village, with a high level of services.

Boxford *(9 miles)*

Boxford, a quaint village, has a stream running past timber framed cottages.

Bury St Edmunds *(11 miles)*

Bury St Edmunds is a busy market town, with excellent shopping and a great variety of eating establishments, quite apart from its many historical connections. Formerly the county town of West Suffolk, it is the seat of the East of England Regional Assembly.

The Theatre Royal in Westgate Street one of the oldest and smallest working theatres in the country, in the care of the National Trust, has recently been extensively restored. The abbey, which had a massive steeple added in 2005, was built on the site of the shrine of the martyred Saxon King Edmund, who became the patron saint of England.

Discovering Bury St Edmunds is a step by step walking guide to the town. The estimated walking time is two hours.

The town is associated with Magna Carta; in 1214 the barons of England are believed to have met in the Abbey Church and swore to force King John to accept the Charter of Liberties, the document which influenced the creation of the Magna Carta. The town was also the setting for two witch trials, the first under the direction of the Witchfinder General, the second used as a reference in the Salem Witch Trials of 1692 and 1693.

Cambridge *(35 miles)*

One of Britain's oldest and finest University cities. A wonderful fusion of the everyday and extraordinary.  Punting on the Cam, numerous museums, botanic gardens, theatres, open-top bus tours and art galleries. Winding streets with glorious university architecture and 'the backs.'

Cavendish *(8 miles)*

Has a lovely church, and a magnificent village green. The Sue Ryder Foundation used to be headquartered there.

Chelsworth *(4 miles)*

Often described as a 'chocolate-box' Suffolk village, with some lovely gardens opened once a year in June to visitors.

201

Clare *(11 miles)*

Has a Country Park with a 13th century Priory and nearby Castle Mote. Visit the small church of the Augustinian Order of the Friars in the former Infirmary. Near the former market place is the great Gothic church of St Peter & St Paul. The Ancient House Museum is opposite.

Colchester *(17 miles)*

The Romans came in 43AD, creating Britain's 'oldest  recorded town'. Visit the award winning museum within the Norman Castle, all set in a lovely park created by the Victorians in 1892. Shopping, Minories Art Gallery, Mercury Theatre, Sports Centre, Tourist Information. Blue badge guided tours of town and castle. Two miles south is the world acclaimed Colchester Zoo.

Dedham/Flatford/East Bergholt

The 'Heart of Constable Country' and birthplace of John Constable.

Hadleigh *(10 miles)*

photo courtesy Hadleigh on the Web

Hadleigh Guildhall, one of three outstanding buildings near St Mary's churchyard, is open to the public for guided tours on Thursday and Sunday afternoons during the summer.

The town has a good selection of shops and eating places and has a leisure centre and swimming pool. There are some great walks nearby too.

Hadleigh was a very prosperous town during the 14th and 15th centuries, has many fine half-timbered buildings, and a splendid church and Deanery Tower.

Ipswich *(22 miles)*

The county town of Suffolk. The waterfront is the East of England's most exciting regeneration project. Offers river cruises, Christchurch Mansion (with works by Gainsborough and Constable), Ipswich Museum, the Transport Museum and a premier regional shopping centre. Guided walks available and city sightseeing tours by open-topped bus.

Kersey *(9 miles)*

A real 'picture-postcard' village, one of the finest of the former Suffolk wool towns, with a lovely church. The ford across the main street is a gathering point for ducks. Kersey Pottery is popular.

Long Melford *(4 miles)*

Whether you are interested in antiques, the latest fashions, good food, life-style shopping or historic buildings, Long Melford's one mile long main street is worth a visit. There are a lot of attractive buildings of almost every period dating back to the Middle Ages.

Kentwell Hall, pictured opposite, is in a romantic, completely moated setting in a tranquil parkland. It features regular Tudor 're-creations'. Melford Hall one of East Anglia's most celebrated Elizabethan houses, has a classic Tudor interior, a fine panelled banqueting hall, Beatrix Potter mementoes and delightful walks.

The magnificent Holy Trinity Church, one of the finest parish churches in England demonstrates, like Lavenham, the wealth that the woollen industry brought to East Anglia during the 14th and 15th centuries. It stands at the northern end of the village overlooking a large, attractive, triangular green.

Newmarket *(29 miles)*

Newmarket has been recognised as the headquarters of horse-racing for over 300 years. There are two complete and highly distinct racecourses — the Rowley Mile (named after King Charles II "Old Rowley") and the July Racecourse. The Millennium Grandstand, based at the Rowley racecourse, has undergone millions of pounds worth of modifications, bringing huge changes and improvements.

The National Horseracing Museum is next door to the headquarters of the Jockey Club, which was founded in 1751. The museum tells the story of the people and horses involved in racing from its royal origins to modern heroes. It is said that King James I was the first to discover that the flat land in the area was ideal for galloping horses.

Sudbury *(7 miles)*

Gainsborough's House — birthplace of Thomas Gainsborough (1727-88), one of England's greatest painters — is now

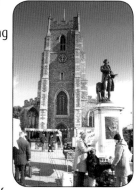

an art gallery and museum with a collection including fine paintings, drawings and etchings from throughout his career.

Sudbury is centred around Market Hill, with its twice weekly market. In front of St Peter's church is the statue of Thomas Gainsborough (pictured above).

The centre of Sudbury has many interesting alleys and streets, including the North Street shopping centre, which was used as a location for part of the TV Lovejoy series.

Stoke-by-Nayland *(10 miles)*

Many of John Constable's paintings featured this area and the bells of Stoke's church of St Mary are famous too.

West Stow *(18 miles)*

125 acres of unspoilt countryside, river, lake and heathland with nature trails and bird hides. Features a reconstructed Anglo-Saxon village, with visitor centre and activity days.

Woodbridge *(30 miles)*

Arthur Mee said of it "one of the most delightful small towns of this enchanting countryside." It has a famous Tide Mill and the Suffolk Punch Heavy Horse Museum.

Lavenham, Manitoba, Canada

www.travelmanitoba.com

The only other Lavenham known to the author is in Manitoba, Canada. It lies on Provincial Road 305 and is part of the Rural Municipality of South Norfolk (main town Treherne) in southern Manitoba, west of Winnipeg and not far north of the Canada/USA border. The First Nation reservations of Long Plains, Dakota Plains and Swan Lake lie between Lavenham and Portage La Prairie.

Surfing the web for Lavenham, Canada was not particularly productive and the best information I found was eventually provided by singer/songwriter Lynda Dobbin-Turner, who also very kindly provided the recent photographs.

Doris Bagnall, President of the North Norfolk—MacGregor Archives Inc., and the Legislative Library of Canada, part of the Culture, Heritage, Tourism and Sport department, based in Winnipeg, also provided information.

The road into Lavenham, Manitoba

Lavenham home, apparently, live outside the town boundaries. There is still a large agricultural base, with a lot of potatoes still being grown in the area due to the ability to irrigate that the Assiniboine River offers. However, the area is also now growing in popularity as a cottage area, due to the beauty of the scenery and landscape and the peace and quiet that it still offers. Many people have actually purchased properties to cottage at because of their love of hunting and the abundance of wildlife locally.

Today

Lavenham today is a lot smaller than in years past. Now there are about 15 homes, for the most part occupied by people who have chosen to return to their roots for their retirement years. The church is still there, though only used for very occasional special services. There is a community hall that hosts two community suppers a year — spring and fall — and an annual snowmobile poker derby. It also acts as a polling station during many of the elections they have.

The majority of people that call

Water rates

Amazingly, one of the first items that appeared on the web in my search

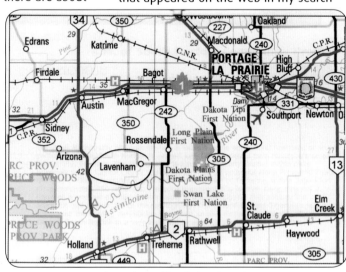

Lavenham, Manitoba, Canada
The nearest city is Portage La Prairie

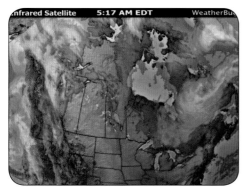

Satellite weather map centred on Lavenham, Manitoba in October 2008

for Lavenham, Manitoba was a report by the Rural Municipality of South Norfolk. In October 2007, setting the water rates for the Lavenham Hamlet Utility for 2008, it was noted that "at the last report there were 19 customers, all except for Lavenham's hall being residential customers; all customers are un-metered." The report went on to say that "raw water is obtained from a nearby well and treated with chlorine. Capital and operating costs were paid for by the co-operative. Drinking water standards were reported as being met."

Name

The entry in the Geographical Names of Manitoba includes: "Lavenham, a Community southwest of Portage la Prairie. The Post Office opened in 1889 as Rosehill. In 1905, the CNR arrived and the Post Office was renamed after Lavenham, a parish and village in Suffolk, England. Garland (1975) noted that before the arrival of the railway, it was named The Henry Settlement. Lavenham School District was on 35-9-10W."

From The North Norfolk—MacGregor Archives Inc. I was informed that the entry in Place Names of Manitoba, written by Penny Ham and published by Western

Erecting a broadband tower in Lavenham, Manitoba in 2008

Producer Prairie Booms (ISBN 0-88833-067-7) states "Lavenham is a settlement, southwest of Portage La Prairie (35-9-10-w). This district was originally part of the Rossendale District and was known first as Henry. The Henrys were among the first settlers and Emmanuel Henry established one of the first stores. After the railway went through Orville Wright, another early settler, named it after his native village and parish in Suffolk, England."

Trails Old and New

The following details are extracted from Trails Old and New: MacGregor and District, 1872—1967, edited by R. L. Taylor, MacGregor History Committee:

"Lavenham district was part of Rossendale and was known as the Henry settlement until the railroad came

Lavenham, Manitoba

through. At that time Oliver Wright named it Lavenham after his home in England. The country was heavily wooded and a number of sawmills which cut rough lumber were established.

The railroad coming through not only meant jobs in construction for the men but it brought business to Lavenham. A boarding house and two stores were erected. The church was built in 1905. Two blacksmith shops and an elevator were there, and a boardwalk down the main street. The first house was built by a nurse, who cared for the sick and attended child-births.

In 1905 the train was snowbound, and again in 1920. Wild horses were shipped in by train for sale and were used to pull

Lavenham, Manitoba old Orange Hall

steam engines and water tanks. Farmers used oxen for heavy work in the fields. Coyotes were reported to have been troublesome.

Homesteads were established starting in 1892/93. An 'Orange Hall', which originally opened in 1902 and moved to Lavenham in 1911, was for the Lavenham Orangemen, and later doubled as a school and community centre. The Orange order was essentially a popular nativist organisation, Irish-Protestant in origin.

Through Fields and Dreams

This publication includes the following details about Lavenham, Manitoba:

"Located about 16 miles south of MacGregor and much higher, because of the nature of the land which is very hilly with many trees of oak and poplar. It is about three miles from the Assiniboine river so the scenery is very nice.

In the early 1900s many businesses were there, including two general stores, a post office, blacksmith shop, pool hall, Massey Harris dealer, grain elevator and brick yard. The CNR ran on the south side of the village and many local people worked for the company as section crews, servicing the tracks. The last of these were removed in 1978.

The house they called the Manse (shades of Lavenham, Suffolk) still stands, though now privately owned. In 1950 there was a Lavenham Playboys (Ice) Hockey team (using an outdoor rink) and as recently as 1968 a thriving Lavenham Ladies Aid group.

above — photographs of Lavenham, Manitoba in October 2008

below — countryside nearby

Lynda Dobbin-Turner

www.musicwriter.ca/

Lynda, country and folk music singer/ songwriter and music composer — a rising star in the Canadian country music industry — (pictured left with her son, Shane, aged 16 in 2008) lives in Lavenham, Manitoba.

Her website says "I'm a mom, a wife, a farmer, a daughter, a sister and a friend. My jobs include raising cattle on one side and providing resources to support adults with intellectual disabilities to live independently on the other. Somewhere in the middle of all of that stuff is Lynda... who is a writer, a singer, a dreamer and a seeker.

The big losses in my life have taught me lessons that push me to do and be all that I can in this short amount of time that I'm given, so I always have my plate way too full, but I'm determined to be and do as much as I can.

I love my life, I love my people, I love my home and I'm grateful for every opportunity I've been given. What can I say....I'm one of the lucky ones, even though my history makes a lot of people think otherwise."

Lynda's view of her yardsite when coming down the road

Lynda Dobbin-Turner

Lynda has not yet visited England, but hopes to do so as soon as opportunity permits, especially to Lavenham, Suffolk.

Lynda and her husband are cattle producers, because the land base around Lavenham is either excellent as in the potato acres or awful, due to all the inclines and steplands, and is only suitable for grazing livestock.

Her grandfather was one of the first teachers at Ladysmith school, just two miles west of her home. He loved the countryside and, when Lynda was a child, would spend most Sunday drives touring though the hills nearby. She says it is a great honour to be able to call Lavenham home, all those years later.

Her website enables the surfer to listen to samples of music from a collection of 15 songs on her excellent first CD, including tracks such as Company of Friends, Learn, Mending Broken Dreams, My Little Corner of the World and Country Charm. Lynda has been singing publicly since the age of 7 and playing guitar and writing since the age of 15.

Other publications about Lavenham

A selection of books and publications about, or with a significant reference to, Lavenham. There may be others, but the following are the author's selection.

2008
LAVENHAM TOURIST GUIDE

Published by Hepworth Computer Services in association with Lavenham Merchants' Guild. Printed by The Lavenham Press.

A tourist guide to the village, with additional information on places to visit nearby.

Available from the Tourist Information Centre, Guildhall gift shop, Church gift shop and several other local outlets.

Price £1.

2008
OUR MEMORIES — Volume 2

by Lavenham Folk. Printed by The Lavenham Press.

Published in October 2008 as a follow-up volume to the first edition, which was published in 2006.

A further look by residents at their memories of the village.

Available from the Village Hall, price £10.

2008
LAVENHAM, LONG MELFORD and the Suffolk Wool Country

Design and photographs by John Curtis. Published by J. Salmon Ltd.

ISBN 978-1-84640-128-3. Photographs of Lavenham's church, the High Street, The Swan, the Market Cross, Little Hall, Wool Hall and the Guildhall.

Also has photographs of Long Melford and other Suffolk villages.

2007
FANFARE FOR LAVENHAM

by Sir Clive Rose GCMG. Published by The Lavenham Press.

An epic poem outlining Lavenham's history from Roman times to the present day, composed in celebration of the 750th Anniversary of The Royal Market Charter for Lavenham, granted by King Henry III in 1257.

2007
LAVENHAM THIS LOVELY VILLAGE IN THE HEART OF SUFFOLK

by Ken Hayward

A true account of what Ken can remember about Lavenham having lived and worked in the village from 1945 to 1969. A very enjoyable read. Available from Lavenham Tourist Information Centre and other outlets, price £6.99.

2006
LAVENHAM REMEMBERS

by Sir Clive Rose GCMG. Published by The Lavenham Press.

Foreword by Field Marshall Lord Bramall KG, GCB, OBE, MC. A Roll of Honour of two World Wars — with facsimile reproductions of individual accounts. For the First World War, 76 names are recorded. For the Second World War, 10 names.

2006

LAVENHAM's PUBS, INNS & BEER HOUSES Past and Present

by Jim Robinson (Blue Badge guide).

An interesting study of the drinking houses of Lavenham, with details of some 15 inns or pubs (past and present) together with information about Lavenham's former brewers. Available from Lavenham Tourist Information Centre and other local outlets.

2006

OUR MEMORIES — Volume 1

by Lavenham Folk. Printed by The Lavenham Press.

Launched at an exhibition on 19th October 2006, this book is the first in a series recording the history of the village as seen through the eyes of some of its older inhabitants "before it is too late". 10 interviews were carried out, by six interviewers (of mixed ages). Specialist advice and support came from Lavenham Photographic, the Crooked House Gallery and Howletts of Lavenham. Available from the Village Hall, price £10.

2005

SUDBURY, LAVENHAM & LONG MELFORD — Francis Frith's Photographic Memories

by Clive Paine. Published by the Frith Book Company Ltd. ISBN 1-85937-849-8 (hardback) and 1-85937-850-1 (paperback).

A fascinating portrait of Sudbury, Lavenham and Long Melford in years gone by, featuring photographs from the world-famous Frith collection. Very interesting.

2004 (*revised 2007*)

GUILDHALL OF CORPUS CHRISTI LAVENHAM

Designed by Rose-Innes Associates, printed by Heanor Gate for National Trust (Enterprises) Ltd. ISBN 978-1-84359-103-0.

A delightful 26 page booklet, with text by Leigh Alston and excellent photographs (some by Lavenham Photographic Studio).

Describes the building, its history, construction, exterior and interior.

Guildhall of Corpus Christi Lavenham

2004 (*2005 and 2006*)

WALKING CLOSE TO THE MIDDLE AGES NEAR LAVENHAM in Suffolk

Walked, written and drawn by Clive Brown.

Ten varied and interesting circular walks close to Lavenham, with simple but detailed instructions and clear concise maps.

2004

HISTORY OF THE 487th BOMB GROUP (H)

by Ivo M. de Jong. Published by Turner Publishing, ISBN 1-59652-018-3. A very detailed history of the U.S. 487th Bomb Group, which was stationed at Lavenham Airfield in 1944/45. A splendid book with many photographs of the airfield and aircraft. The group completed 185 missions, flying 5,242 effective sorties and dropping 141,416 tons of bombs. Sadly, no less than 233 U.S. airmen gave the ultimate sacrifice during that time.

2003

LAVENHAM'S JUBILEE CELEBRATIONS 1935

Compiled by Lionel Baker using photographs taken by F. Lingard Ranson and in collaboration with Freddie Robinson, John Gurling and Eileen Huffey.

This booklet was produced for the Lavenham Carnival, with all proceeds to the Lavenham Carnival Fund.

2003

HISTORIC LAVENHAM in Suffolk

Tourist Guide to Lavenham and the surrounding area. Published by Hepworth Computer Services, ISBN 0-9545938-0-4.

A double-sided fold-out guide in full colour, giving a wide variety of information about Lavenham and nearby places of interest, including a location map and a street map of the village. Out of print.

2003

A RECORD OF THE FIRST FIFTY YEARS AT THE LAVENHAM PRESS

Printed by The Lavenham Press and published by Terence Dalton Limited, Lavenham.

Chiefly intended as an internal document.

2003

LETTERS FROM THE FRONT TO LAVENHAM 1915—1918

By Captain H.C. Wolton MC, 1/5th Suffolk Regiment. Published by John C. Wolton.

2002

LAVENHAM VILLAGE DESIGN STATEMENT

published by the Village Design Statement Association team with assistance (*including financial*) and guidance from many contributors.

The Statement is a record, based on their own words, of how — at the beginning of the new millennium — the people of Lavenham viewed the environment in which they lived and how they saw themselves as a community. The statement was adopted as formal Supplementary Planning Guidance by Babergh District Council.

2001

LAVENHAM GUILDHALL — A BRIEF TOUR

published by The National Trust, text by L.A. Alston, printed by Barnwell's Print Ltd.

An excellent leaflet summarising what one might wish to know about The Guildhall. On sale at The Guildhall.

1998

LAVENHAM CHURCH

Photography by Mike Hodges of Lavenham Photographic, back cover photograph by Robin Golding, designed and printed by Beric Tempest.

A plan and short history of the church and a tour of the building. Well illustrated. Sold out.

1998

HISTORIC BUILDINGS OF SUFFOLK (Volume 1)

Edited by Leigh Alston. The Journal of the Suffolk Historic Buildings Group. Printed by Fuller Davies Ltd, Ipswich. ISSN 1464-6110

Contains an article by Leigh Alston, with drawings by Richard Shackle, about The Old Grammar School, described as the finest merchant's house in Lavenham. Recommended reading.

1995 (reprinted 1997,1999, 2001 and 2004)
SUFFOLK AIRFIELDS IN THE SECOND WORLD WAR
By Graham Smith. Published by Countryside Books, Newbury, Berkshire. ISBN 1-85306-342-8
Lavenham, the home of the 487th Bomb Group, is described in chapter 18. It says that some scenes for the film Twelve O'Clock High were filmed there.

1994
LOOK AT LAVENHAM PARISH CHURCH
by Bessacarr Prints, Thackray House, Manor Road, Hatfield, Doncaster DN7 6SD, ISBN 0-86384-304-2.

Contains many diagrams and questions, to help people — especially children — find out things about the church. Includes sections on the baptistry, tower, aisles, chapels, chancel, porch and outside. Available at the church bookstall.

1993
THE DE VERES OF CASTLE HEDINGHAM
by Verily Anderson, ISBN 0 86138 062 2, published by Terence Dalton Limited and printed by The Lavenham Press.

Contains many references to Lavenham, including planting of a vineyard by Aubrey I in the late eleventh century! Also states that Queen Elizabeth was welcomed to Lavenham in 1578 by Sir William Spring, High Sheriff, and by the Earl of Oxford in his capacity as Lord of the Manor.

1992
FARM, FORGE AND FACTORY
"The life of a village one hundred years ago", by Cliff Hardy, published 1992 by Cliff Hardy, 8 High St, Lavenham and printed by The Lavenham Press. ISBN 0-9519811-0-2. Cliff's experience in farming, as horseman, tractor-driver, herdsman and farm bailiff, combined with his Agricultural Training Board experience and a period as Chairman of the Lavenham Guildhall Museum Committee led to the writing of this book.

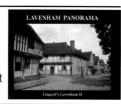

1992
THE FRIENDLY INVASION
By Roger A. Freeman, published by East Anglia Tourist Board in conjunction with Terence Dalton Limited, printed and bound by The Lavenham Press, ISBN 0-86138-103-3. Describes the influence of the large numbers of US servicemen who came to England in World War II. Has three mentions of Lavenham, including a photograph of one of the Nissen Huts occupied by eight officers at the Airfield.

1992
LAVENHAM PANORAMA
Lingard's Lavenham II
Published by Kitty Ranson. Printed by The Lavenham Press.
More of Francis Lingard Ranson's photographs, recording changes brought to Lavenham by the 20th century. Out of print.

1990
LINGARD'S LAVENHAM
Published by Kitty Ranson, printed by The Lavenham Press. A photographic tour of Lavenham past. Francis Lingard Ranson was the village tailor, a keen historian and an accomplished photographer. Kitty was Lingard's daughter and a long-term resident. Out of print.

1989
LAVENHAM INDUSTRIAL TOWN

by Alec Betterton and David Dymond. ISBN 0-86138-069-X (hardback) and ISBN 0-86138-070-3 (limp covers)

Published by Terence Dalton Limited, Lavenham. Originally published as *Lavenham: 700 years of Textile Making* by The Boydell Press, 1982

1986
THE MILITARY SURVEY OF 1522 FOR BABERGH HUNDRED

Published by the Boydell Press for the Suffolk Records Society and printed by Short Run Press Ltd. Edited by John Pound. ISBN 0-85115-438-7. Priced at £15.

One of the fullest surviving returns of its kind. Gives a breakdown of the wealth, population and occupations of Babergh Hundred, including Lavenham, in 1522. It also has information on arms and armour in time of war.

1982
LAVENHAM, 700 YEARS OF TEXTILE MAKING

by David Dymond and Alec Betterton. ISBN 0-85115-164-7. Published by The Boydell Press, printed by St. Edmundsbury Press, Bury St Edmunds.

The book arose from the work of a class in local history, held in Lavenham from 1970-74, arranged by the Board of Extra-Mural Studies of the University of Cambridge. It concentrates on the strong industrial and commercial tradition which lasted for many centuries.

1982
LAVENHAM AND THE CLOTH INDUSTRY

published by The National Trust, written by Alec Betterton, designed by John Allwood.

A very interesting and clearly written and illustrated summary of cloth making in Lavenham.

On sale at The Guildhall.

1976
THE SUFFOLK WE LIVE IN

by Paul Fincham, published by Barbara Hopkinson Books, ISBN 0-9507963-2-8.

A brief and authoritative account of Suffolk's history, with early chapters explaining the shaping of the land and later ones dealing with farming, other industries, communications, religion, natural history and local government. Chapter 11, in particular, is about Suffolk's cloth trade and the Springs of Lavenham, neatly summarising much of the history of that time.

1976 (2nd edition revised 1977, 3rd edition 1980)
SUFFOLK CHURCHES — A POCKET GUIDE

Published by the Suffolk Historic Churches Trust and printed by Baron Publishing, Woodbridge. ISBN 0-950-5385-1-5

Frequent references to Lavenham.

1975 (new edition 1983)
THE GUILDHALL, LAVENHAM, SUFFOLK

by Rena Gardiner, published by The National Trust.

An excellent book, designed and printed from hand-drawn lithographic plates, describing the Guildhall of Corpus Christi, the development of the wool cloth industry, some of the houses and life in mediæval Lavenham. Profusely illustrated and a very interesting read.

1973

LAVENHAM

Published by K. Ranson and printed by J. Salmon Ltd., Sevenoaks.

A reprint of a small book by L. Ranson, date unknown. Interestingly, the map on the back cover has North pointing South-East. The copy I bought was priced at 35p.

1972

LAVENHAM CONSERVATION AND VILLAGE PLAN

Typescript. By James Gorst, County Planning Officer. Published by Cosford Rural District Council, the cover showed a drawing of Lavenham Church & steeple (*described as very curious pieces of Gothic architecture, partly freestone and part flint-work*).

A follow up of Donald Insall's report — a review having regard to changing circumstances to see if modifications were needed. It mentioned a proposed road by-pass along the exposed hillside to the east of the village.

1970

WOOL — EAST ANGLIA'S GOLDEN FLEECE

by Nigel Heard, published by Terence Dalton Ltd, Lavenham. SBN 900963-14-X.

Until the fourteenth century raw wool formed the main English industry and export, but with the growth of the cloth industry the native skills of the East Anglians, combined with the techniques of Flemish settlers, soon placed their region in a paramount position.

1970

LAVENHAM COMMUNITY COUNCIL WELCOMES THE RETURN OF THE 487TH BOMB GROUP ASSOCIATION

A souvenir programme published by Lavenham Community Council and printed by Terence Dalton Limited of Lavenham. Priced at 2/-. The plaque in the Market Place (originally to have been in the airfield control tower, then the church) was dedicated as a reminder of how very much Lavenham owes to the 487th.

1966

SUFFOLK — A SHELL GUIDE, 2nd edition

by Norman Scarfe. Published by Faber & Faber, London. ISBN 0571118216. 124pp. A gazetteer of 500 parishes, with a new chapter on modern Suffolk developments. Understood to have been replaced by The Suffolk Guide, 4th edition 1988 published by the Alastair Press, Bury St Edmunds, first published 1960 by Faber & Faber.

1965 (reprinted 1966/68/72/74)

THE SWAN LAVENHAM

Specially written by Hammond Innes and published by Trust House Forte Hotels. 1968 print by The Stellar Press.

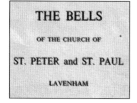

1965

THE BELLS OF THE CHURCH OF ST. PETER AND ST. PAUL LAVENHAM

by Captain G.A.D. Cooper RN Rtd, printed by Kemps Printing Agency, Lavenham. Produced when the Rev. R.A. Bird was Rector. Contains some notes on the bells and bell frame on the occasion of the fitting of a new frame and re-dedication by The Rt. Revd. the Lord Bishop of Dunwich. Also has a drawing of the original bell frame of circa 1525.

1961

LAVENHAM, PAST • PRESENT • FUTURE

by Donald W Insall ARIBA SPDip, dated MCMLXI, published by the West Suffolk County Council and printed by E & E Plumridge, Linton.

A survey and report on buildings of architectural and historic importance in Lavenham, for the County of West Suffolk and the Rural District of Cosford, having regard to those already "listed", making recommendations for the restoration, conversion or improvement of unfit cottages or groups of period cottages which the Architect considered to be falling or likely to fall into a state of decay. Designed as a practical contribution to the special information needed, in addition to that available under existing town planning legislation, by a local authority responsible as guardian of a town of architectural and historic importance to the nation.

1961 (2nd edition 1974, Yale University edition 2002)

THE BUILDINGS OF ENGLAND — SUFFOLK

by Nikolaus Pevsner. Originally published by Penguin Books, 2nd edition revised by Enid Radcliffe. ISBN 0-300-09648-8

One of an unrivalled series of comprehensive architectural guides covering every English county and all periods from prehistoric times to the present day. Frequent references to Lavenham.

1961

VISIT TO LAVENHAM BY MEMBERS OF THE BRITISH ASSOCIATION FOR THE ADVANCEMENT OF SCIENCE

Prepared by the County Planning Department, West Suffolk County Council. Properties for inspection included the Church, the Guildhall and Chapel, Little Hall, several houses in Prentice Street and 20 Shilling Street. The paper also listed numerous other houses that the group were invited to visit.

1958

LAVENHAM BUILDINGS OF ARCHITECTURAL and HISTORIC IMPORTANCE

Published by Cosford Rural District Council and issued under the auspices of the Ministry of Town & Country Planning.

The front cover showed a village plan with all Grade I, Grade II, Grade III and SPAB buildings indicated by shading. It included a provisional list of buildings of architectural interest for consideration. Cosford RDC then applied for conservation status for the village and thence a professional survey was required. This led to Donald Insall's work in 1961.

1956

THE GAYER-ANDERSON HOSTEL FOR ART STUDENTS, LAVENHAM

By Colonel T. Gayer-Anderson.

A short history and guide in two parts.

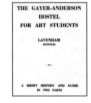

1952

THE CHURCH OF SS. PETER & PAUL LAVENHAM

by M Fountain Page (Rector 1933-1952). Designed and pulblished (*sic*) by The British Publishing Company Limited, Gloucester.

An illustrated guide (*which ran to at least four editions*), approved by the Parochial Church Council and supported by local advertisers. Based on previous publications, it added mainly new matter about the patronage of the living. The Rector described the church as "this fabric which is known wherever a knowledge or appreciation of the indigenous art of England has penetrated."

214

1951
SUFFOLK SUMMER

by John T Appleby, Alastair Press, ISBN: 1870567579.

A nostalgic view of Suffolk during World War II, seen through the eyes of an American serviceman stationed at Lavenham airfield (*and later in Norfolk*). John came from Fayetteville, Arkansas. He loved the East Anglian countryside and, riding an ancient bicycle, explored its attractive villages and ancient churches.

1950, revised 1962
LAVENHAM SUFFOLK OFFICIAL GUIDE

Published by Home Publishing Co Ltd. Text by M. Fountain Page, Rector, Issued by authority of Lavenham Parish Council. Five illustrations.

Contents included a map, Lavenham amenities, a short description and history, weaving, the Guild Hall, a short itinerary and the Church of SS. Peter and Paul.

1949/50
THE LAVENHAM APPEAL

Published jointly by the Lavenham Preservation Committee and the Trustees of The Guild Hall Group of Buildings. Printed by Curwen Press.

An appeal for financial aid, primarily to raise the £4,000 the National Trust required to take on the trusteeship of the Guildhall. Despite some doubters it was a success and raised £6,000. This was mainly due to the support of the Pilgrim Trust. As a result of the appeal the Guildhall transfer was completed in 1951.

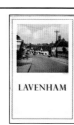

1944
JOINT REPORT ON THE BUILDINGS OF LAVENHAM

JOINT REPORT ON THE BUILDINGS OF LAVENHAM

Typescript. Commissioned by Cosford Rural District Council and prepared by John McGregor of the Society for the Preservation of Ancient Buildings (SPAB), and Marshall Sisson of the Suffolk Preservation Society. Amongst other things this report recommended a bypass for Lavenham!

1939
THE TAYLORS OF ONGAR

by Doris Mary Armitage, published by W. Heffer & Sons Ltd., Cambridge. "A portrait of an English Family of the 18th and 19th Centuries. Drawn from Family Records by the Great-great Niece of Ann and Jane Taylor". The Taylors of Ongar are mainly remembered in Lavenham for their sojourn in Lavenham from 1786 to 1796, first at Shilling Grange and then at Arundel House, both in Shilling Street.

1937 (*and 1947, 1950, 1958 and 1965*)
LAVENHAM, SUFFOLK

by F. Lingard Ranson.

A history of Lavenham, a history of and visitor's guide to the church, wills of clothiers, visitors guide to the town and some notable people of Lavenham. Mr Ranson was part founder of the Suffolk Preservation Society and, in 1944, co-founded the Lavenham Preservation Society which, with others, virtually saved the village from almost complete demolition.

1929
LAVENHAM CHURCH and TOWN

by the Rev. G.H. Lenox-Conyngham, Rector of Lavenham, printed by Marten and Son Limited, of 17 Market Hill, Sudbury. Photographs by F.L. Ranson of Lavenham.

He writes about the Rev. J.M. Croker (*1855—1891 and also an expert carpenter and stone mason*) who made many changes to the church, about the ravages of the death watch beetle to church timbers and about the de Vere and Spring families, who were instrumental in the building of the church.

1925

LAVENHAM PARISH CHURCH — REPORT ON THE CONDITION OF THE ROOFS AND OTHER WOODWORK

By F.E. Howard, Architect, Oxford, who examined the roofs, he described as very fine specimens of English carpentry of the sixteenth century, as far as possible without undue disturbance of the lead or the erection of extensive scaffolding. He found considerable evidence of the ravages of the Death Watch beetle.

1924

THE SPRINGS OF LAVENHAM
and the Suffolk Cloth Trade in the XV and XVI Centuries
by Barbara McClenaghan, Girton College, Cambridge.

Printed & published by W.E. Harrison, The Ancient House Press, Ipswich. Written in 1921 to obtain a Historical Research Certificate from the University of Cambridge. The author only attempted to treat the subject in so far as it affected the noble family of Springs.

1915

FORMS OF PRAYER FOR PRIVATE AND PUBLIC USE IN TIMES OF WAR

Issued by Authority, published by the Society for Promoting Christian Knowledge, London and printed by Harrison & Sons, London.

Taken away from the church (*despite the clear admonition not to do so*) it included a Form of Intercession; Supplementary Forms of Prayer; Prayers for Family Worship; Private Prayers; and a Form of Humble Prayer to Almighty God. The handbook was priced at 2d a copy.

1910

LAVENHAM: THE CHURCH AND ITS BUILDERS
by W.D. Caröe MA FSA (a reprint from *The Church Builder* of October 1910), printed by William Clowes and Sons, Limited, London.

This is the script of a lecture delivered in Lavenham Church on July 5th, 1910, by special permission of the Right Reverend the Lord Bishop of Ely. Sold for 6d a copy

1908

THE CHURCH OF S. PETER AND S. PAUL, LAVENHAM

Printed by William Clowes and Sons, Limited, London.

A reprint, with some additional matter, from *The Church Builder* of October 1908. The pamphlet details the work that the eminent church architect Mr W.D. Caröe MA FSA considered should be undertaken as soon as possible. The estimated cost of the entire work was £1,650!

1897 (*2nd edition 1903*)

THE VISITORS GUIDE TO LAVENHAM AND ITS CHURCH
by the Rev. Canon Scott, Rector of Lavenham, published by F.T. Groom, Bury St Edmunds. Printed by Adlard & Son, London.

The Rev. Scott (*formerly Vicar of West Ham, & Rural Dean*) takes the visitor on a walk about the town and church, assuming that the visitor has arrived by train — about two hours from London. (*The passenger service ceased in 1961*). Appendices, include details of Lavenham and the Great Rebellion of 1642-43.

216

1830

AN INQUIRY INTO THE BIRTHPLACE, PARENTAGE, LIFE AND WRITINGS OF THE REV. WILLIAM GURNALL

by Hugh McKeon. Printed and published by S. Loder for the author.

An early study about William Gurnall (author of *The Christian in Complete Armour*). Hugh McKeon lived in Lavenham and was an antiquarian of considerable research. The book was dedicated to the master, fellows, scholars and students of Emmanuel College, Cambridge (Rev. Gurnall was a former scholar and MA of that college).

1829

AN INQUIRY INTO THE RIGHTS OF THE POOR OF THE PARISH OF LAVENHAM, IN SUFFOLK

by Hugh McKeon, printed for Baldwin and Cradock, London.

"with historical notes and observations; being the result of a long and laborious investigation, to which are added biographical sketches of some of the most distinguished natives of Lavenham, from the earliest accounts to the present time." The price, to subscribers only, was five shillings. It is understood that Mr McKeon died in 1832/3 and is buried in Lavenham.

1796 (MDCCXCVI)

SPECIMENS OF GOTHIC ORNAMENTS FROM THE PARISH CHURCH OF LAVENHAM IN SUFFOLK

Published by I & J Taylor, 56 High Holborn, London.

Comprises 40 plates, from sketches taken about 1790, originally for the amusement of an artist who then resided at Lavenham, when the parts generally were in good repair.

1596

SURVEY OF THE BOROUGH OF LAVENHAM

A book of the common lands belonging to the borough of Lavenham in the county of Suffolk.

There are 19 pages to the document.

1585

MANORIAL SURVEY OF LAVENHAM (HA 505/1/23)

It includes numerous references to all Lavenham's gildhalls.

It begins (written in Olde English) "Twentyeth year of the reign of our sovereign Lady Elizabeth, by the grace of God, of England, France and Ireland, Queen, Defender of the faith, etc."

There are 22 pages to the document.

1086
THE DOMESDAY BOOK

The Domesday Book (*also known as Domesday, or Book of Winchester*) was the record of the great survey of England completed in 1086, executed for William I of England (*William the Conqueror*). The survey was similar to a census by a government of today. While spending Christmas of 1085 in Gloucester, William "had deep speech with his counsellors and sent men all over England to each shire ... to find out ... what or how much each landholder had in land and

livestock, and what it was worth" (Anglo-Saxon Chronicle). The Domesday Book is really two independent works. One, known as Little Domesday, covers Norfolk, Suffolk and Essex. The other, Great Domesday, covers the rest of England, except for lands in the north that would later become Westmorland, Cumberland, Northumberland and County Durham (*because some of these lands were under Scottish control at the time*).

There are also no surveys of London, Winchester and some other towns. The omission of these two major cities is probably due to their size and complexity. Despite its name, Little Domesday is actually larger — as it is far more detailed, down to numbers of livestock. It has been suggested that Little Domesday represents a first attempt, and that it was found impossible, or at least inconvenient, to complete the work on the same scale for Great Domesday.

For both volumes, the contents of the returns were entirely rearranged and classified according to fiefs, rather than geographically. Instead of appearing under the Hundreds and townships, holdings appear under the names of the local barons, i.e.. those who held the lands directly of the crown in fee.

Lavenham is mentioned in Little Domesday as: "among the Terrae Alberici de Ver." It is also stated that on the manor there were 25 cattle, 65 hogs, 200 sheep, 80 goats and 6 hives of bees, besides an acre of vineyard — the whole being valued at £15 a year.

Publications whose dates are not accurately known

198.. ?

A SHORT HISTORY OF THE SWAN, LAVENHAM

by Peter Rushton and Michael Grange. Published by The Swan Hotel and designed and printed by Kindaim Ltd., Stowmarket.

Opens with a brief description of the village's past and some of its notable buildings. Describes various features of The Swan at the time, including the Wool Hall, dining room, bar and fine mementoes of Lavenham's and England's early history and lounges. The hotel was, then, one of the Trusthouse Forte group.

---

believed to be between 1971 and 1975
LAVENHAM CHURCH

Produced by Photo Precision Ltd., St Ives, Huntingdon, with a preface by Rev. Rex Bird, Rector of Lavenham, with text by Derek Wilson.

A well illustrated and detailed description of the church, intended for visitors. It describes a tour of the church, pointing out all features of interest, starting with the de Vere porch.

197.. ?

LAVENHAM — THE SWAN

Written, illustrated and produced by SPAN, Wendover, Bucks.

A detailed description of the inn, the village and places to visit nearby. It includes quite a lot about the history of the village and particularly refers to the wool trade, the Springs and the de Veres. The church, too, receives good attention.

---

believed to be between 1965 and 1971
THE CHURCH OF SS. PETER & PAUL, LAVENHAM

Designed and published by The British Publishing Company Limited, Gloucester, with photographs by Richard Burn, Sudbury.

An illustrated guide (5th edition), approved by the Parochial Church Council, with some minor alterations from previous editions. It has a foreword by Rev. M. Fountain Page, Rector 1933—1952. It was supported by local business advertisers. Priced at one shilling.

circa 1935 ? (5th edition is signed Fountain Page October 1950)
LAVENHAM, SUFFOLK — THE OFFICIAL GUIDE

Issued by authority of Lavenham Parish Council, 'Laneham', Church Street (3rd edition). Designed and published by The Home Publishing Company (property Publications Ltd), Croydon.

Priced at 6d, the guide was supported by local business advertising. It included sections on a description and history of the village, weaving, the Guildhall, a short itinerary, the church and a map, plus illustrations.

---

date unknown
A BRIGHT IDEA

Publisher unknown. Two photographs by Ranson Photo, Lavenham.

A brief (four page) leaflet about how to get to Lavenham, and then a suggested tour of the village, pointing out the many landmarks, with brief additional notes about historical personalities.

Publications whose dates are not accurately known

date unknown
WHERE TO GO, LAVENHAM AREA
By B.A.J. Baker, printed by The Lavenham Press.
Suggestions for making the most of a 5 day visit to Lavenham (or possibly 14 days). Suggested walks around Lavenham, indoor activity suggestions, recommended inns, pubs and restaurants.

---

date unknown
LAVENHAM SUFFOLK
Published by L. & K. Ranson and printed by Kemps Printing Service, Lavenham
Gave a brief history of the village, a description of the Guildhall, the Church and the Woolhall, and a suggested walk around the village with suggestions for countryside tours. An outline street was included, and three photographs.

date unknown
THE GUILDHALL LAVENHAM SUFFOLK
Published by The National Trust, printed by Metchim & Son Ltd. Price sixpence.

---

date unknown
THE GUILDHALL LAVENHAM SUFFOLK
Published by The National Trust, printed at The Lavenham Press Ltd.
Cover photograph by John Bethell given by The National Trust.
A brief history of the village and a description of the Guildhall. The back cover describes The National Trust and how to become a member.

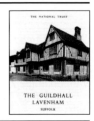

Another publication of interest

1999
REGINALD BRILL
By Judith Bumpus, published by Scolar Press in association with Kingston University, ISBN 1-80414-696-6. The first major study of Brill's life and work.
The four pages of endpapers are a selection of illustrated envelopes (wage payments) presented weekly by Brill to his housekeeper Nellie Smith, of Lavenham.

Publications updated regularly

A WALK AROUND LAVENHAM

Published by the Suffolk Preservation Society.

(Originally written by Dr David Dymond)

Describes a walk from the Market Place to the Parish Church and back again by a different route — just over one mile. Available at Lavenham Tourist Information Centre and other outlets. Recommended.

LAVENHAM/ALPHETON AIRFIELD — STATION 137

Prepared by Lavenham Tourist Information Centre staff.

A brief history of the Lavenham/Alpheton airfield, so that anyone who has an interest in the airfield, or its links with the past, may find it of some use. Available to purchase at the Tourist Information Centre.

FOOTPATH MAP OF LAVENHAM

Surveyed, researched, compiled, drawn and published by Wilfrid George. Original survey 1982, latest revision 2000 (7th edition).

The hand drawn map shows public footpaths, bridlepaths, roads, byways and other tracks. Available at Lavenham Tourist Information Centre and other outlets.

WALKS LEAFLETS

Published by Suffolk County Council and usually available from Lavenham Tourist Information Centre.

One features the Lavenham Circular Walk (3.5 miles) and another features walks in the Sudbury/Long Melford/Lavenham area. A third, produced by Lavenham Rambling Club, Community Council and W.I., with SCC and Countryside Commission financial assistance, features walks in Lavenham and adjoining parishes.

GUIDED WALKS AROUND LAVENHAM

Published by the Babergh District Council Leisure Division.

Gives information about guided walks around Lavenham with a qualified Blue Badge guide. Walks available from Easter to the end of October. Start 2.30pm on Saturdays, 11am Sundays and Bank Holiday Mondays. Group bookings at any other time by arrangement. Tickets and start from the Tourist Office in Lady Street. Adults £3.00, children under 14 free.

221

Afterword

Most books have a foreword, so I decided to have an afterword to sum up my thoughts, opinions and feelings just before the book went to press. I've spent over two years on the project, though not full time at first.

Credit crunch and beyond

What extraordinary times we live in — taxpayers bailing out profligate banks and financiers with eye-watering sums of money, house prices falling fast and a recession upon us.

Amazing amounts of cash are being borrowed to fund a variety of political goals and the bill is going to come home to roost sooner or later, meaning we and our children will pay for it. Suggestions that the money will be repaid by the banks is, in my opinion, complete rubbish. Taxpayers and bank customers will pay.

The wider picture

Wars in Iraq and Afghanistan drag on and, having served thirteen years in the Middle East myself, I don't see an easy end to them. Reading the history of military intervention in that region does not fill one with confidence.

I took part in one illegal war myself — the Suez affair. When you read the history afterwards you realise what a gigantic con-trick the whole affair was. And I saw some of my compatriots die during the beach landings. Luckily, I myself was only shot at by inaccurate snipers.

Much hot air is spent by politicians on appearing tough on immigration. Every country has a limit on the number of people it can support. The whole social structure of Britain has changed rapidly over the last twenty years and it will, in my opinion, take very many more years before a more stable state appears.

This is not to say that all immigration is bad — my Anglo-Saxon ancestors were immigrants in the past. The history of Britain is littered with bloody conflict, religious and otherwise. We need to be aware of the possible consequences.

Cooperation

Again, I would like to record the really wonderful cooperation from the people of Lavenham and others who have helped to make this book possible.

Time was given generously and with minor exceptions drafts were turned round quickly. It has all confirmed for me what a splendid place we live in — not just pretty houses but a great group of people who work together.

Cancer

During the book's gestation I was diagnosed with cancer. Like many men this was in the prostate, but had spread to the whole of the pelvic area and up the spine. Interestingly, for about a year previous to the correct diagnosis being made I thought I had severe sciatica.

Having been diagnosed I was then 'fast-tracked' at West Suffolk Hospital with regular blood tests, scans and so on. Mr Colin Kennedy was my consultant — how lucky can you be! Fortunately it was decided that hormone treatment was the solution and at the time of writing it certainly works. I feel much better and have not had to have chemotherapy or radiotherapy. I honestly do not consider myself to be ill — merely that I have a condition which is being successfully treated. I can only thank everyone for their support and prayers and for the excellent treatment from the NHS.

I feel incredibly fortunate.

Annexes

1 Extracts from the *Lavenham Village Design Statement*, dated 2002

2 Extracts from Lingard Ranson's book *Lavenham, Suffolk*, last edition dated 1965

3 Extracts from the Donald Insall report about Lavenham, dated 1961

4 Extracts from Rev. Canon Scott's book *Visitor's Guide to Lavenham and its Church*, published in 1897

Annex 1 — Extracts from the
Lavenham Village Design Statement 2002

Author's note: I felt it would be useful to include a summary of some of the main points from the 2002 Lavenham Village Design Statement (VDS). It is a very interesting document, well produced, and illustrated, in full colour.

Readers requiring more information are recommended to read the full Statement. The extracts are included here with permission.

What is a Village Design Statement?

(as shown on the Natural England website at www.countryside.gov.uk)

Many people feel that they have no say over what development takes place in their community; but Village Design Statements offer a constructive solution to this dilemma.

Local communities have an unique appreciation and understanding of their own place, and a VDS is based on this knowledge. It describes the qualities that residents value in their village and its surroundings. Around 200 English communities have completed Design Statements to date (February 2008).

A Village Design Statement sets out clear and simple guidance for the design of all development in a village, based on its character. It is an advisory document produced by the village community, not by the planning authority. It will not stop change from happening, but it can help effect how any new building fits in to the village. VDSs are intended to influence the operation of the statutory planning system, so that new development is in harmony with its setting and makes a positive contribution to the immediate environment.

What does a VDS cover?

- It describes the distinctive character of a village and its surrounding countryside;
- It shows how character can be identified at three levels:
  - the landscape setting of the village,
  - the shape of the settlement,
  - the nature of the buildings themselves;
- A VDS sets down design principles based on the distinctive local character;
- Production of a Statement fosters working in partnership with the local authority, engenders understanding of current planning policies, and offers the chance to influence future policies.

Design Statements have been completed by villages in all parts of England — from Cumbria to Cornwall, and from Shropshire to Suffolk. They are of value to residents, planners, designers and developers. There should be broad involvement of local interests so that the finished design statement is a representative document, and one that presents ideas for stimulating and sustaining community involvement in planning issues. It is important that the parish council, plus planning authority councillors and officers are drawn in to the VDS process. Preparing a Village Design Statement doesn't demand design or planning knowledge — the only requirement is an interest in the future well-being of your village. But it will need time, energy, imagination and determination! An effective Village Design Statement:

- is developed, researched, written and edited by local people;
- reflects the representative views of a community;
- involves a wide cross-section of residents in its production;
- describes the visual character of the village;
- demonstrates how local character and distinctiveness can be protected and enhanced in new development;
- is compatible with the statutory planning system and its local application;
- should be accepted as supplementary planning guidance (and thereby influence developers and decisions on individual planning applications);
- is relevant to all forms and scale of development, and
- is about managing change in the village, not preventing it.

A Village Design Statement is unlike any other planning document. It gives planning advice directly applicable to the statutory planning system and is entirely community based.

The complete design statement includes the following sections:

- Introduction
- A little history
- Settlement and housing (with aims and objectives)
- Employment (with aims and objectives)
- Shopping and amenities (with aims and objectives)
- Countryside (with aims and objectives)
- The built environment and conservation (with aims and objectives)
- Village access and communications (with aims and objectives)
- Conclusion
- Appendix of Aims and Objectives
- Acknowledgements

The Lavenham statement includes an excellent map (*drawn by Rachel Bodiam*), showing details of the village (including countryside, agricultural land, permanent grassland, the village envelope, special landscape area, county wildlife site, conservation area, public open spaces, public footpaths, public bridleway, St Edmunds Way and World War II pillboxes) and the parish boundary.

LAVENHAM VILLAGE DESIGN STATEMENT (2002)

Those involved

Those acknowledged in the statement were:

Members of the Village Design Statement Association team, including: Geoff Brace, Jane Balchin, Neil Clayton, John Commander, Jean Chantler, Sylvia Eden, Philip and Wendy Gibson, Will Gockelen, Jane Gosling, Alan Glasspoole, Carole Harr, Melvyn John, Pam Johnson, Lucy Koserski, Jaki and Stefan Labedzki, Iain Livingstone, John Moore, Adrian Palmer, Bryan Panton, Barbara and Carroll Reeve, Eve Ranzetta, Sir Clive Rose, Clare Santer, Josie and Tony Sheppard, Julia Spenceley and Donald Whitton who acknowledged with thanks the professional assistance of the staff of Suffolk ACRE and the Planning Officers of Babergh District Council.

Assistance and guidance was also received from The Lavenham Society, Suffolk Preservation Society, Suffolk County Council and Cllr. John Roberts.

The Lavenham Village Design Statement was produced with the financial assistance of the Community Fund Awards for All Programme, a Suffolk ACRE Millennium Award, The Lavenham Society, Wendy Matthews, Rosemary

McRobert, Jane Gosling and Sir Clive Rose. It received encouragement from Lavenham Parish Council.

Most importantly, without the co-operation, participation and support of the people of Lavenham the Village Design Statement could not have been produced.

Introduction

This Village Design Statement is the record, based on their own words, of how at the beginning of the new millennium the people of Lavenham view the environment in which they live and how they see themselves as a community. It gives expression to their concerns, hopes and perceived needs and sets out a vision for the future which, while preserving the fabric and values of a unique heritage, will ensure that Lavenham remains a vital and varied society in which people of all ages and conditions can live and enjoy fulfilled lives.

In July 1998 a well attended and fully representative meeting of Lavenham residents overwhelmingly endorsed a proposal to prepare a Village Design Statement. A comprehensive questionnaire (the Village Survey) 'How do we live in Lavenham?' was circulated to every household: no less than 546 households, representing some 62% of residents, responded. The evidence was clear that people from all parts of the community share concern for the well-being of the village and welcomed the opportunity to express their views. Further community involvement was encouraged by workshops, exhibitions and public meetings, and by again delivering to every house in the village a synopsis of the facts, figures and views gathered from the questionnaire. Lavenham Merchants' Guild carried out a related survey of local businesses.

The present document presents a summary of what has been learned

from the detailed and in-depth study undertaken over three years. It has been prepared with the approval of Lavenham Parish Council and, with the exception of those paragraphs of Aims and Objectives marked with an asterisk, has been **adopted as formal Supplementary Planning Guidance by Babergh District Council. This Village Design Statement is thus directly relevant to all planning applications, whether by individuals or by industrial and housing developers.** While the District Council has indicated that the document does not bind the Council other than in the determination of planning applications, the points not adopted as Supplementary Planning Guidance are acknowledged by the Council.

More generally, but no less importantly, it embodies policies which are outlined in the Babergh Local Plan which will:

- retain and strengthen the sense of shared identity within the village;

- restrict expansion of the village beyond the present village envelope and maintain the population at about the present level;

- help correct the present age imbalance by providing more and better facilities for younger people and creating conditions favourable to young families;

- require new housing to include social and local needs dwellings and encourage economical letting of smaller properties.

Settlement

The population of Lavenham is about 1800, living in some 880 households. About 45% have lived here for 16 or more years, but only one-sixth of the population is Lavenham born and bred. At least 45% have moved in during the last 15 years. Women outnumber men by a ratio considerably higher than the national average, particularly in the 65+ age bracket. More than 60% of the population is older than 45, and of these more than half are over 65. There are about ten times as many people over 60 as there are children under 10. People under 40 comprise less than a quarter of the population.

More than one-third of Lavenham residents are retired. About 45% are in work or self-employed, 80% of these locally; only about 5% work in London. Some 9% are in training or full-time education. Unemployment is gratifyingly low at 2%.

The life of the village depends on many services and activities, including shops, which provide for day-to-day needs. We are lucky still to have a good variety though many have closed over the years and supermarkets in Sudbury and Bury St Edmunds pose a continuing threat to our shops. There is still the Post Office, which is expanding its services to include banking facilities. There is an active Merchants' Guild representing businesses in the village. The Medical Centre provides facilities at GP level and there is a Dental Practice.

The handsome Primary School, built in the village centre 100 years ago and still in excellent order, currently has 41 pupils with some coming from outside the village. There is room for an expansion in numbers to ensure that the school continues to provide a shared experience for our young people. Nursery groups cater for under 5s, but for Middle and Upper Schools the children must travel away from the village.

Community and recreational activities have several focuses. The Guildhall (given to the National Trust in 1951 to be held for the village in perpetuity) houses a branch of the County libraries, a museum and tea room, and is available for meetings of the Parish Council, societies and other gatherings. The Parish Church and Salvation Army together with the Roman Catholic community provide the framework and impetus for much communal activity. Groups and societies include: Scouts, British Legion, Bird Club, Rambling Club, Cambridge Extra Mural Centre, Women's Institute, Gardening Club, Music Society, Theatre Club, Natural History Club, Tennis, Cricket and Football Clubs and many others. The Lavenham Sinfonia's concerts, held in the church, attract appreciative audiences from a wide area. The Community Council is the umbrella group for sport and recreational activities and organizes three popular annual events: the August Bank Holiday Carnival, the Christmas Street Fair and Hidden Gardens, in June.

The village is however short on public premises for its activities. The Church Rooms are acknowledged to be inadequate; the Guildhall's largest room holds only 65 people; the School is not always available or suitable. The Community Council has therefore developed plans for a new Sports Pavilion on the Recreation Ground (currently under construction with the participation of much voluntary labour and skills) and with the Parochial Church Council has put forward ambitious proposals for a new Village Hall on a central site. These will be the first new public buildings in Lavenham for many years.

Employment

Lavenham, with a population of some 1800 has a thriving local economy comprising some 100 businesses ranging from sole traders to nationally recognized hotels and companies. The village is well served with shops and services catering for local needs and providing facilities for a large catchment area. The majority of overall trade is derived from the local area and county.

There are approximately 330 full time and 160 part-time jobs (2002 figures), the largest contingent being in hotels, public houses and restaurants. Some 30% of all employment is provided by three companies and 50% by six companies. Tourism generates about a half of all trade and supports hotels, B&Bs, holiday lets, galleries, antique shops and the like. The District Council recognizes Lavenham as part of a strong local tourism industry. In addition, although local businesses consider that the historic levels of tourism have been constant, increasing competition from elsewhere makes it necessary to promote the village.

It is essential that the existing wide range of businesses in Lavenham be maintained so that the level of employment and self-sufficiency of the community can be sustained.

Aims and Objectives:
- To recognize that tourism, light industrial and local retailing businesses are vital to the local economy.
- To provide opportunities for the development of the local economy, by which employment can be sustained and new jobs created.
- To ask the Lavenham Merchants' Guild and others to produce a marketing strategy for Lavenham.
- To ensure that any future commercial development in and around the village is carefully, planned and designed and compatible with this Statement.

Shopping and amenities

Lavenham is unusual for its size in being virtually self-sufficient in all the amenities necessary for comfortable living. Most residences are within ten minutes walk of good shops (groceries and household goods, butcher, baker, fruit and vegetables, pharmacy, wines and spirits, newsagent and tobacconist). The Post Office offers a full range of facilities and the village enjoys good collection and delivery services. There are well-run, friendly pubs offering good food and accommodation, an internationally renowned hotel with extensive facilities and an outstanding smaller hotel with a highly regarded restaurant. There are B&B facilities to suit every pocket. A modern medical centre provides comprehensive facilities at GP level, well supported by the village pharmacy and pharmacist on duty. The Lavenham Dental Practice provides dentistry for the village and surrounding area. Perhaps surprisingly, given the preponderance of older residents, there is no residential retirement or nursing home or day-care facility within the village, though there is warden-assisted housing.

Retail facilities in the village are vulnerable to intensifying competition from supermarkets and stores in Sudbury and Bury St Edmunds — both easily accessible to the 80+% of households with, or having access to cars. Out-of-village shopping has been encouraged by the loss in recent years of a filling-station and banking facilities. Conversely, and fortunately, tourism accounts for nearly 50% of all retail business and supports a number of galleries and shops selling gifts and non-staple commodities. To date, the village has largely escaped the more tawdry manifestations of the tourist industry.

The absence of banking facilities is seen by nearly 90% of residents as a major lack, despite the widespread availability of 'cash back' in shops and personal banking facilities provided at the Post Office.

Aims and Objectives:
- To maintain and sustain the existing wide range of shops and amenities.

In conclusion

Lavenham runs the real risk of following other famous villages in many parts of the country where shops no longer cater for local residents, and the fabric of society is eroded until the village is turned into another beautifully preserved museum. Indeed, Lavenham Parish Council believes that this process has already started with the closure of some light industry and the bank.

As work on the Village Design Statement proceeded, it became apparent that a number of initiatives had come from Central Government in this whole area of grass roots participation. These led to the Vital Villages Initiative and a Green Paper on proposals to introduce fundamental changes to the planning process. This process of change is unstoppable and its effects as yet unclear. What is clear is that the community must therefore be alert to ensure that urgent and effective steps are taken both to preserve the integrity of the village and its environs and to make housing and related amenities available for all the people of Lavenham.

It is hoped this Statement will play its part in meeting our shared goal of living in a varied and sustainable community.

Lavenham Village Design Statement Association July 2002.

The published work of the association

- Village Survey 'How do we live in Lavenham?'
- Lavenham Merchants' Guild's Local Business Survey.
- 4 separate Working Group Reports on:
  Countryside Perspective,
  Planning and Design,
  Village Character, and
  Village Needs and Perspectives
  Statistical analyses and feedback from

the Village Survey can be viewed at the Lavenham Library, Suffolk County Council and Babergh District Council.

APPENDIX of AIMS and OBJECTIVES

SETTLEMENT

1 It is vital that existing social activities and facilities should be fostered by community, participation, co-operation and support.

2 The success and maintenance of the proposed Village Hall and Sports Pavilion similarly, depend on the active participation of the community.

HOUSING

1 Lavenham Parish and Babergh District Council are encouraged to produce, when resources allow, and in consultation with the residents of Lavenham, a long-term strategic plan for the future development of the village. The wealth of evidence, information and sentiment contained in the Village Survey, which has been made available to these Councils, gives a good starting point for such an exercise. This information should also prove a useful tool when considering planning matters of both a general and specific nature.

2 At both the Outline and Detailed Planning stages, residents, builders and developers must work together with the Parish and District Councils. Any new dwelling or extension must not be a successful design within its own plot, but also in relations with neighbouring properties and with the prevailing character and layout of that part of the village.

3 The current proposals by Babergh District Council to meet the local and particular needs of its residents, and the creation of sustainable residential environments should be applauded.

For Lavenham these factors are particularly relevant and must be implemented.

4 There is an expressed need for 2 and 3 bedroom housing provision for young families.

EMPLOYMENT

1 To recognize that tourism, light industrial and local retailing businesses are vital to the local economy.

2 To provide opportunities for the development of the local economy, by which employment can be sustained and new jobs created.

3 To ask The Lavenham Merchants' Guild and others to produce a marketing strategy for Lavenham.

4 To see that any, future commercial development in and around the village is carefully planned and designed, and compatible with this Statement.

SHOPPING AND AMENITIES

1 To maintain the existing wide range of shops and amenities.

COUNTRYSIDE

1 The permanent grasslands adjacent to the village should be preserved as an essential element of the views into and out of the village.

2 Existing hedges and woodland are also important to the views and every effort must be made to retain and improve their contribution to the landscape.

3 District Council should be urged to join together the two Special Landscape Areas.

4 Historic features, even when not officially classified, ought to be recorded and conserved.

THE BUILT ENVIRONMENT AND CONSERVATION

1 Babergh District Council must ensure that alterations to existing buildings should be undertaken sensitively, with due regard to both the character and location of the property Local and natural materials are preferred.

2 Likewise, the District Council must insist that future housing developments take advantage of the best of what is new rather than just imitating existing building forms. They should continue to consult as early as possible in the planning cycle with the Parish Council especially where exceptions to policy are envisaged.

3 Babergh District Council's *Design Guidance Note for New Housing in the Babergh District* and the Suffolk Preservation Society's *Patterns for Suffolk Buildings* indicate and illustrate styles, features and practices which are relevant to Lavenham. Both publications provide an objective and useful basis for establishing an agreed understanding of best practice which can be referred to in any future discussions of planning applications for Lavenham.

4 Alterations to individual houses in terraces should be avoided when these lead to the fragmentation of the terrace facades.

5 Babergh District Council is encouraged to pursue its objective of surveying the listed buildings in Lavenham.

6 The Parish Council and other interested parties, are encouraged to participate in the proposed District Council initiative to produce a Guidance Note on criteria against which the development would he considered.

7 Street furniture and signs should be kept discreet and in character with existing village architecture in line with the Suffolk Conservation Manual.

8 Babergh District Council has identified the need to remove telegraph and electricity poles and the 'undergrounding' of cables. The District Council must give this a high priority, and in liaison with the Parish Council agree an order of priority of the streets concerned.

VILLAGE ACCESS AND COMMUNICATIONS

1 Ensure that any road developments are in keeping with the village's rural character both in scale and design.

2 Encourage the Suffolk Highways Authority and Police, to consider introducing restrictions on certain streets and ensuring speed limits are enforced.

3 Babergh District Council should widen the remit of The Lavenham Car Parking and Traffic Management Working Party to include traffic movements and the needs of pedestrians and cyclists.

4 It is essential that car parking in Lavenham should remain free.

5 The Lavenham Merchants' Guild should agree drop-off points with tourist coach operators.

6 The proposed community bus providing a feeder service to direct bus routes and/or 'Dial a ride' operation will meet many perceived needs and should be actively supported within the community.

7 The Highways Authority is urged to act to provide a pedestrian crossing at First Meadow.

Annex 2 — extracts from
Lavenham, Suffolk
by F. Lingard Ranson

Lingard Ranson's book was first published in 1937. Two impressions followed in 1947, a third edition in 1950, a fourth in 1958 and a fifth in 1965.

The book featured a Foreword by Lieut.-Colonel Montague W. Douglas CSI CIE. Colonel Montague was President of "The Shakespeare Fellowship" and Lingard was a member of that group. The colonel's kinsman and school fellow was the Rev. G.H. Lenox Conyngham who was Rector of Lavenham from 1917 to 1933. As a third link with the village, the colonel had been invited to unveil a memorial to the late Sir Francis Spring, a descendant of the famous Thomas Spring, in the Chantry of St Catherine (the Spring Parclose) in Lavenham Church.

Foreword

Amongst other things, the colonel wrote "Lavenham, with its Saxon and Roman beginnings, Norman de Veres, Lords of the Manor; its wide flung trade in wool, blue cloth, fine yarns; its Flemish weavers and looms; its Trade Guilds, ancient Inns, Tudor architecture, and — a land-mark from afar — the great Church on the hill; its Royal progresses; its anti-taxation riots, sympathy for the Puritan cause, religious movements, even to bull baiting (1842); lastly, its sacrifices for the Great War, and recent (1936), if tardy, introduction of pipe water and electric light, is a concise History of England, in miniature. As suggested by the author (*Lingard Ranson*), the question of its transfer to the State as a mediæval preserve, deserves consideration.

Mr. Ranson writes out of the fullness of his heart, and Lavenham and its church of "Seynt Peter and Pawl" means much to him."

Author's Note 1947

Mr. Ranson, in his Author's Note of 1947, wrote that he believed the village to be not only of National, but of World importance. He recorded his heartfelt gratitude to Divine Providence that lovely Lavenham survived the horrors of war, almost untouched, but regretted to add that there was a possibility of a worse fate in store for our unique heritage. He noted that many of the ancient cottages, for lack of repair during the war years, were in a sad condition. So much so that many might be considered unfit as dwellings. He earnestly hoped that every effort would be made to preserve for posterity, those relics linking Lavenham with its glorious past.

Preface 1965

In the preface to the last edition of his book, Lingard Ranson said the object of his book was to give to lovers of Lavenham an outline of its history, from the earliest times — through the prosperous mediæval period — to the present day (1965). Also to record some of the events which marked its rise and decline, and to give some account of the people who gave Lavenham its beautiful Church and buildings.

Chapter I

Records the principal events which affected the social and business life of Lavenham past and present.

Chapter II

A detailed explanation of the Church and those involved in rebuilding it, together with restorations carried out between 1825 and 1964.

Chapter III

A visitors guide to the Church, pointing out items of interest, and details of charities.

Chapter IV

Wills of Lavenham clothiers, etc. with some extracts of gifts left to the church, poor, roads, etc.

Chapter V

The visitor's guide to Lavenham, describing buildings in many of the streets at the time.

Chapter VI

Describes notable people of Lavenham who — apart from the Spring family and the de Veres — included Thomas Lavenham, an author at the beginning of the 13th century and Richard de Lavenham, a professor of Divinity who was murdered by the mob during the Wat Tyler rebellion.

He also mentions one William Blair, born in the village in 1766, who became a celebrated surgeon in London.

The book is now out of print, although copies can sometimes be bought on the second-hand market.

These extracts are published with permission from the copyright holder, Mary Webster.

Annex 3 — extracts from
Lavenham Past • Present • Future
by Donald Insall

This annex gives extracts from a report prepared by Donald W. Insall, Architects & Planning Consultants, London & Bristol for the County of West Suffolk and the Rural District of Cosford in MCMLXI (1961). It was published by the West Suffolk County Council, printed by E & E Plumridge, Linton, priced at 19/6.

LAVENHAM
PAST • PRESENT • FUTURE
by
DONALD INSALL

FOREWORD

'Those of us who live in West Suffolk have a great sense of pride in the traditional beauty of our small towns and villages, and in particular in the one and only Lavenham.

The members of the West Suffolk County Council and of Cosford Rural District Council felt that there was a note of challenge in the introduction to the report on the Buildings of Lavenham, prepared by the Minister of Housing and Local Government, which read:

"Lavenham is the most complete example of a small medieval town in East Anglia. Its general plan remains unspoilt, and its wealth of medieval buildings unrivalled."

We were conscious that many buildings were falling into disrepair and there was a grave danger of many of them being lost unless steps were taken by private and public enterprise to carry out a well conceived plan of restoration.

Both authorities agreed to consult the Ministry of Housing and Local Government and the Society for the Protection of Ancient Buildings, and we were advised that as a first step a detailed survey should be undertaken by an architect with special knowledge and experience.

Mr. Donald W. Insall, A.R.I.B.A., S.P.dip., was recommended to us as one who was greatly experienced and I have great

pleasure in writing this brief introduction to his authoritative report to the County Council, which follows his painstaking and careful analysis of buildings of architectural and historical importance and includes his recommendations for the future of the town of Lavenham.

(signed) G. Falconer.

PREFACE

This report is a pioneer study, made possible by the imagination and initiative of the County of West Suffolk. It is designed as a practical contribution to the problem of providing the special information needed, in addition to that available under existing Town-Planning Legislation, by a Local Authority responsible as guardian of a Town of architectural and historic importance to the Nation.

We have been greatly honoured in being invited by the County and the Rural District of Cosford, on the nomination of the Society for the Protection of Ancient Buildings, to undertake this signal task. In submitting our Report, we would like to acknowledge with gratitude the valuable assistance so freely given by all concerned, particularly the County Planning Officer, James T. Gorst, M.T.P.I., M.I.Mun.E., and his staff. Our special thanks are due to Alan F. Skinner, O.B.E., Clerk to the West Suffolk County Council, M.P. Statham, M.A., County Archivist, and to Mrs. T.R. McGeorge, Chairman of the Cosford Rural District Council, C.A. Durrant, Clerk to the Council, and G.H. Hine, M.I.Mun.E., Surveyor to the Council. We are also most grateful to Canon H.W. Stapleton Cotton, M.A., Rector of Lavenham, to A.E. Baker, J.P., Chairman and Miss. K. Ranson, Hon. Secretary of the Lavenham Preservation Society. We have much appreciated the valuable interest and support of the Press, and especially of the Bury Free Press and the East Anglian Daily Times.

We are especially conscious of the work already done for the Town by Marshall Sisson, C.B.E., A.R.A., F.S.A., F.R.I.B.A, and John E.M. Macgregor, F.S.A., F.R.I.B.A., and the Society for the Protection of Ancient Buildings. Also by the Historic Buildings Section of the Ministry of Housing and Local Government whose chief Investigator at the time was S.J. Garton, O.B.E., F.S.A., L.R.I.B.A., and especially Miss F.M. Blomfield, M.A., F.S.A., who prepared for Lavenham, the list of buildings of special architectural and historic interest under Section 30 of the Town and Country Planning Act 1947.

I would like warmly to acknowledge the help and inspiration throughout of my Associate, Peter E. Locke, A.R.I.B.A., and of all the team, in carrying through so taxing but stimulating a programme.

Above all, we should like to thank the people of Lavenham, for their warm welcome and great kindness in inviting us inside so many homes, and for all the valuable ideas discussed and now included in the pages which follow.

As well as being of interest to all who know and love Lavenham, we hope that this Report may prove of practical value to the County of West Suffolk and to the Cosford Rural District; and that further, it will help others entrusted with the special responsibility of those historic county towns and villages which are the crown not only of Suffolk, but of England.

(signed) Donald W Insall

TERMS OF REFERENCE

1. To prepare for the County Council an overall Survey and Report on buildings of architectural and historic importance in Lavenham, having regard to those already "listed" by the Minister of Housing and Local Government under Section 30 of the Town and Country Planning Act, 1947.

2. To make recommendations for the restoration, conversion or improvement of unfit cottages or groups of period cottages which the Architect considers are falling or are likely to fall into a state of decay.

THE HISTORICAL BACKGROUND

The Town of Lavenham is one of England's richest architectural treasures. Her supremacy springs from two chief sources: the riches of the wool trade, and the skill of her builders. These met at their zenith; and the result lives on, as an exceptional and pure example of English domestic architecture in the Middle Ages.

Early Lavenham

Of pre-Mediæval times we know little. Pre-historic mammoth tusks, teeth and bones, flint weapons and implements have been discovered during excavation. The Iceni inhabited the district in Roman times; and there was a small Roman settlement near the town. Coins of thirteen Roman Emperors have been ploughed up: and graves, ovens, bricks, and tiles of the period have been unearthed, including a hypocaust now in the garden of "The Grange".

The name of "Lavenham' is said to have originated in Saxon times as the "home of Lafa". At the time of the Conquest, principal landholders were Ulwin and Alwius. By 1086 Ulwin had been succeeded by Aubrey de Vere as Lord of the Manor, and Alwius had been succeeded by Frodo. By the 14th Century there were two manors, Overhall and Netherhall, both held by the de Veres, who retained their large estates in Lavenham until the late 16th Century.

References to Lavenham in the Middle Ages provide fascinating glimpses of mediæval life. The Market Place was formed in the 13th Century, when it is said that large brick culverts were built under the main streets; some of them remaining still. In 1275 Edward I passed through Lavenham in state, and in 1290 granted to Robert de Vere a charter to hold a Whitsun Fair. His son, another Robert, obtained by 1330 a special charter from Edward III authorising all his Lavenham Tenants to pass free of tolls throughout England. This charter is said to have been confirmed by Queen Elizabeth in 1585. According to a persistent local tradition, Flemish weavers settled in the Town in the early 14th Century.

The Golden Fleece

For the next two hundred years, references to the Town are almost entirely concerned with the wool trade. By 1300, the export trade in wool was at its zenith; but it was later surpassed by the export of cloth; and by 1450, Lavenham was second only to Hadleigh as a centre of the cloth trade in Suffolk. Guild restrictions, which made it difficult to co-ordinate production soon led to the migration of the industry from the older and larger towns to the small towns and villages; and the market town of Lavenham benefited especially from this movement.

Typical of the Lavenham families who made their fortune in the cloth industry was that of Spring. The business careers of the three Thomas Springs, father, son and grandson, epitomise the growing new industry of the late 15th and early 16th Centuries, It was the third Thomas who was generally known as "the rich clothier": and he became so powerful and respected that his family entered the ranks of the nobility, his daughter becoming mistress of Rushbrooke Hall.

The magnificent Church stands as a monument to the prosperity of Lavenham in late mediæval times; and to the industry of Thomas Spring, Simon Branch (another rich clothier) and John de Vere, 13th Earl of Oxford, who between them financed its construction. The superb tower was built by the gifts of Spring and other local clothiers, work being started in 1486 and completed in 1525.

Three Guilds were powerful in Lavenham at this time: Corpus Christi founded by one of the de Veres; Holy Trinity, with a Hall in Prentice Street, and St Peter, with its Hall in the High Street. These Guildhalls were destined to be degraded to wool halls and even workhouses, for the end of the 16th Century saw Lavenham diminishing. The last Town pageant was the Royal Progress of Elizabeth through Lavenham with all her Court in 1578. Soon afterwards, Edward de Vere alienated the Manor to Thomas Skinner; and many of the Merchants and Clothiers are said to have left Lavenham, their fine timber-framed houses falling empty and in some cases derelict and ruinous.

The decline of the cloth industry was due mainly to fluctuations of foreign markets, upon which the industry depended, and the competition of new fabrics. It is recorded in 1618 that the weaving of blue cloth had almost ceased. But then the decline began to be offset by the alternative employment of wool combing and spinning fine wool yarns, a new move of prosperity being evidenced by the opening of the Grammar School in 1647. The Guild Halls became Wool Halls; and the economic importance of Lavenham was helped by the fact that the main road to and from Bury St. Edmunds ran through the Town. But nothing could replace the wool trade, calculated to have been worth £150,000 a year to Lavenham. By 1732, Kirby lamented that "the poverty and wretchedness which the loss of the trade has occasioned to only three towns in this part of the country, Lavenham, Sudbury and Glemsford, is incalculable".

Plague struck the Town in 1699, when small-pox broke out, and twenty-seven people died. In 1712, 180 people succumbed; and the final death-roll from the disease when its ravages died down in 1713 was 282.

John Kirby mentions in 1732 that a Fair was held annually on the 29th of September, and was much frequented for the sale of butter and cheese, and the hiring of servants; and horse and cattle markets were also held. In 1873, however, Bayne's "Royal History of Eastern England" notes that the butter and cheese fair had been recently discontinued, and the traditional Tuesday market was "almost disused".

By the late 18th Century, commercial decline had finally set in. For centuries the Town had been governed by six capital burgesses, known as Headboroughs; and these dignitaries were appointed by the Lord of the Manor for the last time in 1775. The Guildhall of Corpus Christi was closed in 1787, and was bought by the people of Lavenham for £105, for use as the Parish Workhouse.

19th century Lavenham

In 1826 and 1827 references to Lavenham appear in early guide-books. Bolton Street was then Boughton Street, after a family of that name. Barn Street was called "Hockrill" or "Lynch's Street", and the River Brett remained as the Breton; but where were "Shimpling", "Searl's and "Bellrope Piece"?

Of the later 19th Century, we have more detailed records. A town lock-up was built in 1833, the Market Place School in 1861, and the Gas Works opened in 1863. The Great Eastern Railway arrived between 1863 and 1865. Factories for the manufacture of coconut matting, and for horse-hair weaving, were built in 1861; a steam flour mill in 1865; and the first sugar-beet factory in England in 1866, this being demolished in 1961. Weaving and wool spinning were now largely a memory, crippled chiefly by the introduction of machine production in Lancashire and the North. Lavenham did, however, benefit temporarily by the migration of the silk industry from London. A new industry, noted in 1873 as the chief local source of employment, was straw plaiting for bonnets. Brisk local trades were being carried on in corn, malt and seeds, as well as in finished woollen articles.

Though Ranson is enthusiastic for his "aspect of crooked timber houses all huddled together", Bayne is disparaging: "the streets

The typical fate of a "Hall"-type house
diagram opposite page 12 of Mr. Insall's report

are small and narrow, and the houses of mean appearance". Civic pride now became tempered by Victorian 'progress'; the Guildhall in Prentice Street was demolished in 1879; and St.Peter's Guildhall followed in 1896. The Free School closed in 1887; and old weavers' cottages in Lady Street were taken down and re-erected at Walberswick. Later, in 1911, a magnificent timbered building dating from about 1440, previously used as a Wesleyan Chapel, was also pulled down.

Today (*1961*)

A slump followed the first World War; and in 1930 the last of the factories closed down, and for the first time for 600 years no textile industry of any sort was carried on in the Town: but electric power lines arrived in 1934, and a mains water supply in 1936, and Lavenham revived. Population statistics illustrate the Town's fluctuating prosperity. In 1732 there were 1,776 inhabitants; and after dropping slightly, the population rose to 1,870 in 1838. With the Victorian rise in the birthrate, the peak of 2,018 was reached in 1901; an abrupt and violent slump followed and the population fell to 1,400 in 1936. It stands now at a little under 1,500; an encouraging sign that Lavenham is beginning to prosper once more.

RECOMMENDATIONS

1. SUMMARY OF PROPOSALS
Whose Concern?

Lavenham is unique. Described in the Ministry of Housing and Local Government's statutory lists as "the most complete example of a small mediæval town in East Anglia", the Town is a remarkable survivor of the lost towns of mediæval England. To the fortunate townspeople, Lavenham is a good place to live in; to tourists from home and abroad, her charms are a magnet; to all who love old buildings, she is a source of delight. There is no question whether or not proposals for her future are worth while. How can they best be achieved?

It should firstly be said that the only panacea is daily interest and care. A living town cannot be mummified, or made into a museum exhibit. While all may agree and suggest that one day, pounds should be lavished, it is only by penny spending today on her penny problems that in the end, sterling results can be achieved for Lavenham.

But "everybody's job is nobody's job". Unless each of the daily attentions, which are her birthright, can become the concern of someone specifically responsible, the town must perish by default. What major cares are necessary; and who will undertake them, if Lavenham is to be saved for posterity?

Householders and Occupiers

No amount of intervention by the Authorities can replace daily care. Decay accumulates at compound interest; and there is much truth in the old tag about "a stitch in time". Lavenham is a house-proud town; and with a little encouragement, gutters and gullies will be cleaned as automatically as windows. To live in a house is to know best its weaknesses and defects; and only prompt attention to these by householders can avoid and overcome the mounting costs of decay and neglect.

Landlords

Many landlords have exemplary tenants, who look after their houses as their own.

237

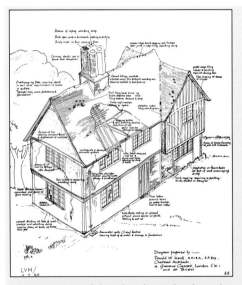

Some common defects found in timber framed buildings of the XV & XVI centuries

diagram opposite page 21 of Mr. Insall's report

A very few do not have the interest and experience to notice and recognise incipient troubles such as the onset of dry-rot. The institution of a service of regular property inspections would greatly help owners in achieving a proper standard of building care. It is altogether in the interests of each landlord that his building property should receive the same regular and well-advised attention as his other assets. Common sense dictates that a well-maintained house will attract good tenants, willing to pay a sensible rent. It is the practical approach, firmly based on sound economics, which must ensure the future of the old buildings of Lavenham.

Speculators

The world is often jealous of the property speculator; but it cannot be gainsaid that many of the good buildings in Lavenham would have perished, had they not, when first abandoned, been bought and held for a few critical years against decay. On the other hand, derelict houses have sometimes changed hands purely for their site values; and some, still neglected, remain an eyesore and a scandal in the town today. In these cases, a speculator should decide to sell to the Authorities at a fair price.

In preparing conversion schemes, speculators can advantageously consult the Planning Authority, who are anxious to co-operate and give expert guidance.

"Chelsea in Lavenham" is the tempting danger in preparing a building for sale; obviously, houses must be attractively reconditioned to find purchasers. But the market is such that the honest exploitation of a building's own intrinsic merits, allied with "all mod. cons.", will always find a ready sale.

The Local Authority

The Local Authority's role is manifold — part watch-dog, part family doctor, wholly the firm and decisive but sympathetic arbitrator, on all matters of detail affecting Lavenham. Its officers must have a most delicate part to play. At all levels, confidence must be fostered in the Council's aims and actions.

Sympathy with the buildings and the problems of their owners springs naturally from detailed local knowledge. This must be expressed in common-sense interpretation of of the Bye-laws, which are necessary and advisable but not always kind to old buildings if too rigidly enforced. It is too easy to find faults and to criticise; while the real need is always for constructive suggestions, with the emphasis upon the positive health of buildings. Patience and helpfulness to the householder, backed by detailed knowledge and understanding, can achieve much. Financial aid by Improvement Grants and repair loans will help both the houses and and their occupants, and strengthen the Council's hand in guiding the works. The key is encouragement by a positive approach, instead of the negative attitude so often taken towards old property.

At the same time, the Local Authority must be prepared to act decisively against undesirable proposals, and by watchfulness curb them before they become fact. Compulsory purchase of derelict sites and properties, for example, will place the Council in a strong position for their proper development. Delay until someone else acts immediately places the Authority in a defensive position, if proposals have to be resisted. Preservation is so often regarded as both negative and 'precious' for this reason.

Above all, the Local Authority must lead by example. At Lavenham, the Council's excellent conversions and recent housing estate do just this, and are a model to others. With sensitivity as the guiding principle, and firm and helpful daily guidance, the future of Lavenham can be assured.

The County Council

In the minds of many people, a County Council is a distant, all-powerful and mysterious outer planet controlling their destinies, and only occasionally materialising in an approachable form. This is inevitable and to an extent necessary; since decisions must be made at County level, in which proposals for a town may be part only of a master plan.

In Lavenham, most admirably, Shire Hall has materialised in the Market Place, and the present Survey is the result. Nothing but general good can come of this, and the contact now made must be strengthened.

Both overall and in detail, the County can help Lavenham in countless ways. Planning control is as much needed in the insertion of a single window in a listed building as in the development of a large new site. Either may be of equal importance to the Town; and as much care is needed in their control and guidance. A very high degree of public watchfulness is called for in the common interest. Specialist advice must also be available where required, together with positive, decisive action when needed.

Architectural building materials, the road surface underfoot, or power lines overhead, may seem minor points; but their sum total is a formidable influence in Lavenham — a Town in which attention cannot be too detailed. Similarly, new development and its siting and design could make or mar this as a place where people like to be.

The County Council's guidance, now so clearly manifested, is the most potent force in ensuring that Lavenham will become a model for the whole of the Country.

2 • FORMAL RECOMMENDATIONS TO THE COUNTY OF WEST SUFFOLK AND THE RURAL DISTRICT OF COSFORD

Implementation : A Lavenham Advisory Committee

We recommend:-

1. That in view of the National importance of Lavenham and the variety of responsibilities concerned, and of the need for special care in co-ordinating them, the County Council should convene a special Lavenham Advisory Committee to consist of representatives of the Ministry of Housing and Local Government, the executive Departments of the County Council, the Rural District Council and the Parish Council, with powers of co-optation; this Committee to meet at frequent and stated intervals and with provision for delegated interim action.

2. That with the aid of the foregoing Report, this Committee should prepare a Preservation Programme implementing the following further recommendations:-

Town Improvements in Lavenham

We recommend:-

3. That the Rural District Council should purchase available vacant "gap" sites, and build thereon suitably designed houses to maintain the essential street continuity of Lavenham.

4. That in planning for the future, the County Planning Officer should, after giving priority to the infilling of gaps in street frontages, thereafter allocate suitable land for the modest future growth of the Town.

5. That in considering development applications, the County Planning Officer should be empowered to retain specialist advice; and that a special degree of attention to architectural detail is necessary.

6. That a comprehensive Survey and Report should be made at least twice annually by an officer of the County Planning Department on foot, for the purpose of ensuring adequate development control.

7. That the County Council should approach the Eastern Electricity Board and the General Post Office, seeking the removal of the present unsightly overhead wires and poles which deface the Town, and the undergrounding of all services.

8. That the County Highway Department should prepare and carry out at an early date, a comprehensive scheme of resurfacing pedestrian areas in Lavenham, limiting tarmacadam to traffic ways, and elsewhere retaining and re-introducing paving materials appropriate to the Town.

9. That in view of the importance to Lavenham of its trees, the County Planning Officer should prepare an immediate Survey, followed by the issue of Tree Preservation Orders; and that the Council's officers should also be instructed to exercise special restraint in public tree lopping.

10. That the Parish Council should campaign actively for the removal or improvement of "eyesores" in the Town, with aid from the Rural District and County Councils where appropriate.

11. That the Parish Council should promote the establishment of a store of valuable building materials (e.g. oak, handmade tiles, doors, etc.) salvaged from any properties past repair, for re-use in Lavenham.

12. That the Rural District Council should seek the advice of the Civic Trust in carrying out a street tidying scheme.

13. That a new street lighting scheme should be commissioned by the County Council (e.g. by competition) to show the Town and its buildings to the best advantage.

14. That in view of the high proportion of timber buildings of importance, the County Fire Service should investigate the possibility of providing a readily available fire service in Lavenham.

The Improvement and Repair of Buildings in Lavenham

We recommend:-

15. That the Advisory Committee should confirm at regular intervals a short-list of endangered buildings in Lavenham, allocating responsibilities and formulating specific recommendations for their rescue and rehabilitation.

16. That owners of these buildings should first be encouraged by all possible means in initiating repairs and improvements, by means of Repair Loans and Improvement Grants under the 1958 and 1959 Housing Acts, the statutory limit where desirable being waived with the consent of the Minister.

17. That certain neglected buildings in divided ownership, or whose owners cannot even, despite such aid, contemplate essential repairs, should at the same time be acquired by the Local Authority, repaired and improved under contract, and made re-available by sale or lease.

18. That in repairing these buildings, the Local Authority should seek the assistance of a block grant from the Historic Buildings Council for England.

19. That the Local Authority should establish a service of informed Property Inspections for ratepayers, advising by the early diagnosis of defects, on repairs needed for the fullest economy in property maintenance,

20. That to this end, the Ministry of Housing and Local Government and the Ministry of Works should be asked to give special guidance in training Local Authority officers in positive building care.

By promoting this Survey and programme for its implementation, the County of West Suffolk has pioneered a way which it is hoped may serve as an inspiration to all who bear the responsibility of guiding the future of England's historic country towns and villages. Many of them are of the greatest architectural importance - although none more than Lavenham. By realising the value and necessity of providing for sympathetic, practical and detailed analysis of these special problems, the future of a unique national heritage can be assured, and our trust handed on to posterity. Our historic towns and town-centres increasingly deserve new and detailed study; and the County hopes in its present survey to have made a real contribution to the techniques so vital to this end.

Annex 4 — Extracts from the
Visitor's Guide to Lavenham and its Church
by The Rector: Rev. Canon Scott
(formerly vicar of West Ham, and Rural Dean)

published 1897 by F.T. GROOM, BURY ST. EDMUNDS and printed by ADLARD AND SON, Bartholomew Close, E.C. and 20 Hanover Square, W.

"LAVENHAM, well known for its magnificent Church, is a picturesque little town in West Suffolk. It has a station on the branch line of the Great Eastern Railway from Mark's Tey to Sudbury and Bury St. Edmunds, and lies about halfway between the two. It is sixty-six miles from London, and the journey from Liverpool Street — *the main line being left at Mark's Tey* — takes about two hours. December 1897."

So wrote Canon Scott as the introduction to his book, in the closing years of the 19th century. The railway, sadly, closed in the middle of the 20th century, but the Canon's observations remain of interest today. He went on to write:—

WE may take it for granted that the visitor has reached Lavenham by railway. If he have come from London he will probably have been inclined to grumble at the slow pace at which he has travelled since leaving the main line at Mark's Tey. But he should remember that we have only a single line of rails, and that in Suffolk we are not often in a hurry, but prefer to take things quietly. Anyhow, he has at last got to Lavenham, after catching sight of the tower of our noble church just before the engine began to shut off steam.

On leaving the station the visitor sees the road to the town before him, and may notice, a couple of hundred yards or so to the left, across some allotments, the disused factory where more than one attempt was made to produce beetroot sugar. **THE SUGAR FACTORY.** The sugar was excellent, for the soil suits the root; but it did not pay, and so for many years the doors have been shut, and a large quantity of costly machinery lies idle and profitless.

Before we have gone many yards an old plastered house may catch the eye. There are many such in the town, and they are mostly not white-washed but pink-washed, and some are so far out of the perpendicular that one wonders why they do not fall. On this house — and it may be seen on many others — is embossed the French fleur-de-lis surmounted by a crow, or possibly it is a bishop's mitre. What can it mean? It probably has to do with days long gone by, when French weavers came over after the Revocation of the Edict of Nantes in 1685. The mitre (if it be a mitre) may belong to Bishop Blaise, the patron of woolcombers, elected to that dignity (the Patronal, not the Episcopal) in memory of the sad fact of his own flesh having been combed from his bones during one of the persecutions of Diocletian. St. Blaise's day (February 3rd) was kept here as a holiday, and with a procession of emblematical figures, till within comparatively recent years. **BISHOP BLAISE.**

This may remind us that Lavenham was an important centre of the cloth trade at the time — it was much earlier that the supposed date of the crown — when the Eastern Counties were the chief manufacturing districts of England. In the Middle Ages the great source of England's wealth was wool. **THE WOOL CLOTH TRADE IN THE MIDDLE AGES.** The woolsack on which the Lord Chancellor sits (*used to sit*) is a memorial of this. Wool had been at first exported, just as it came from the sheep's back, to the Low Countries and even to Italy, and when there manufactured into cloth was brought back again. Thus, in one of the Colloquies of Erasmus (The Uneasy Wife, Uxor), where two ladies are talking, one of them says "You have one of the prettiest suits I ever saw in my life; it is as soft as silk. It is English cloth, I suppose?" The other replies, "It is indeed of English wool, but it is Venetian dye." Edward III was one of the first to see that this was an uneconomical way of proceeding, and he set himself to work to introduce Flemish weavers **THE FLEMINGS.** to settle here and teach the English to manufacture their own cloth. He promised them, as old Fuller tells us, that "if they would come over, bringing their mystery with them,. they should feed on fat beef and mutton instead of herrings and mouldy cheese, till nothing but their fulness should stint their stomachs." They accepted the invitation but preferred to go no further from home nor further inland than could be helped. Norwich became the centre of the cloth trade, and the third largest city in the kingdom. But from this centre the manufacture spread outwards, and some of the villages where it settled, such as Worstead, and Kersey and Lindsey, gave names to special articles which have survived to this day. Lavenham for many years had a large share in the cloth manufacturing, and probably was a much busier place four centuries ago — and a richer — than it is today. In 1397 loans were demanded by the Crown from seventy of the more important towns in England. Among them was Lavenham, which had to pay £20, being the same amount as Bath, Derby, Lichfield and Plymouth) Cunningham's "Growth of English Industry and Commerce during the Early and Middle Ages, p. 343)

After this long digression we must go on with our walk. Passing the Congregational Chapel, built in 1827, though the Independents have had a congregation here for almost exactly 200 years, and on the opposite side of the road a shop famous in all the neighbourhood for antique furniture (it is not the only one in town), we come to another factory, where horsehair from Siberia and elsewhere, and cocoa-nut fibre from Ceylon, are made up; the former into seating for chairs, and perhaps into material for penitential shirts, and the latter into mats and matting of all sorts and conditions. This, happily, unlike the sugar factory, is a very busy

LAVENHAM STILL A MANUFACTURING TOWN. place, and gives employment to a large number of men, while the women in their own homes — for every third cottage in the parish has its loom — weave horsehair for one or other of two firms (Messrs. R.W. Roper and Sons, and Messrs. Laycock) which divide the trade between them, and have several other factories in the town. "What would Lavenham do without weaving?" is a commonplace remark; for work "on the land", as they call it here, would not employ half the people. But as things are, and with the additional employment which are the roller-mills and maltings of Messrs. Baker afford, it is a rare thing to find an able-bodied man or lad out of work; and to confess the truth, for a country place, spite of agricultural depression, we are fairly well-to-do.

But we must go on with our walk. The street — we call it the High Street, though the name has not yet been put up, the authorities having exhausted

ON THE WAY TO THE CHURCH. their energies in the recent numbering of houses — is hilly and picturesque. We have gone up one little hill, and half down the other side, when we come to the first side street. Unlike any other in the parish, it displays its name, Hall Road. We will turn up it, first noticing a chimney nearly opposite the turning, which is said to date from the time of Henry IV. Going up Hall Road to the end of the orchard wall, a white gate on

the left invites us to take a path which promises to bring us to the Church, which now for the first time has come into sight. A few yards beyond the gate we shall find that the view of the Church standing on the rising ground, with the foreground of water and trees belonging to the Hall, is exceedingly

THE CHURCH. pretty; and if I were an artist, this is the view of the Church which I should sketch in preference to any other. The view also from this point of the Hall, the home of Mr William Biddell, formerly MP for the Western Division of Suffolk, with its well-kept gardens, is very pleasant.

But now we must follow the path to the Church (dedicated to St Peter and St Paul), the glory of Lavenham. Let us stop as soon as we have passed the churchyard gate. the massive Tower first catches the eye, with its buttresses reaching to the very top.

THE TOWER. It is 141 feet high and yet seems as if it had never been completed; for the twenty-four coats of arms (they are those of Mr. Spring, "the rich clothier of Lavenham," who was one of the two chief builders of the church) come so exactly to the very top of all as to suggest that at least a few feet more were meant to be added. Tradition says that the architect (whose name is unknown) was killed by falling from the tower when it had reached its present height, and that it was thought unlucky to continue his work further. Below each window of the tower, built into the beautiful flint-work, we may notice a star. A herald would call it a mullet;

THE DE VERE "MULLET." and it is the cognizance of the de Veres, the Earls of Oxford; one of whom, the thirteenth Earl, was, along with Mr. Spring, the builder of the church. After noticing the inscription over the chapel at the eastern end of the aisle, "Simonis Branch et Elizabethe uxoris ejus qui istam capellam fieri fecerunt" — the words which have been erased were probably "orate pro animis" — we continue our walk past the low "Vestibulum, as it is called on the founder's monument inside. It now serves

THE VESTRY. as the Vestry , and very probably has always done so. It was part of an earlier church, as was also the Chancel, where the east window and the adjoining window on the south side belong to the Decorated period of Gothic architecture. The rest of the church is of late Perpendicular, and is said to have been considered by Pugin the finest specimen of the style in existence. Just as we turn the south-east corner of the church we can hardly fail to notice a monument erected only a few years ago (remember this was written in 1897 !), and which we shall afterwards find to be an imitation of the ancient cross in the Market Place. ....

CONTENTS OF APPENDIX

APPENDIX

I. RECTORS OF LAVENHAM

1302.	Nicholas de Wytcherch.
1312.	Robert de Elmham.
1334.	Richard de Stoke.
1354.	William de Lavenham.
1361.	John de Pelham.
1386.	John Poland.
1400.	John Pygot, jun.
1416.	John Saddle.
1444.	William Fallam.
1459.	William Morton.
1459.	George Vere.
1462.	John Walter.
1475.	Henry Boost.
1477.	Thomas Ashby.
1486.	John Gigles.
1497.	Thomas Appleton.
1508.	Thomas Stackhouse.
1529.	William Basse.
1558.	Christopher Chapman.
1559.	William Day, D.D.
1571.	William Rainolds.
1578.	Henry Copinger, D.D.
1622.	Ambrose Copinger, D.D.
1644.	William Gurnall.
1679.	Roger Young.
1688.	Charles Turner.
1710.	William Kinnerley.
1729.	Thomas Wright.
1730.	John Squire.
1763.	John Davy.
1792.	James Buck.
1825.	Richard Johnson.
1855.	Joseph M. Croker.
1891.	Thomas Scott.

....

VIII. LAVENHAM AND THE GREAT REBELLION, 1642—3.

It was during the early part of the Civil War between the forces of Charles I and the Parliament that the latter formed the famous Eastern Counties Association, which was destined to keep its own borders free from the worst evils of the war, and to help furnish the sinews of war which carried the Parliamentary cause to victory on other fields.

Lavenham took its full share in supporting the Parliament in its struggle against the king, as the following extract from the Tanner MSS. in the Bodleian Library, Oxford, shows:
"Lavenham in Suffolke.

"Herein is subscribed the names of those that Find Voluntarie Armes and who Serve in the Same. All which are all redy Sentt to Cambridge with a month's pay acorrding to the Ordenance of Both houses of Parlamentt for the defence of the Five Counties as Expressed in the Association.
"they went under Captaine Richerson of Hadely.

and all the names are recorded ....

IX. GEOLOGY OF LAVENHAM

By the Rev. E. HILL, M.A., F.G.S., Rector of Cockfield, Suffolk

Boulder Clay. — The clay generally called the Great Chalky Boulder Clay, which hides all older formations through so large a part of Suffolk, extends over the whole of the parish of Lavenham. It consists of a matrix of grey clay, often weathering red, containing occasional pieces of Lias and Kimmeridge limestones, many flints, and countless chalk fragments of all sizes down to microscopic dust: it has been estimated that more than 100 may be visible in a square foot of surface. The pieces of chalk are always somewhat rounded: and the larger masses of it, and the limestones, are frequently covered with scratches such as are attributed to the action of ice. This clay is unfossiliferous; the shells so often reported in accounts of well-sinkings are all derived from older formations, and often are merely shelly portions of the limestones noted above. The parish is intersected by a valley whose bed is less than 160 feet above the sea, while some part rises to 270 feet; so the clay seems more than 100 feet thick. A well sunk 30 feet in the bed of the valley did not reach the chalk.

There is no opportunity in Lavenham for studying this clay, except by chance in a new ditch or well.

High-level Gravel. — While the valley above mentioned was much shallower than it is now, powerful and irregular currents seem to have run down it; for we find high up along its western slope masses of a peculiar gravel. This differs from other gravels of West Suffolk by the great size and roundness of its flints, and by the red clay which is mixed with them. It agrees with descriptions of the "cannon-shot gravel" of Norfolk. It has been traced along the west slope of the valley, generally from 30 to 50 feet above the present stream, from Bradfield to Stanningfield, through Cockfield, to Lavenham. At Cockfield patches or thin sheets of Boulder Clay have been seen overlying it, (possibly slips from higher levels).

This gravel may be seen on the west side of Bear Lane, about 300 yards south-east of the Church; in a field north-west of Mr. Biddell's house (Lavenham Hall); and in a field east of the Bury St. Edmunds Road, a quarter of a mile north of the railway station. At this last spot it overlies other gravels, free from clay, and containing sand and chalky material, which are also seen 200 yards west, on the other side of the road.

Newer Gravel and Brick earth. — When the valley had been excavated to its present depth (perhaps deeper), sand and other gravels were deposited, usually of smaller, more angular, and cleaner materials. Such may be seen here and there in the bed of the stream, and are worked by the side of the road south-south-east of the sugar factory, in the field which contains the brick-works. Some of the gravel here, however, is rather coarse; it may perhaps have been washed down from the older beds just described. As these workings appear to go lower than the present stream, it would seem that the valley was at one time somewhat deeper than it is now.

Rain would wash down the sides of this valley the finer portions of clay. Such seems the origin of the beautifully stratified deposit, some 15 feet thick, which is worked for brick-making on the east of the town. A beginner in geology must not think that the inclination of the strata is due to upheaval or earth-movement; the beds were deposited on a hillside, and follow its slope. In this brick-earth, tusks, teeth, and bones of elephant, hippopotamus, &c., occur. A fine tusk, about 4 feet long, was found in 1897 at the bottom of the deposit, resting on the top of the Boulder clay below. This deposit appears to overlie the gravels last described.

Human Period. — Flint implements, so common north of Bury, seem rare or unknown from the Clay plateau of Suffolk and its valleys. We have no pre-historic materials for the history of Lavenham.

The town stands on the west bank of the valley. Various wells have been sunk, but none have reached the under-lying chalk, though this is seen at Monks Eleigh, three miles down the valley to the east, as well as at Sudbury, six miles to the south. It is recorded that while sinking a well at the "Greyhound" in 1827, at a depth of 50 feet "mephitic air" was met with, "which put out candles and killed chickens" (see Geological Survey Memoir, on Quarter Sheet 50, S.W. Neighbourhood of Stowmarket.)

These extracts are reproduced with permission from Suffolk County Council

Index

251